The Countess of Carnarvon lives at Highclere Castle, best-known to millions worldwide as the setting for the popular television programme *Downton Abbey*. As an author, Lady Carnarvon has written several bestselling books including *Lady Almina and the Real Downton Abbey*, *Lady Catherine* and *At Home at Highclere*. She is also the author of *Seasons at Highclere* and *Christmas at Highclere*.

T0364546

Also by the author

Lady Almina and The Real Downton Abbey:
The Lost Legacy of Highclere Castle
Lady Catherine and The Real Downton Abbey
At Home at Highclere: Entertaining at The Real Downton Abbey
Christmas at Highclere: Recipes and Traditions from The Real Downton Abbey
Seasons at Highclere: Gardening, Growing and Cooking Through the Year at
The Real Downton Abbey

The Earl and the Pharaoh

From The Real Downton Abbey to The
Discovery of Tutankhamun

THE COUNTESS OF CARNARVON

WILLIAM
COLLINS

William Collins
An imprint of HarperCollins*Publishers*
1 London Bridge Street
London SE1 9GF

WilliamCollinsBooks.com

HarperCollins*Publishers*
Macken House
39/40 Mayor Street Upper
Dublin 1
D01 C9W8, Ireland

First published in Great Britain in 2022 by William Collins
This William Collins paperback edition published in 2023

1

A catalogue record for this book is available from the British Library

ISBN 978-0-00-853177-5

Set in Granjon by Palimpsest Book Production Limited, Falkirk, Stirlingshire

Printed and bound in the UK using 100% renewable electricity
at CPI Group (UK) Ltd

This book is dedicated to the 5th Earl,
the current Earl and Edward

CONTENTS

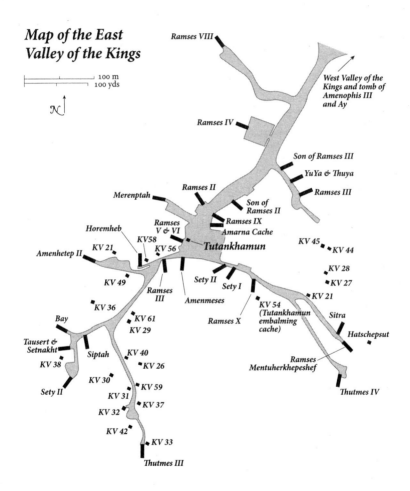

Map of the East
Valley of the Kings

100 m
100 yds

N

Ramses VIII

West Valley of the
Kings and tomb of
Amenophis III
and Ay

Ramses IV

Son of Ramses III

YuYa & Thuya

Ramses III

Ramses II

Merenptah

Son of
Ramses II

Ramses V & VI

Ramses IX

Amarna Cache

Horemheb

KV 45

KV 44

Amenhetep II

KV 21

KV58

KV 56

Tutankhamun

KV 28

KV 27

KV 49

Sety II

Sety I

KV 21

Ramses
III

Amenmeses

KV 54
(Tutankhamun
embalming
cache)

Sitra

KV 36

Ramses X

Hatschepsut

Bay

KV 61

KV 29

Tausert &
Setnakht

Siptah

KV 40

Ramses
Mentuherkhepeshef

KV 38

KV 26

Sety II

KV 30

KV 59

Thutmes IV

KV 31

KV 37

KV 32

KV 42

KV 33

Thutmes III

3rd Earl of Carnarvon = Henrietta Howard (known as Muddy)

The Hon. Alan Percy Harty Molyneux Howard Herbert

The Hon. Auberon Edward William Molyneux Howard Herbert

Eveline Alicia Juliana Howard Herbert (who married 5th Earl of Portsmouth)

Evelyn Stanhope Earl & Countess of Chesterfield (who lived at Bretby)

1 =

4th Earl of Carnarvon

2 =

Elizabeth Catherine Howard (known as Elsie whose family lived at Greystoke Castle)

Winifred eldest sister

1 = Cpt. Alfred Byng

2 = Herbert Gardner

5th Earl of Carnarvon

Margaret Herbert

Victoria Herbert

The Hon. Aubrey Nigel Henry Molyneux Herbert

The Hon. Mervyn Robert Howard Molyneux Herbert

Alfred de Rothschild and Maria Wombwell

=

Almina Victoria Maria Alexandra Wombwell

Evelyn Leonora Almina Herbert

6th Earl of Carnarvon

PREFACE

THIS IS A book about a man whose life and death became front-page news throughout the world between the autumn of 1922 and the spring of 1923 when, with his colleague Howard Carter, he discovered the tomb of Tutankhamun and then, shortly afterwards, died. The media circus that accompanied the opening of the tomb latched onto the glint of gold, the extraordinary treasures and, of course, the superstitious world of ancient Egypt. The back story of hard work, the acquisition of experience and knowledge in an inhospitable climate, was overlooked in a welter of excited prose.

Carnarvon did not seek the world of celebrity. Born to a position of great responsibility, the eldest son of one of the pre-eminent Victorian statesmen, Carnarvon had a restless and enquiring mind that was held back by a lifetime of illness and injury. An avid race-goer and horse breeder, he was also involved in both the worlds of aviation and of automobiles in their earliest days. His health compromised by a serious car accident, he then discovered the joys and frustrations of excavating an ancient civilization when he spent winters in Egypt for the benefit of his health.

Working from source where possible, this book has been a different journey, far richer and more diverse than I expected when I set out. From contemporaries, from his family, from his own records and from snippets in archives throwing up shafts of light, it has been a journey of discovery about a different man from the one I thought I would find.

To quote his beloved sister Winifred, it is a 'story that opens like Aladdin's cave and ends like the Greek Myth of Nemesis and cannot fail to capture the imagination of all men and women'.

I

IN MEMORIAM – 26 DECEMBER 1874

How do I love thee? Let me count the ways.
I love thee to the depth and breadth and height
My soul can reach, when feeling out of sight
For the ends of being and ideal grace.

L ORD CARNARVON HAD just requested the footman, Williams, to
bring a further screen into the sitting room to make sure his
wife, Evelyn, would not suffer from the slightest draught, given it
was so intensely cold outside. He was fussing gently but the fire was
well built up and Lady Carnarvon was trying to find a comfortable
position in which to sit, expecting her fourth child in just two or
three weeks.

Lord Carnarvon had removed his wife from Highclere Castle to
their house at 16 Bruton Street, Mayfair, London, well before her
lying-in, desiring to be near all the best doctors, and he had engaged
Sir William Gull and Dr Farre to be in attendance.

It had been such a sad and melancholy Christmas. Poor Mrs Laverick, Highclere Castle's housekeeper, had left on Christmas Eve to stay a few days with her mother but there had been a dreadful railway accident near Oxford. About thirty people died and at least seventy were injured. Carnarvon had sent David Thomas, the butler from Highclere, up to Oxford to find out what news there was and, as it emerged, to identify Mrs Laverick's body. It seemed that a pneumatic tyre had failed, and one railway carriage pulled the others down an embankment into the freezing, snowy fields. Despite local brave efforts to assist, there was little to be done and Mrs Laverick had, if it was any comfort, died instantaneously. A week later she was buried at Highclere in the cemetery in the park with many of the estate staff standing by, heads bowed against the weather and the tragic loss.

Evelyn was very much shocked and overcome at the news. She asked her husband to organize a wreath for the coffin as a heartfelt gesture for a much-loved member of the household. Carnarvon noted in his diary that he would write on behalf of them both. 'I cannot help but feel it very much – she was one of those old-fashioned and faithful servants . . . a heavy shadow seems to have fallen over the whole house.' He had then received a letter from Her Majesty Queen Victoria about an entirely different, political matter. It was written in her own hand, and he read it out to Evelyn to offer, as much as anything, a momentary distraction. Looking out of the first-floor window into the grey London dusk, the thawing snow, now turning to liquid mud, was fading into the dark obscurity and he hoped the children were able still to enjoy the winter weather in Devon, where they were staying with his mother.

Ten days before, Lord Carnarvon had travelled down to Pixton Park with Winifred, Porchey and little Margaret, who were to spend Christmas there along with their governess Petit and nurses Emma and Mary. His youngest sister Gwendolen was also staying at Pixton, and, although not in the best of health, kindly ensured their beloved mother was supported. For his own part, he had thoroughly enjoyed some excellent walks and shooting, as well as catching up with his sister Lady Portsmouth who had arrived a couple of days beforehand. Their mother, known to all as Muddy, was giving them occasional cause for anxiety over her health this winter, which he supposed might be expected given she was now 71 years old. Two of her sisters had sadly died but she and her younger sister Charlotte were still flying the flag.

It was a happy household high on Exmoor, a muffled white world with the newly made snowmen and quick shouts of laughter as snowballs thrown by Porchey or Winifred found their mark. Carnarvon spent some precious time away from cares of government, pulling the children across the lawns on a sledge, helping build their snowmen and enjoying their chatter and stories. Porchey seemed stronger for being outside; his parents were often concerned for his health as he was very slight and tended to suffer too readily from chest ailments.

Lady Portsmouth returned home to Eggesford, a large, rambling Gothic house only twenty-five miles away, albeit a challenging journey across the wintery moors. She had, however, her mother's calm practicality, which was much needed as she had twelve children, the youngest of whom was only 4 years old, and a busy and noisy household to run. This very much revolved around her husband's timetable of hunting and shooting, though her eldest girls had reached the stage where they were more intent on attending every local dance. In between, all of them were out riding ponies and playing with dogs or hiding to fire snowballs at unsuspecting family and staff.

Shortly afterwards, Lord Carnarvon left for London bearing stories, drawings and good news about all three children's health for their mother.

Unaware of the loss of Mrs Laverick, the three children spent a lovely Christmas with their grandmother and were excited about meeting their new brother or sister. The days passed quickly on Exmoor until a telegram was delivered to Muddy with the happy news that they had a new little sister, born quite quickly on Wednesday 30 December 1874. Eve was exhausted but overjoyed, in tears as she held the darling little baby in its swaddling clothes. Evelyn's mother Anne, Countess of Chesterfield, seemed quite annoyed it was another girl and not a boy, but all the newspapers gladly reported that mother and baby were doing well, and Lord Carnarvon received congratulations from his friends.

The plan had been for the children to return to London in January by train and ten days later they set off. They arrived in Bruton Street exhausted but excited, tumbling out of the carriage eager to see their parents and new sister. They were quickly borne off to wash their hands and straighten themselves up after the journey. Their mother's bedroom was snug and warm and the heavy fringed brocade curtains were pulled back around the bed, several lamps allowing some pale light into the high-ceilinged room. Winifred was just 10, her younger brother Porchey 8 and Margaret 4. Wide-eyed, they could see their mother leaning back on the white pillows. Their father had told them she was tired but, reassured by her smile and her gentle voice, they tiptoed into the bedroom, clutching their nurses' hands. Winifred, being the eldest, gently reached across to wind her fingers through her mama's hand, which was always so pale and delicate. Their father leaned over the other side of the bed, smoothing the pillows.

'Here is Baby as well, my darling, doing so well,' said C, 'and all our other angels.' Porchey and Winifred tried to smile but felt frightened: their mama seemed so faint. Little Margaret tried to climb up onto the bed, but her brother gently pulled her back, his face creasing up in happiness as their mother smiled encouragingly. 'Darlings, I am feeling a little tired, but I will be better soon. I love you so much.

Tell me about your snowmen. Who made the biggest one?' Relieved, Porchey said he had sledged the fastest, he had flown off over a stump, but the snow was so deep it was a huge cushion. She turned her head and asked after Muddy, their grandmother. Winifred said she was resting as she had a cold but really wanted to see Baby. Winifred said they all wanted to know what she was going to be called. Soon they tiptoed out of the room to let their mother rest.

Evelyn did gain a little strength but when Benjamin Disraeli, the leader of the Conservative party, dined with Lord Carnarvon in Bruton Street on 15 January he felt most concerned and wrote to Lady Bradford, Evelyn's aunt: 'I partook of a Bretby turkey in Bruton Street – rather a melancholy repast, for Lady Carnarvon had a relapse in the morning and Lord C was very nervous and depressed. Gull (the physician) came in the evening and was not discouraging, and C told me at cabinet today that her pulse had again subsided.'

It was less than a week later when Lady Portsmouth read a most painful account of dear Evelyn from her brother Carnarvon and she gathered herself promptly to leave for the train, arranging for Lady Duckworth to chaperone her daughter Cathy at an upcoming dance down in Devon. She heard from Eve's mother Lady Chesterfield that her doctors were more encouraging, but she was soon ensconced on the 11.40 train from Exeter to London with a thoughtfully provided basket of provisions.

The next day she spent the afternoon with her brother and Lady Chesterfield. The doctors thought Eve was a little better. While standing in the hall of Bruton Street talking to her brother as he left, dear little Margaret ran to her for a hug and, stroking her brown curls, she suggested she took her off for a cheerful tea at Batt's Hotel in nearby Dover Street, the nursemaid following along behind. Meanwhile, Lady Portsmouth determined to ask the doctor herself for an account as her brother worried dreadfully and she found it hard to determine the truth of the news.

The Dowager Lady Chesterfield was struggling to hold herself together. Her son, Philip, had died barely three years ago. He had been one of the party accompanying the Prince of Wales to Scarborough and they had both contracted typhoid. The Prince of Wales recovered, although it was touch and go, but her Philip, her beloved boy, a first-class cricketer and a politician, had died. Now she was sitting with her daughter, the kindest, best of daughters and the possibility that the normal order of nature would again be reversed with her child so desperately ill.

January the 21st brought some good news for Lady Portsmouth in that her mother, who had kept to her bed since the New Year, was feeling much better. However, the next moment brought a note from her brother saying that darling Eve had suffered a relapse, though she had in fact slept the night before and her temperature was not as high.

Very anxious for news, Lady Portsmouth walked round to Bruton Street and into the saddest, most desperate house. Everyone knew that Eve's life was ebbing. She had been both Lord Carnarvon's love and his companion, a woman of excellent judgement whose influence over him in political matters was invariably both sensible and good.

The children filed back into their mother's bedroom and Winifred solemnly bent closer to her mother to hear 'love each other, my darlings, you are my eternal gift, and I will always watch over you, please always help each other'. 'Yes, Mama' was all they could say.

During the last hours, Lady Chesterfield rarely left her daughter's room, sharing the precious time at the bedside with her son-in-law. On Sunday Lady Portsmouth 'prayed hoped feared trembled hoped again all day' and, on a more practical note, suggested that their brothers, Alan and Auberon, who had arrived for the deathbed, stay with her and not Lord C.

Evelyn died on 25 January surrounded by her family. Lady Chesterfield was white with exhaustion while Lady Portsmouth cried out 'for my dearest C – my darling Eve'. However, she wrote in her diary on 26 January that there was some blessing in even painful certainty.

Carnarvon was utterly devastated and spent the following days in despair, walking aimlessly with friends through the London parks. Their words and letters helped keep her alive for him and gave her value despite the too-early death. Augustus Hare wrote: 'The news of dear Lady Carnarvon's death came . . . as a shadow over everything. Surely was there never a more open, lovable, unselfish, charming, and truly noble character, apparently radiant with happiness and shedding happiness on all around here [the West Country].'

More formally, Lord Derby wrote, 'Lady Carnarvon who has been dangerously ill for a fortnight died this morning, a great loss to the party. She will be regretted by many, being hospitable and sociable in disposition.' Even the Queen had felt the greatest possible anxiety about Lady Carnarvon's illness – a telegram of enquiry from her was sent in the early hours of the 25th, perhaps indicating that she was thinking of the Carnarvons while watching at the bedside of her son Prince Leopold, who was dangerously ill – and on Eve's death said she would become sponsor for the late Countess's motherless infant.

The children had their nurses, who loved and hugged them and tucked them up in bed with hot chocolate, making sure they were never alone. The nursery maids were with Margaret as they helped look after Baby in the nursery and the routines continued. Winifred, stoical and serious, wanted to do what she could to help her father, while Porchey, small and thin, not the strongest of children, became rather silent and wrapped up in his own world.

Soon afterwards, Lady Chesterfield left for her home, Bretby, in Derbyshire, and the family prepared to leave for Highclere. A few days later, on Friday morning, Porchey peered out of the train windows, Margaret leaning over him. The train was slowing, puffing, with squealing brakes as it drew to a halt in an overcast cold, snowy Newbury. The stationmaster hurried forward, dressed respectfully in black like everyone else, and Lord Carnarvon stepped down. Given the circumstances, Carnarvon managed wonderfully, full of thought for everyone, rallying around his brothers: Auberon, married and living in the New Forest, Hampshire, and Alan, who lived in Paris where he practised as a doctor, working in a hospital, as well as the precious children. His sister gathered the children around her and hurried them all up the steps into the carriage, which soon pulled away, the horses impatient in the cold weather.

The children craned their necks, curious, and saw the end of their mother's coffin being carried from the train. It was a monochrome scene, from the graphite sky to the black coats, hats, dresses, veils, mufflers.

The next morning Lady Portsmouth was up in good time and went into the library in case her brother was there. Eve had adored these new rooms. The Castle had been remodelled by the architect Sir Charles Barry for his client, the 3rd Earl of Carnarvon, who had died before it was finished so it had been partly Eve's life work. She had thought so much about how to decorate the rooms, how to dispose the furniture and yet now was instead lying in state in her coffin.

Later that day, the coffin left the Castle and the family walked together down the hill, holding the children's hands, past the silent estate workers, to the cemetery chapel in the middle of the park which had been so recently completed. Lady Portsmouth held tight to little Porchey's hand while Thomas (Lord Carnarvon's house steward) bore the late Countess's coronet and the tradesmen and tenantry formed a close line on each side of the road. The coffin was taken into the mortuary chapel, followed by the mourners, and Lady Portsmouth watched as 'dearest C' placed a wreath of white camellias from her mother on the coffin, before carefully placing one from himself and their children. Evelyn was buried to one side of the chapel built by the 3rd Countess of Carnarvon. She had said she wanted to be buried in the light.

The following day, Sunday, was the last day of January. It was a bright day and after they had sung Evelyn's favourite hymns and received the sacrament, Lady Portsmouth wrote, 'we all walked with the beloved children to her grave and covered it with flowers. In the afternoon Mr Waters preached to a crowded church a true and loving sermon of our darling . . . alas alas.' Auberon left that day, and on the following day Cousin Robert and C's brother Alan also left.

Over the next few days Lady Portsmouth walked a great deal with Carnarvon and visited Evelyn's grave, feeling very anxious about Eve's children. Linking her arm with her brother, she said that night and day he and his children were in her thoughts as she asked herself what would Eve have wanted? . . . 'my heart is so very sore. I loved her like a beautiful very unique jewel and then I loved her for my dear Carnarvon's and for her darling children's sake and oh how I long for her back.'

2

THE CHRISTENING

IN THE INITIAL period following his wife's death, Lord Carnarvon withdrew from public life to look after his family and cope with his bereavement. He walked continually, desperately wanting to share his stories and grief, especially with his sister, who had stayed on. 'We walked and visited her grave, all newly turfed and we thought the hard frost dealt gently with the flowers (I found the gardener covered them with matting every night). Dear Little Porchey was kept in with a slight cold.' Lady Portsmouth spent a lot of time with 'the dear children'. 'Winifred and Porchey (often) with me walked round for their exercise and I told them stories.'

Eventually, it was time to return to London for the christening of the baby, rather grandly named Victoria Alexandrina Mary Cecil Herbert. This took place in the Chapel Royal of the Savoy, an ancient church near the Thames much loved by their mother. As promised, the Queen was one of the godparents and was represented by the Marchioness of Ely along with the Marquess of Salisbury and the

Countess of Derby. Lady Portsmouth and her sister Lady Gwendolen were there to support their brother. It was a moving service and Evelyn's uncle, Canon Forester, took the opportunity to pay tribute to the rare intelligence of a very special, kind woman who touched so many people's lives in such a positive way.

Queen Victoria was true to her word and did not neglect Lord Carnarvon. During the year she asked him to stay both at Windsor and at Osborne House, followed later by Balmoral. While conversation may have been about political affairs, he also wrote that 'her genuine kindness touched me most greatly'. She also asked Lord Carnarvon to bring the children to Windsor and he noted that, although 'they seemed rather frightened and shy, the Queen was so kind that they finally lost their fright and became at home and very much interested. She ended by giving them each a present.'

During the next few years much of the children's life was spent between Highclere and one of Lady Portsmouth's noisy households, whether in Devon or in Hampshire. Kind friends such as the Marquess of Salisbury asked Carnarvon to stay and Porchey remembered at one point being pulled round Hatfield on a bearskin by his sister. His father took them sailing along with their aunt and cousins. Lord C had bought a new yacht which he described as 'very good but, like all other things, just short of perfection'. Porchey in particular loved being on the water: he enjoyed being with the crew, learning about the art of sailing and watching and listening to the sound of the waves.

On 7 May, probate on Lady Carnarvon's will was granted and the family was reminded sharply once again of their loss. Lord Carnarvon sat down in the library with his son to read out what his mother had written: She 'begs her son Lord Porchester to look on the said estates, which he would thereafter succeed to, as a solemn trust not to be used for his own gratification or pleasure but for the glory of God and the honour of those who have gone before him'. She had also made provision from her brother's estates – the late Earl of Chesterfield – for her younger children.

Winifred and Porchey were much loved, living between Highclere and their aunts, going out for rides, being fed sugar wafers and hoping for toys. They adored their aunt Gwendolen, a frequent visitor from her home in Putney, who in return loved her motherless nieces and nephew. She was something of an invalid, a little figure sitting on a sofa or going round in her donkey cart, but there was always room for the children, and she always saw the upside of their adventures.

Most importantly for Porchey, she was there to intercede with irate housekeepers who found water cannons aimed at oil paintings or dogs hidden under the bed covers. Porchey spent weeks explaining to his aunt that a spear would help him understand ancient history and early battles most awfully well. She arranged for one to be made and, in some ways rather luckily, it was soon thrown and wedged by its happy owner in a rather important engraving. It was not returned to Porchey who then thought that a saw would be most useful to learn how to cut up logs and trees. Diplomatically removed from Porchey's grasp, this in turn was hung on a blue ribbon from the schoolroom wall as a work of art.

A cricket ball sailed through a window in the library and Porchey was crestfallen and hopelessly worried about what would be his punishment. Gwendolen consoled him with half a crown, and he ran off in a much happier frame of mind. He was a gentle boy, a terrific tease, loving to play practical jokes from a young age, and, given that he grew up in a family of sisters, very relaxed and amusing in the company of the fairer sex.

That autumn their father was not very well, tired and with a nagging cough. He had thrown himself back into his government work in his role as colonial secretary with a feverishness that was neither quite healthy nor natural. Porchey and Winifred spent a certain amount of time with their aunt Lady Portsmouth. They were happy with her, and she had written to her brother, 'Porchey has grown very sweet and handsome looking'. Her Devon home was all about the outdoor life and Porchey and Winifred spent their days hunting, shooting and riding across the moors with their cousins. The hunt meets at Eggesford were full of characters from all walks of life and Porchey spent days with them, waiting in spinneys, cantering across the moors, or simply chatting. The equanimity with which he treated anyone in his future life was perhaps a result of this upbringing with his aunt. Then, in the evenings, the children would sit entranced as their aunt read out loud from books such as *Ivanhoe*.

At other times, to try to stem her loneliness, Lord C would send the children up to Bretby to stay with their grandmother, Lady Chesterfield. She lived in an enormous house and ran the estate herself, even if Lord C tried always to be available to help. Bretby was a house of much antiquity, remodelled to a design by Sir Jeffry Wyatville in 1812 and was famous for its gardens and park, which had been completely restyled by the 2nd Earl in the late seventeenth century, so that some even compared them favourably with the gardens at Versailles. Over the next few years, Lady Chesterfield became especially close to Winifred and Porchey.

Just as the family were learning to cope with their new way of life, in May 1876 Lord Carnarvon received a telegram to say that his mother's strength was waning fast. He rushed down with Sir William Gull, the royal physician, to Pixton, in Somerset, where she lived. Her three sons and two daughters were by her side as she peacefully left them, an indomitable, wise, shrewd and kind woman they affectionately called Muddy.

Muddy had taken much pleasure in all her grandchildren, playing the piano for them to sing and dance to and encouraging them in all they did. Her coffin was brought back to Highclere, and she was buried with her husband in the graveyard in Old Burghclere. Alan, Carnarvon's brother, took some time away from his hospital in Paris to help with all the arrangements and, in any case, he much enjoyed spending time with his nieces and nephew at Highclere. A most courteous man, he enthralled Porchey and Winifred with fascinating stories of the Siege of Paris that had taken place five years earlier and said that he looked forward to welcoming the children to Paris whenever they were deemed old enough.

3

THE RELUCTANT SCHOOLBOY

Porchey's cousins had been sent to a preparatory school, Cambridge House at Belmont, near Brighton, so he was sent there, too, the school chosen perhaps more for its reputation than its suitability for each child. The headmaster was a Mr Sibthorpe and the school reports tended to be rather average and not quite what Lord C hoped for; a boy who was often not very well and who should not eat so many sweets – although he could give credit where it was due, writing in November 1878: 'It is most gratifying to see the earnestness with which he applies to his studies. The change is so satisfactory that I thought you would be glad to participate in the pleasure.'

Porchey missed his father very much and found the whole experience hugely challenging. His well-written letters always expressed the hope that his father would come and visit and the cheerier news invariably included an outing with Mrs Walker or Mrs Sibthorpe. Looking back, the experience probably ingrained in him a measure of reserve and personal withdrawal. Unhappy, he used to tell his sister Winifred how homesick he was and the only positive outcome as far as he was concerned was that he survived it. His cousins tried to look out for him as he was neither strong academically nor a good sportsman, although he did enjoy cricket. During the holidays, his father took various recommendations as to good Latin tutors, which seemed to haunt his life and yet, by the age of 10, he was reasonably bilingual in French with a good working knowledge of German, some Latin and less Greek. He played the piano and had a charming voice.

Like many children, the school holidays were the most important dates of the school year, whether they were spent in Devon, Highclere or Bretby. Whatever the circumstances, Lord C very much enjoyed taking his son out shooting, especially when they spent the day walking together; in turn, Porchey enjoyed the stories and companionship of his father. There was nothing better than sitting with their father in the evening by the fire and persuading him to tell them a ghost or a fairy story. The children were entirely entranced: nobody did it better.

In January 1878, Lord C was again unwell. At work, he was at odds with Disraeli (now Lord Beaconsfield), not wanting to repeat the mistakes of the Crimean War and refusing to sanction sending the British fleet to the Dardanelles. Both Lord C and Lord Derby resigned in protest, to the fury of Queen Victoria, who had wholeheartedly given her support to Lord Beaconsfield. In fact, the Queen would not even shake hands when he returned his ministerial insignia to her.

At this point Porchey managed to persuade his father that he could leave school and be tutored at home. Winifred often interceded on her brother's behalf and in many ways her academic leaning and reading were more like those of her father than Porchey's; in later life she would write biographies of several seventeenth-century figures. When Porchey returned to school, his father later went to stay by the sea, too, which made his sister Winfred happy. She was a caring, kind child, writing with as much home news as she could to her brother.

Lord Carnarvon had begun to find a family rhythm through the year with his young children, Winifred was now 13 years old, Porchey two years younger, Margaret 8 years old and Baby was 3. It was nevertheless not easy, given his work and social commitments, and he relied heavily on his sisters. Nevertheless, he wrote regularly to the children when they were apart and was always concerned about their health and welfare.

Lord C's mother's family were the Howards who lived at Greystoke Castle in Cumbria and the sadness of Muddy's death had brought forth more family invitations. During the holidays Greystoke was often filled to overflowing with children of all ages, which was fun for his own children. Days were spent on the shores at Ullswater, and Lord C described how glorious he found the huge skies, mountains, and water, 'much too beautiful for mortal man'. From riding and boating by day, evenings were spent with music and stories. He had also met a rather serious, elegant young cousin called Elsie (Elizabeth) Howard and a new chapter in his life was about to open. He was conscious that she was twenty-five years younger than him, and he wrote to her aunt saying that he was aware of what he 'was asking dear Elsie' but she had decided to accept him.

It was not long before his sister Lady Portsmouth received a letter which she read out loud to her husband – her brother was to marry. 'I do not think you will be surprised . . . I am engaged to be married to dear Elsie.' He had so much 'admiration as you know for her charming character'. She wrote to her brother Alan, 'all is settled between Carnarvon and Elsie'. His daughter Margaret wrote to him at Greystoke to say Aunt Gee (Gwendolen) explained to her he was going to be married and she was very happy and had been allowed half a day off school, too. 'When are you coming back that I may see and talk to you all about it?' Winifred had met Elsie already and sent her 'best love', and she had also written to Porchey saying she was sure he would like her.

Elsie and Lord C were married from Greystoke Castle on Boxing Day morning 1878. Alan Herbert was best man and the bride arrived to the 'Bridal March' from Wagner's *Lohengrin*. The wedding breakfast was served in the great hall, and they were surrounded by family and friends. Winifred was so excited to wear such a beautiful dress and she and Porchey thoroughly enjoyed themselves. It was very cold with deep snow and a hard frost so Porchey thought they would be able to sledge or skate the following day. In the end, he helped build an igloo and, on the 29th, Lady Gwendolen wrote from Greystoke to Lord C, who was by then at Pixton, 'Porchey in good health & spirits & everyone is most kind & fond of him. He & Esme [Elsie's brother] descend a bank of snow on tea trays', but he ended up with a cold before spending New Year with his cousins and Aunt Eveline at Eggesford in Devon.

After his departure from Greystoke his aunt Gwendolen wrote, 'Esme says he shall feel quite dull Porchey made him laugh so much.' A few days later she wrote, 'I could not help feeling glad he had shown his real self to them even if sometimes one might have had a fear of his spirits growing too high', commenting that 'the shy silent Porchey is after all only a make believe & so long as his spirits are not allowed to run away with him the boyish side of his character is very taking'.

Lord and Lady Carnarvon went first to London and then to Pixton for their honeymoon. Back at Highclere, Elsie scooped Vera and Margaret into her arms and thereafter they just called her mother. However, Elsie was only 22 and so thought Winifred and Porchey were different, and it was for them to find their way together rather than for her to dictate.

Lord C hoped for the best and wrote to his sister that Winifred saw Elsie as a central figure in her life and 'Porchey is evidently captivated by her'. He would even agree to sing if Elsie accompanied him on the piano. In the spring, Lady Portsmouth kindly agreed to present the new Countess at court: 'I shall be delighted to present Elsie and very proud' and Lord C hoped that Highclere could now be a real home again for his children.

An old friend, Lady Phillimore, wrote of the newly married couple: 'They are happy together those two and make sunshine around them.'

Lord C kept a study on the top floor of the Castle. It was lined with a gilded painted leather wallpaper similar to that in the saloon and had outstanding views. It was not far from the nursery which in the past had been useful. With careful thought he noted in his diary on Tuesday 23 September 1879, 'Porchey's last day at home. Tomorrow, he begins his Eton life – and walks alone. He goes in good heart hoping and expecting for more than he fears . . . and a sense of emancipation probably greater than he knows . . .'

Together with his father and stepmother, Porchey caught the train from Highclere to Eton smartly dressed in a tweed jacket. His trunk had been sent ahead of him. Like so many parents, Lord C thought 'parents could do nothing so good for their children as to give them a good . . . education.'

His father had carefully chosen G. E. Marindin as Porchey's house-master. Marindin had attended Eton as a boy himself before returning in 1865 as a master, remaining there for twenty-two years. Cotton Hall House was built for him in 1870 by William White in the 'Domestic Revival' style and Marindin carefully superintended the plans until it was finished in 1871. By reputation, he ruled entirely with kindness and spoke with gentleness and humour even in moments of reprimand.

The Carnarvons arrived in time for tea; Porchey was shy and uncertain while his father sought to strike the right balance of encouragement and fortitude before he and Elsie left for home. Porchey returned to his room which would not really change throughout his career at Eton: a shut-up bed, a burry (bureau), washstand and sock cupboard in which his tea things were kept. Over time Porchey acquired some nice racing prints and some obligatory schoolbooks.

Just as in his father's time, Eton was a school full of ceremonies, acronyms and tradition. The early morning challenge for each new boy was to be up on time, dressed in tails and starched collars. Then it was down to breakfast, the first time wondering what your fellow students would be like. Porridge and eggs or kippers, mushrooms and grilled sausages were all on offer as the menu was rotated through the week.

The first few days were exhausting as Porchey just tried to be in the right place on time, beginning with Lower Chapel and later finding his way around the campus with the right books. Every lesson was in a different building, and he had to plan all his books before returning for chambers, a mid-morning break, for half an hour with toast and tea. More lessons followed before lunch and then the prospect of games. All the boys had to share some of the domestic duties and to run errands and tidy for the older boys – a duty known as 'fagging' – in addition to tidying their own rooms.

Just four days later, Porchey found himself faced with some comprehensive exams. These really did not go very well in his father's eyes as he was ranked in the lower half of his year. As usual on his side, his aunt Eveline wrote to her brother at Highclere that 'dear Porchey . . . is only 13 and a quarter, . . . He may have been very nervous . . . his own greater readiness to work is worth everything. You took so high a place at Eton . . .' In Eveline's view he just needed to be encouraged. Her two eldest sons were also at Eton, though further up, while John Francis would join the next year, so Porchey had some support and, given time, she felt he would find his own level. Porchey himself, however, was acutely aware that he could not produce the exam results his father had found so easy. He could feel his father's disappointment and he missed his home and sisters.

The 4th Earl was intellectually extremely able. He had read Homer, Virgil, Horace and Herodotus before he went to Eton and, at a similar age to Porchey, had written to his own father that: 'I do four different kinds of verse Elegiacs, Sapphics, Alcaics and Iambics of which Sapphics are my favourite.' He took a first at Oxford in Literae Humaniores (known as Greats) and had travelled for a few years before returning home and marrying.

Rather like London cab drivers who must learn 'the Knowledge' (i.e. know their way round London's streets), so Porchey and every other new boy had to learn and pass the 'colours' test, which meant they knew where every house was, the housemasters by initials and the house games colours.

The school prided itself on sporting prowess and the success of the boys was judged on the field or on the water, but such absorption in sport did not suit every young man. Happily, Marindin was also no athlete although he sought to inspire those in his house. While neither football nor rugby were appealing to Porchey, his cricket was sufficiently good enough to win him his cricket house colours.

However, the best time of the day for most of the boys, whatever the term, would be late afternoon back in their houses, when they would split up into 'messes' of two or three boys within each year and tea would be set out and taken in one of their rooms. The house provided bread, butter and milk but otherwise they could bring in a cake or cook eggs or even a pheasant, after which they would help clear it away. It was a time when real friendships were formed before 'late' school. The formal evening meal was then taken in the company of the Dame and the tutor.

Porchey's father, visiting him at the end of October 1879, commented, 'he gets on well with the other boys . . . I think he is also desirous of working up to a higher place in the school', and that his son was 'a good dear boy'.

Lord C was trying to create a nurturing home but was still acutely aware of the children's loss of their mother. Nevertheless, he noted in his diary that Porchey 'is very fond of Elsie and she is quite charming to him'. End of year reports were encouraging and Porchey had made good progress with the piano as well.

The family went down to Devon and the two youngest children, Margaret and Vera, set off in a coach with their aunt Eveline to cross Exmoor to Pixton where they would join their father and siblings for Christmas and New Year. All the family enjoyed walks across the moors and Porchey went out with the keepers to enjoy some walked-up birds. His father had been suffering from gout so rested with Elsie, who had just shared the happy news that she was expecting a baby. Despite her own youth and the hard work of trying to oversee an inherited family of young children, Elsie had also organized gifts, sweets, fruit and cakes for eighteen children from the Dulverton workhouse.

Too soon the return to school loomed, never an inviting prospect especially in the dark, cold winter months. Porchey tended to suffer from bronchitis and spent some of the following term in the sick bay.

Like many other boys, Porchey tended to begin each lesson with enthusiasm, concentrating briefly on what the tutor was writing on the blackboard before subsiding into a daydream as his interest in turning out Latin verse and construing Latin sentences waned. Fortunately, Marindin was always on hand to help. Despite his father's joy and commitment to learning, Eton was not necessarily regarded as a school for scholars. It did produce very self-possessed and polished pupils but the education itself focused, in time-honoured fashion, on the 'dead' languages of ancient Greek and Latin.

There was little flexibility in the timetable and more practical subjects such as Geography, Modern Languages and Mathematics only occupied more of the timetable further up the school years. Porchey much preferred them for their practicality but was little encouraged. Perhaps inevitably, he naturally sought out the more idiosyncratic opportunities. His friend Charlie Newton Butler had started to help keep the Eton Beagles and organize drag hunts, while the attractions of Windsor Racecourse, just across the river, were soon identified and formed an integral part of his career at Eton.

A new boy started at Eton in the Lent term, the son of His Highness the Maharajah Duleep Singh. He entered Manor House (A. C. James) but was in the same year as Porchey. Prince Victor's father enjoyed a special relationship with the Queen and was staying with her at Windsor Castle, handily close to Eton. He had become the Maharajah of the Punjab at the age of 6, but the Punjab had been annexed by the British and, in 1849 under the third Treaty of Lahore, both the young Maharajah and the Koh-i-Noor diamond were sent to England. Queen Victoria and Prince Albert entertained him at Osborne House on the Isle of Wight and Queen Victoria was swift to insist to her courtiers: 'With regard to the Young Maharajah. The Queen wishes to observe to Lord Aberdeen that he should be treat as a Prince in whom the Queen took an interest and we accordingly treated him just as we do all Princes . . .'

Queen Victoria thoroughly enjoyed his company and included him and his family in both her private and public life. The Koh-i-Noor diamond was formally presented to Queen Victoria on 3 July 1850 at Buckingham Palace to mark the 250th anniversary of the East India Company. Put on display with its mysterious history, this huge, flawed and asymmetrical diamond failed to bring the expected rapturous applause from the public and Prince Albert decided to commission a skilled diamond cutter brought in from Amsterdam to cut it. From its original 186 carats, 'the Mountain of Light' (the translation of Koh-i-Noor) became a polished stone of some 105 carats.

Some months later, the Maharajah was staying with the Queen when she commanded a brightly arrayed group of Beefeaters to bring the jewel from the Tower of London to be admired once more by the young Maharajah.

The casket was ceremoniously brought in. 'Maharajah I have something to show you.' He stepped across and was stunned into silence when he saw the diamond. It was not the mythical, symbolic Mountain of Light he had once held. With supreme effort he held it once more, walking towards the light by the window while the Queen watched him anxiously. After some time and a deep sigh he walked back across and with deferential reverence placed the diamond into the Queen's hand, tendering it as a gift and offering his loyalty to her. Not all the assembled courtiers were entirely happy as they did not consider it was the Maharajah's to gift.

Queen Victoria welcomed him as one of the family. 'I was quite sorry to see him go,' she wrote after one visit. 'I take quite a maternal interest in him.' She also paid time and attention to the young Maharajah's education. A tour around England was organized to inspire the young Maharajah to settle down to an English country life and it was repeated to the Queen that he was 'one of the most charming young men'. Queen Victoria wrote that he 'sat next to me at a dinner dressed in his beautiful clothes and wonderful pearls and emeralds'. He was also a favourite with Prince Albert as well as the royal children.

It was no surprise therefore that in 1863, with such encouragement, he bought an estate in Norfolk called Elveden and it was there that he would bring up his family, having chosen his own bride, Bamba Muller, whom he had first seen in Cairo, Egypt. She was the illegitimate daughter of a German father and Ethiopian mother, living in a Cairo mission, whose life was now transformed into that of a Maharanee.

The Queen wholeheartedly welcomed his new wife, giving them both precedence at royal occasions, invariably placing them next to her. Later in 1866, she insisted on christening their son. 'I have never beheld a lovelier child . . . I named him Victor Albert . . . the Dean of Windsor performed the service . . .' Frederick was born two years later followed by three more children, both boys following in their father's footsteps and attending Eton.

By the end of the Lent term, Porchey and Prince Victor had become firm friends as they equally and consistently found themselves at the bottom of most classes. Both were also slightly different from the consensus of pupils at Eton. Victor wore his dark hair far longer than was usual and displayed a certain elan and sense of style in his manner; he had, of course, also arrived in the middle of the school year, which is never easy. Porchey was a shy and skinny boy who often required medical exemptions from many of the usual school activities.

Eton broke for the Easter holidays, always most welcome to Porchey after the mud and wintery weather of the Lent term. Both boys went their separate ways, Porchey returning home to Highclere to be there when his stepmother, Elsie, gave birth to a brother, Aubrey, on 3 April (the name Aubrey having perhaps been chosen because it was the childhood diminutive of his uncle Auberon).

Lord Carnarvon was thrilled, for 3 April was also the birthday of his distant kinsman, the seventeenth-century poet George Herbert. Aubrey, however, was always called Hereward by his parents after the Anglo-Saxon hero Hereward the Wake, to whom his parents fondly thought they were also related.

Porchey's father had just given him a George Hare mahogany plate field camera as a present and the boy was thrilled. He became both intrigued and fascinated by the effort it took to operate the camera successfully and loved the results. He immediately began by taking photographs of two sides of the Castle and his father was very proud of his efforts, writing 'Porchey's first photograph' alongside the result in April 1880, and 'Highclere Photographic Company'.

In early summer, the whole family settled into their London house in Bruton Street, as Lady Winifred was to 'come out' for her first London season. Porchey, however, returned to Eton, but always found the Summer term much easier, not least because cricket was the one sport he was reasonably good at. This year, however, he found a new outlet. Both he and Duleep Singh very much enjoyed slipping away to watch the races whenever possible. At Eton, the boys traditionally organized a lottery on the horses running in the Derby, but any other betting was usually inhibited by a lack of funds. However, this consideration did not apply to the young Prince, and Duleep Singh caused something of a sensation when he placed a bet of £5 on a certain horse, by far the largest wager ever accepted.

Lord Carnarvon remained unaware of his son's extra-curricular activities and was once more immersed in politics, developing an initiative to take forward the idea of National Insurance to support unemployed workers and those who were sick or elderly.

Meanwhile, the Queen had commissioned a splendid painting of Prince Victor by Sydney Prior Hall to be displayed at the Royal Academy in May. Prince Victor was dressed for his portrait in a beautiful red silk tunic, a foil for all the jewels and strings of pearls as well as an historic embellished belt and sword. On Thursday 27 May his parents attended one of many royal events, a State concert in Buckingham Palace with all Queen Victoria's family gathered together. Outside the immediate royal family, the next place of honour was, as usual, given to the Maharajah and Maharanee Duleep Singh. The Earl and Countess were also invited and looked appreciatively at the couple in Indian dress covered in splendid jewels and pearls as well as admiring the Maharanee's sweetness of expression and very fine eyes.

Elsie was still not well, suffering from post-natal complications, and after a brief visit with Lord and Lady Sefton to Royal Ascot, the family travelled to Wildbad in Germany to take the cure and rest. Winifred was particularly excited as she had never been abroad before. They set off on 23 June but after only two weeks away returned to London. Elsie had become increasingly unwell, and they wanted the reassurance of a London doctor with whom they were familiar, Dr Gull. Porchey had not accompanied them but instead was staying with his beloved aunt Gwendolen in Putney, who was not only well disposed to welcome his school friends but who enjoyed their somewhat spirited company very much.

When the Carnarvons returned to the fresh summer air at Highclere, they found Porchey really very unwell with a terrible sore throat. Dr Douglas of Newbury had been using his laryngoscope to inspect the throat and prescribing gargles, but Gwendolen swore by sage tea interspersed with teaspoons of honey.

Elsie was at last feeling better and taking drives around the park enjoying the lovely weather. A constantly revolving stream of friends and family, picnics, riding and boating made for the best of the summer idylls and Porchey felt far better being outside in the warm weather. Reality soon intervened, however, and the last week of the holiday was spent at Bretby, the family house in Derbyshire, with his tutor Robert Harrison, whom his father had engaged to try to get Porchey's second year at Eton off to a better start academically. Porchey himself, though, was far more interested in a trip to Newmarket with his grandmother, always on the lookout for a tip and already happily familiar with several bookmakers. Again, his father was not necessarily aware of all that was going on.

During the autumn both Elsie and her husband felt under the weather and decided to avoid the damp, cold weather at Highclere and spend the worst of the winter months in Madeira. They sailed with the other children on 26 October, leaving Porchey and one of his Wallop cousins to sail out later in December.

Lord C had thought that he might spend the time learning Portuguese, improving his German and translating the *Odyssey*. It was not, however, the warm, restful time that he'd hoped for, and bad weather and mishaps dogged the entire expedition. Everyone went down with colds and even bronchitis and Elsie slipped on 'some stones . . . thank God no real harm . . . foot and ankle sprain', meaning that Dr Graham, who was based in Madeira, was in almost constant attendance.

Meanwhile, Porchey sailed from Southampton on 16 December without his cousin, who had caught the measles. His father noted he had 'much enjoyed the voyage. The captain and the officers had been very kind to him, and everything had gone well', but his return journey was delayed until 16 January due to high seas and challenging weather. En route back to school, Porchey stayed with Lord C's close friends the Phillimores at Henley; they wrote to his father, 'you will have heard how charmed we were with Porchey, a pleasant better-bred boy I have seldom seen.' In turn, Winifred kept Porchey up to date, writing regularly to him and very proud, too, that she and Elsie had sailed to the Canary Islands and returned to Madeira after a brief exploration without mishap.

4

'I am always ready to learn although I do not always like being taught.'

Porchey's Easter school holidays were often spent at Bretby. Lord C was now editing the eminent 4th Earl of Chesterfield's *Letters to his Godson*, dating from the 1760s–1770s, a sequel to the already well-known *Letters to His Son*, written over a period of thirty years from 1737 to give perceptive and nuanced advice for a gentleman based on his own calm diplomacy, gentle tact and linguistic dexterity. His godson and heir, who became his adopted son and succeeded him as the 5th Earl, was a favourite companion of George III, accompanying him on his morning rides and joining his whist parties on the royal yacht. In 1798 he was appointed Master of Horse to His Majesty, and he took a great interest in agriculture, being considered a good judge of horses and cattle, while his Home Farm at Bretby was held to be one of the most complete establishments in Derbyshire.

Sadly, the 6th Earl of Chesterfield did not follow any such advice and quickly dissipated a large fortune on the turf and in the hunting field. He paid astonishing prices for his racehorses and gave his name to the Stanhope, a carriage driven by a four-in-hand team. He won the Ascot Gold Cup in 1829 with Zingaree, for which he paid 2,500 guineas, and had purchased another good horse, Priam, for the then record price of 3,000 guineas. With this he won the Goodwood Cup in 1831 and again in 1832. Another horse, Don John, picked up at a bargain price of 110 guineas, won him both the 1838 St Leger and Doncaster Cup.

He won the Oaks twice and in 1843 the Grand National with his horse Vanguard. The outlay, however, was unfortunately far above any return and he fell heavily into debt before retiring to live entirely at Bretby Hall. Nevertheless, he did construct a gallop of some two miles to exercise his horses and much enjoyed his shooting before dying aged just 61. One month later his grandson Porchey was born. He would very much follow in his grandfather's footsteps with his twin passions of racing and gambling.

Chesterfield's widow Anne continued to live at Bretby and was very fond of her grandchildren, sharing with her grandson a love of horses and racing and, even at 72 years old, she was often to be found at Newmarket. Prime Minister Disraeli was a regular guest at Bretby and even proposed marriage, to no avail, although they remained friends and regular correspondents.

Whilst Porchey had returned to Eton in January, the rest of his family left Madeira to return to England in time for Easter, when the whole country and the Queen were plunged into mourning by the death of Disraeli. It marked the end of an era and Lord C wrote of him: 'a large character disappearing off the stage . . . a man who will be a puzzle and a subject of wonder. I am . . . very glad I returned in time to call and to send him a message.' He was laid to rest on 26 April in Hughenden churchyard with his wife Mary Anne.

Disraeli's great friend Alfred de Rothschild helped organize the funeral and its procession and Queen Victoria sent a posy of primroses. A few days later, in private, she visited his tomb with her daughter Princess Beatrice. They walked the route the funeral cortège had taken and laid a beautiful porcelain cross of camellias and other flowers on the tomb.

That summer, Lord Carnarvon and Elsie went to Eton for the 'Fourth of June' (the school sports day). Happily, the weather was good and there were fireworks, the procession of boats, luncheon in Hall, Chapel services and a promenade in the playing fields. The guests of honour were the Maharajah Duleep Singh and his Maharanee, who occupied with oriental dignity two venerable, if not splendid, armchairs on either side of the Provost. Sir Frederic Roberts, the Duke of Buckingham and many other notable Old Etonians were also present, so it was something of an occasion and the Carnarvons were delighted to meet Porchey's great friend Prince Victor. On an academic note, happily the housemaster Marindin gave good and encouraging reports.

The summer heralded a marvellous round of parties in London. The Prince and Princess of Wales held a garden party at Marlborough House to which they invited Lord and Lady Carnarvon. Every night hostesses from the Salisburys to Lady Portsmouth competed to welcome guests to every type of entertainment, from small, exclusive dinner parties to large extravaganzas. Lady Holland began the season with a huge garden party for all the children as well as '1,200 persons of distinction' in her home, Holland House, Kensington. With beautiful gardens and lawns, refreshments for all and a Punch and Judy show, it was much enjoyed. Among the young guests was a beautifully dressed young lady, Miss Almina Wombwell, who arrived with her aunt Lady Julia Wombwell.

Exhausted, the Carnarvon family retired to Highclere for the month of August and later in the month hosted a Saturday garden party with bands for three hundred guests. A number of family and friends were staying, among them Sir John and Lady Macdonald, one of the founding fathers and Prime Minister of Canada.

The state rooms were open to be viewed and admired while the garden improvements and winding walks newly meandering across the lawns were a great success. A novel event was the arrival of a cow decorated with a necklace of flowers and led onto the lawn outside the library. The milk produced there and then was immediately made into a syllabub, to the huge enjoyment of the children. With a marching band and old English country dances, all of which Porchey and his sisters joined in with, the afternoon gave much pleasure to all. Lady Carnarvon had engaged a conjuror who entertained guests in the saloon and later a buffet was served from the dining room.

Now 15 years old, Porchey was a more relaxed individual. He was happy to spend time riding, fishing and boating with his sister Winifred, and cousins and friends were always coming to stay. His camera was still of huge interest, and he loved the dogs and pets, which were as much as possible smuggled in upstairs. The harvest had been brought in early and the hay was great fun to jump down into, the woods offered new trails to canter through and they were all trying out tennis on the east lawns with rubber balls and wooden-framed racquets. His tutor Harrison was supposed to undertake structured tutorials with his pupil every day but there were many distractions and escape routes.

The return to school soon dawned and Porchey had a major crisis – he could not find his pet snake, a present from his friend Duleep Singh. His sisters all helped him look for it and eventually one of the footmen found it hanging behind one of the curtains in the library. Retrieved and safely contained within a box, it returned to Eton, where it lived in his desk.

In discussion with his house tutor, Lord C agreed that space and time, as well as leaving less important matters be while standing firm on academic achievement, would be a sensible approach. Both his father and housemaster sought to provide adequate supervision. As every parent, Lord C had to remind himself that at this age a young man's treble voice cracks, bristles compete with blemishes and attitudes swing between indolence and annoyance. Porchey did not fight the rules and regulations as other boys did, so much as simply avoid them where he could. He was innately restless and keen to discover the amusements of life for himself. The house could not run without rules and therefore Porchey tended to be somewhat permanently in trouble for being out of bounds and charmingly evasive about fulfilling the demands of school.

Porchey began to receive an increasing number of letters from his father, which required some careful invention and tone on his part in order to compose suitable replies. Despite his allowance his father had been called on: 'I have just paid another bill – a very overdue account – and would be glad if you in fact would a make a contribution' was a not untypical example. It seemed to have become some sort of competition as to whether Porchey or Prince Victor could make the larger bet and their allowances were certainly not spent on simple luxuries such as Fuller's Walnut Cake in Windsor. Furthermore, if it was not the horses, then they were losing at cards.

Having attended the wedding of his brother-in-law where Winifred was one of the bridesmaids, Lord C went to stay with the Phillimores in Henley to seek their advice before visiting his son at Eton. When he next saw Porchey, he had stern words with him:

'I cannot pretend that your career at Eton has been anything less than a source of anxiety . . . never forget, however, that I remain your forbearing father.'

As the term continued Lord Carnarvon became ever more concerned. His letters noted that he was sorry to hear that Porchey was unwell and suggested he abandon some of his more vigorous night-time activities and his smoking, neither of which seemed to be Porchey's answer to the problem.

In October 1881, Porchey came home from Eton for a few days knowing he would have to face his father. 'I tend not to hear from your tutors unless you have been absent or late. However, you may not be surprised to hear I have had far too much correspondence from them.' Winifred was academically diligent and able to divert their father a little by seeking his interest in her studies, but she was a girl and not the heir.

Some of the happiest times for Porchey and Winifred were when they went off exploring Highclere, albeit with a groom in tow. They knew the names of all the fields and woods, from springtime watching the brown, stony fields filling with the delicate green shoots of wheat or barley reaching towards the white wool-studded sky, the hedges of hawthorn flanked with nettles, buttercups and bluecaps, fallen elms offering perfect trees to jump. The tiny delicate leaves of the oaks marked the advent of summer, and all at Highclere competed to see who heard the first cuckoo. And now, as summer faded, the mosaic of autumn colours painted a rich new world; the crisp air spurred on their rides around the fields and murmurations of starlings marked the turning year.

Often they would stray towards the centre of the estate and of the farm, to the extraordinary expanse of Beacon Hill. The ancient hill fort fascinated them; walking along the remains of the houses or lines of the protective walls which had once stood perhaps thirty foot tall, they imagined the people who had lived here. Now tall grass covered the embankments. At the foot of the hill scattered across the level pasture were twelve barrows, large tussocked mounds a hundred foot in diameter, which they could clamber up looking for secret openings (the burial grounds of Bronze or Iron Age people).

Their father had shown them a letter and drawing from his great-grandfather, the 1st Earl, who had looked inside one barrow.

The 4th Earl was Patron of the Newbury and District Field Club and President of the Society of Antiquaries, as well as a well-regarded expert and speaker on British archaeology. His two eldest children had read his reports with much interest and their bedrooms were named for the old Anglo-Saxon kingdoms.

Now there were exciting plans afoot: the careful excavation of two barrows which were about to be intersected and thus removed for the new railway line from Didcot to Southampton. Porchey and Winifred were determined to be there: Porchey offered to be photographer and Winifred of course to take the notes. In fact, Mr W. Money was the lead excavator and assiduously recorded the works. They found the remains of cremation, some flints and a bronze brooch but thought it had already been 'tapped' (opened) before. The other barrow contained some pieces of ancient pottery, some bones and a palaeolithic flint axe but, overall, the burials suggested that, while these barrows represented the resting place of distinguished members of the tribe, there was little wealth in the area. Other barrows, in Wiltshire for example, had yielded objects of gold or silver.

In November 1881, the barrows had been mentioned in a lecture, 'Highclere, 1800 years ago', given by Lord C at the Highclere and Woolton Hill Club, in which he commented on the English people as being neither British nor Saxon, Danish nor Roman, but a composite, a blending, of them all.

Lord C agreed with his housemaster at Eton that for the time being his son would travel with him and his wife, hopefully returning to school after Easter to complete the year. Therefore, on 17 December the family, including Winifred, Porchey and his tutor, left for the Continent while the youngest two girls and the baby went to stay on the Isle of Wight.

From Biarritz, they travelled to Pau and Lourdes. There was time to talk, and Lord C acknowledged that he was not sure that Eton was now an option. By mid-January, Porchey was ill with flu, delaying their departure for Avignon. Later, they travelled to Cannes and on to Menton, close to the Italian border. At this point Winifred and Porchey went back to Paris to see their uncle Alan before making their way home, shepherded by the valet Wiener.

Their father and Elsie went on to Italy, looking for a plot of land to buy: 'we have had the most glorious weather', they said, and commenting, 'there are endless nooks along this most lovely shore where nature is really divine'. The search was crowned with success and over the next few years an Italian villa fondly named Alta Chiara, an Italianization of 'Highclere', rose up on the almost landlocked harbour of Portofino. They shipped across Portland stone and planned their house together.

Porchey returned to Eton for a final few weeks before leaving for good at the end of the Lent term. Prince Victor stayed on and by now had been joined by his younger brother Frederick. He had made a niche for himself and, if not very sports-orientated, did show a voice of 'much promise and remarkable sweetness' in the song 'The King's Highway'. His career at Eton continued after a fashion and he gave much attention, theoretically and practically, to music. He studied counterpoint and orchestration under Sir Joseph Barnby, which later stood him in good stead in the drawing rooms of London.

Harrison was once more in charge of Porchey's education while Lord C pondered on whether his son should attend a different school, such as Winchester. Both student and tutor spent some time in London but it wasn't all work: they helped at a large evening party for some three hundred people held at 43 Portman Square. Then it was back to Highclere and the parties and sport there. On 22 July Lord and Lady Carnarvon entertained 260 local children with various games and both Porchey and Winifred helped take out the tea to the children while the Highclere cricket team played against the local West Woodhay team.

While Porchey spent much of the autumn with his grandmother at Bretby and, of course, his tutor Harrison, he was asked by his father if he had spent much time studying or in fact on shooting or riding and discovering local racecourses. Porchey did feel very humbled; he loved his father dearly and expressed every good intention for the future.

Just after Christmas 1882, Elsie gave birth to another son. Lord C fussed as usual, remembering the problems the last time and the death of his first wife, and noting that he was simply glad that all his family were around him as they began another year. Porchey's study hours were limited by his enjoyment of taking his gun out or his latest fad, a new machine called a treadle tricycle. It had two very large rear wheels and a smaller one in front with the direction of travel finessed (or otherwise) through a sort of joystick.

Going too fast down Dog Kennel Hill towards the chapel, he was inevitably thrown quite badly and one of his legs was badly scraped. Rescued and helped up to his room, the doctor was called and, as a precaution, one of his legs put in splints. Confined to barracks, he managed to complete some studies and was well enough to go to his baby brother Mervyn's christening at Highclere church at the end of January.

Porchey continued to charm Harrison and both of them to irritate Lord C, who could only perceive minimal academic improvement. Both he and Elsie were planning to leave for the South of France for a few weeks and he noted in his diary: 'I had a talk with Harrison on the subject of our previous conversation . . . he seemed to have forgotten a great deal of it . . . the matter was left on the [same] footing . . . but at Easter we should consider the whole position.'

After his earlier mishap, Porchey was sufficiently recovered to go hunting with his Portsmouth cousins, enjoying riding as fast as he could. Given that Harrison was not with him, he would take the opportunity to slip away to meet up with Prince Victor at various racecourses. Lord C inevitably found out and decided to send his son and his tutor on a walking tour to Germany, to improve his health and his German before going on to various French spas where Porchey's French could be further advanced.

Student and tutor returned on 4 August and Harrison parted company with the household while Lord C considered how to find a tutor who might help his son go up to Oxford, as he had. Porchey, however, would be unlikely to emulate his father's academic achievements.

In the end, Lord C enrolled his son at a crammer run by an eminent clergyman, Dr Mandell Creighton, who was also an historian and would later be a professor at Cambridge and Bishop of Peterborough and of London. Places at Dr Creighton's were in high demand and normally the young men were slightly older than Porchey, who was only 17 years old. Nevertheless, he went to board with the family at Embleton Vicarage, not far from the north-east coast of England, halfway between Newcastle and Edinburgh. Certainly remote, it was half a mile from the sea and a links golf course. There were scattered farms and long walks along beautiful beaches as well as an ancient castle, Dunstanburgh, to explore – and no racecourses.

The students were encouraged to study and to reflect on their deepening understanding on their future roles in life. Porchey's older Portsmouth cousins also attended, and Mrs Creighton found many of them somewhat trying: 'Young Stopford Brooke and Lord Porchester irritated me by their untidy slovenly ways.' They in turn found her somewhat bossy.

Porchey felt his life was once more being interrupted by textbooks and, despite the best intentions on all sides, Porchey succeeded at undertaking more smoking than Latin verse. His father had taken him up to Embleton just before he embarked on a successful Canadian tour with Elsie. Returning on 10 October, both parents had gone first to Greystoke Castle to see their sons before Lord C went on to visit Porchey. Sitting down with Dr Creighton, the news was not good.

'Thank you, Dr Creighton, for your letter, I felt I wished to hear your views and thoughts in person before I make any decisions.'

'Lord Carnarvon, as in my letter, I just want to tell you frankly that I do not think Lord Porchester will pass the examinations for Oxford. I entirely understand should you decide to remove your son from my establishment.'

'May I ask if you think a few more months' study, more time, might be advantageous? Am I without hope?'

'My Lord, not at all, and if Lord Porchester studies hard he might get into a college, perhaps not Christ Church, but there are many [other] excellent colleges.'

'I wonder if I might recommend Porchester's efforts to Balliol and Benjamin Jowett, whom I know, and I might put his name down,' remarked Lord Carnarvon, and Dr Creighton agreed that he would help if that was the next proposal.

In the meantime, father and son spent a few more days staying at the Chesterfield Arms, an inn near another family estate (Bingham in Nottinghamshire) with some excellent shooting. From there they both returned to Greystoke and thence to Portman Square. By early November Porchey was once more back with Dr Creighton for another month and his father had his name down for Oxford for a little under a year hence.

December in London, however, was rather too much fun. He very much enjoyed the theatre, music and opera life, as did Prince Victor, and then, of course, cards and clubs. Lord C found himself in receipt of a letter from his younger brother Auberon offering advice on Porchey's London and gambling tendencies at the card table. He suggested Carnarvon promote some sort of moderate stakes betting rather than none at all so that perhaps Porchey would not be quite so extravagant at the London tables.

Porchey felt even less inclined to return to the wilds of Embleton and came up with the brilliant idea of joining the Army instead. He returned to Highclere for Christmas ready to convince his father.

As usual, Highclere was filled with family and friends. They all gave a very successful concert in a local village hall: Lady Carnarvon played a duet with Winifred as well as singing to the great admiration of the audience. Elsie's sister played the violin and Porchey sang and was commended as a very fine vocalist.

Afterwards, feeling a little cast down, Lord C went up to London with his son to meet Captain Walter James, who had retired from his regiment – the Royal Engineers – and two years before had set up a crammer college in Lexham Gardens, South Kensington, which specialized in preparing applicants for the entrance examination for Sandhurst.

Porchey told his father that he should be allowed to take independent lodgings near the college rather than live at home. Lord C agreed to a compromise: he could stay with a friend, Lady Antrim. The Carnarvons were about to leave for Italy as their new villa was nearing completion and, for his own peace of mind, Lord C wanted to create some sort of safety net around his son. He therefore asked Schomberg Kerr McDonnell, Lady Antrim's tenth and youngest son, to Highclere to meet Porchey in the hope that he would agree to take charge of his son and act as tutor and minder.

Lord C hoped Porchey might have discovered his passion in life and, before he left, wrote to him: 'I wish you every possible success in passing the exams and hope you will join the army. I am sure you will settle in well and you have courage, enthusiasm, and a strong sense of humour all of which should suit the army. I rather think you get on with all sorts of people too.'

Portofino was to become a much-loved part of the Carnarvons' life but, perhaps not unexpectedly, their return was greeted by the news from both McDonnell and Captain James at Jimmies that

Porchey was often enjoying a few too many late-night drinks and card parties and smoking so much that his health was really compromised once again.

Porchey was hunting with his cousins down at Eggesford and, on the way back, he stopped at Highclere. Porchey's philosophy was to charm, to ask forgiveness and to say he would try better, and he assured his father he wished to do well and still wanted to try for the Army. Porchey was now 18 and both McDonnell and Captain James suggested that the best option, once again, would be to remove him from the clubs and cards. On the recommendation of various friends, Porchey was now to go and study for his Army exams with Dr Wilkin in Hanover, Germany. He set off from Highclere in August although, prudently, this time his father paid for just one term.

Returning in December Porchey joined his aunt and uncle Lord Portsmouth at Eggesford, and they arranged some horses and hunting – 'two good hunters at 2 Guineas a week each'. His uncle was most 'pleased to have his hunting pupil back again and we are all most charmed'. Lord Carnarvon noted that Christmas at Highclere was a success and that Porchey seemed very well. He 'played his banjo, sang a song or two and helped much at a tea for many of the older women and wives of the cottagers'. In fact, 'Nothing can be more amiable or pleasanter than his whole conduct since he has been at home. It is a marvellous transformation and gives me more delight than I can express. Whatever the cause – Germany – growth of good sense and good feeling, it is a breath of sunshine that is indescribable.'

Porchey went up to Bretby to see his beloved grandmother in January and his father noted how everyone missed him very much and that he would then return to Germany while the Carnarvons departed for Portofino. Unfortunately, this was not to be. Porchey discharged himself from Dr Wilkin and returned to London where

Prince Victor was still studying at Jimmies in London to enter the Army. They enjoyed themselves immensely and were both rather in debt and so, returning from Portofino, Lord C took his son down to Pixton Park to spend time with his Portsmouth cousins. He rather missed Winifred, who was very calm and loving with both the father and brother, but she had been delighted to set off for the Continent with Elsie's sister Maud, their mother and Esmé Howard, of whom Lord Carnarvon thought very highly and an excellent influence: Esmé was very cultured and an excellent linguist. They had a wonderful time, went to a Wagner opera, saw Graf von Moltke, Chief of the Prussian General Staff famed for his acute intelligence, across a Berlin Street and even went to have their fortunes told.

In June 1885 Lord Salisbury's Conservative government regained power and as Prime Minister and friend he pressed Lord C to accept the post of Lord Lieutenant of Ireland. Carnarvon was not in robust health but as Lord Salisbury had 'put the matter to [him] on public grounds . . . [he did] not feel at liberty to decline the Office'. Ireland had long been a personal preoccupation. He had spoken in the House of Lords, saying, 'Nature has bound together these two islands in an unhappy ill-assorted union' and was very critical of the past capriciousness of policies towards Ireland when it was on the verge of civil war.

Carnarvon accepted Lord Salisbury's offer and a seat in the Cabinet on the condition that 'they would consider the whole future policy to and government of Ireland'. Firstly, though, he wished to ascertain the conditions on the ground and on 29 June he arrived in Ireland and was cheered on the road into Dublin by a large and good-humoured crowd. He travelled in a state carriage with his wife and a small team including the Lord Chancellor, the Under Secretary and an ADC, Captain the Hon A. Byng. Lady C began to settle into the Viceregal Lodge and made various excursions with Winifred and Margaret, often accompanied by Captain Byng but otherwise without a formal escort. Lady Carnarvon charmed those whom she met at hospitals, museums, the Zoological Gardens and schools. Meanwhile, Porchey was staying with his grandmother at Bretby before joining his father in Dublin.

Barely a week later, Porchey and his father were back at Bretby having received a telegram that the Dowager Countess's sore throat had moved to her lungs. Her sister Lady Bradford and cousin Colonel Forrester were both at her bedside when she died at the age of 82. Lady Dorothy Nevill, a frequent guest at Highclere, wrote of her friend as 'a highborn lady of the old school'. Both son-in-law and grandson were acutely aware of the loss of the last emotional link with Evelyn and stood together as she was buried in the family vault on Friday 31 July 1885, her coffin entirely submerged under the innumerable and exuberant wreaths.

Thence, Lord C travelled down to London with Porchey, where he had a private meeting, off the record, with Charles Parnell, an Irish Nationalist politician, at Lady Chesterfield's London house in Hill Street, Mayfair. Carnarvon informed Lord Salisbury of the meeting, but otherwise the matters discussed remained within the four walls.

Travelling back to Ireland together, Lord C and Porchey agreed it would be best to let Bretby. Fortunately, they found an ideal tenant, Mr Hamar Bass, the local MP, who was a keen cricketer and race-horse owner and who was rebuilding his own house at that time.

Foreseeing how busy the role in Ireland would be, Elsie persuaded her brother Esmé Howard to become an assistant private secretary to Lord C. He had just passed the Diplomatic Service Examination and, being only a little older than her stepson, was good company and very much a pillar of family support in Ireland. He organized some salmon fishing for both Porchey and himself in Galway, which was extremely successful. They both enjoyed riding out in Phoenix Park and later took the opportunity to shoot woodcock.

As ever, it was a critical political time in Ireland and Lord C had shortly to navigate a dangerous Irish banking crisis, which he did with swift and calm reassurance. In terms of the pressing social iniquities, he wished to hear as many views as possible, both initiating meetings as well as hosting several dinner parties at Viceregal Lodge. Throughout the next six months many family members came over to Ireland to explore and to support Lord C, including his brothers Alan and Auberon Herbert, as well as Elsie's family.

Lord Randolph Churchill commented: 'It is the first time that I can recollect that a Lord Lieutenant has been able to emancipate himself from the Treasury shackles so as to translate generous promises into generous acts.'

Lord C returned to London in November for a Cabinet meeting before travelling to Windsor at the request of the Queen. On 28 November, the whole family was in the drawing room at Viceregal Lodge for the presentation of the Order of St Patrick, and Aubrey was a very sweet page. But the highlight to end the year was an invitation to dine and stay with the Queen at Windsor Castle before the novelist Henry James came to stay at Highclere. It had been a busy programme and Lord C felt exhausted.

Christmas was spent at Greystoke Castle and on Boxing Day Lord C wrote in his diary: 'seven years ago Elsie and I were married and . . . [they] have been a time of most blessed happiness.' Having given up on Oxford and the Army, after Christmas Porchey left for Trinity College, Cambridge, to read Modern Languages and Mathematics.

Lord Salisbury's government fell on 28 January 1886, and the Carnarvons left Ireland on the same day. They decided with much pleasure to set off for Portofino once more but went up to Cambridge to visit Porchey before leaving. 'His rooms are nice ones, and he seems to be settling down fairly and doing some work, the tutor Rev A Stanton seems a good quiet man.'

Porchey was reasonably fluent in both French and German but did need some support in mathematics as he found Mr Prior's lectures quite exacting. This was arranged with a competent scholar, Mr Gerdard. Unfortunately, Porchey's main concern seemed to be that the beauty of the wooden panelling in his college rooms was utterly spoiled by layers of paint, which he asked if he might remove at his own expense in order to return the rooms to their original elegance. Sadly, the offer was refused but Porchey did his best to continue to enjoy student life.

At the end of term Porchey set off to Portofino as well, arriving in time for Easter. Elsie had not been at all well with 'a great deal of fever and a bad cough', and Porchey was quite exhausted. His father despaired: Porchey 'arrived about midnight having walk'd all the way from Rapallo. He had mistaken the station and missed the boat . . . exhausted and famished and with a troublesome cold . . . but he slept on to 12 o'clock today and revived.'

Sadly, their visit was cut short when the wife of Auberon Herbert, Lady Florence, died in April. She was brought back to Highclere to be buried next to her son Rolf, who had also recently died aged just 9 years old. Once more the family was united by a funeral. The three surviving children, aged 6, 8 and 10 years old, and their father stayed on for a while, lodging in a cottage by the lake before returning home to the New Forest.

Porchey returned to university and once again fell back into his rather hedonistic ways. He was surrounded by a group of friends with a not dissimilar attitude, among them Prince Victor, Prince 'Eddy', Lord Hawke, Lord Francis Hope, the Studds and Charles Wright. Cricket took up quite a lot of the time – Porchey played for the Athenaeum. Even more fortuitously, both Chesterfield Park Races and Newmarket were not too far away. Overdue college bills were sent to his father having, rather too often, seemingly slipped his son's attention, while college reports drew attention to Porchey's lack of scholastic enthusiasm 'and disinclination to study'.

While Prince Victor also attended Trinity Cambridge in very much the same spirit as his school friend, he was even more frequently absent than present. His father was now in a perilous financial state and, as a result, had put the magnificent contents of Elveden Hall up for sale, publicly challenging the forfeiture of the Punjab with Lord Salisbury through letters and legal arguments in the newspapers. Naturally, in India the Sikhs cherished the memory of the Lion of the Punjab and thought the heartless treatment of his son and heir cast a slur on their loyalty and honour.

The Maharajah set off for India on the steamer *Verona* with his wife and children, including Victor and Freddy, who became rather popular on board. Concerned that he might promote revolutionary activities against the British Empire, the Maharajah was intercepted rather than openly arrested when the family arrived at Aden. They were 'disembarked' and, except for the Maharajah, were all politely forced to return to England. The Maharajah reverted to the religion of his ancestors, becoming a Sikh, and, in the end, sailed for Marseilles. Queen Victoria, seemingly oblivious to the hypocrisy, wrote that her 'godson she must see should not be ruined'.

At the end of July 1886, after a month of entertaining and cricket at Highclere, Porchey and Victor left for Canada where they wanted to see Niagara Falls before travelling on to the USA in early October. Both were back in time for the Christmas examinations in December, with Porchey hoping to negotiate a move into lodgings away from college with both the college and his father. Unsurprisingly, the Rev. Stanton had certain reservations. First, given the short notice, Porchey would still have to pay for the college lodgings as well as the lodgings in town. Then, while he thought the other young men who would be in the lodgings were 'reasonably quiet and sensible', he wondered whether it would be conducive to study for someone who already struggled with discipline.

Porchey had assured his father that he was regularly attending his tutorials, although he had said he was not well enough to take part in early lectures and had been excused. Winifred knew her brother rather too well and feared that 'he was more often seen at Newmarket than at lectures'. He had also managed to spend some delightful afternoons in the shops in Cambridge to add prints and drawings to the walls of his rooms, had found time to attend various balls and had much enjoyed a race meeting at which his pony Limerick won. The inevitable consequence was that he was listed as achieving only a 'IV' at Cambridge at the end of term. This was a far lower result than even his father had feared.

5

SHIP AHOY

LORD AND LADY Carnarvon had acquired a new, larger house in London in Portman Square in which Porchey was currently lying rather ill and from which Lady Winifred Herbert was to marry Captain the Hon. A. Byng. The service took place at the Chapel Royal of the Savoy, Aubrey and Mervyn were pages, Winifred's sisters and husband's sister were the maids of honour and Elsie looked beautiful in a ruby red velvet dress. Mr Byng was such an amiable man, and they all knew him quite well.

Porchey could not have been happier for his sister but decided he wasn't well enough to attend the service, appearing instead at the reception in his silk dressing gown. Later the bridal couple took a train to Newbury to spend their honeymoon at Highclere Castle, where the Highclere band had been engaged to play that evening. The Carnarvons left immediately for Portofino and Porchey followed two weeks later via Paris, Monte Carlo, the theatre and more colds and flu.

On the advice of his father, Porchey bought himself a sailing boat. He already had learned to sail a little as it was the only way to reach the house in Portofino, but he now spent most days learning with a local crew, coping with the sudden gusts of wind which swept down from the mountains around the coast. He learned to stay calm and was soon able to take charge when the local fishermen fell to praying to the Madonna in the worst squalls rather than attend to the rigging.

This was a precursor to further travel. In June, Porchey attained his majority, and his father was too sensible to allow his son to pursue indefinitely a further lacklustre course of study. Lord C had himself not been much older when he had set off with a university friend, Viscount Sandon, to visit Nineveh and Babylon, travelling along the borders of Persia and through Armenia.

In early July, Porchey bought a 100-foot yacht, *Aphrodite*, from Sir R. N. Bulkeley. Even though it was regarded as a fine schooner with magnificent accommodation, reports noted that it was being refitted in Cowes, in the Isle of Wight. By August, Porchey was based in Cowes, where he was elected a member of the Royal Yacht Squadron. While Lord and Lady Carnarvon set off for Australia at the end of September, Porchey left Cowes for Lisbon, then Madeira and thence to the West Indies.

The idea was to sail around Cape Horn to meet up with his father, but the weather was too rough. The Hon. A. Macdonald and Mr Sutherland were sailing with him under the hugely experienced guidance of the captain, Mr Cawes, but Prince Victor had not been allowed to be part of the voyage. He was confined to barracks once more as he was studying for the Army at Sandhurst.

The two young boys, Aubrey and Mervyn, as well as their sisters, were sent to Lord Carnarvon's sister Lady Portsmouth, along with Nanny Osmond and their German governess.

For all the tutors and classroom failures, Porchey had, at long last, discovered a passion for reading amid the long days of solitude at sea. His sister had always been a devoted reader but she would henceforth tease her brother for always being lost in a book and no sooner finishing one, than beginning another. Winifred wrote: 'the once idle undergraduate flung himself with avidity into the pursuit of knowledge, and especially of history, certain periods of which he studied with the meticulous research of a professor preparing a course of lectures.' He would often say that the sea taught him the acceptance of circumstance, of the seas and the wind, and he made decisions accordingly. It was not so much about solitude as independence.

In the meantime, the newly married Lady Winifred Byng very much enjoyed the jubilee festivities celebrating fifty years of the reign of Queen Victoria. Porchey had agreed with his father that Winifred and Alfred should make Bretby their home for the time being and, while she was happy giving direction to the gardeners, her husband oversaw the agent's work. Porchey was never a consistent letter writer, but he did write when he had some news. There had been some frightening storms, they had all been tumbled around at sea and at one point Mr Cawes, the captain, was desperately ill, delirious, and unconscious for well over a day. Consequently, Porchey had had to take the helm in the high seas and, with the help of the good first mate, bring the boat safely into harbour. Another time, when the ship's doctor had to operate on one of the crew, Porchey had to administer the chloroform and be the anaesthetist which, he reported, he did with calm efficiency but closely following instructions.

Aphrodite eventually berthed in Buenos Aires where they found a prosperous city with a skyline of spires and cupolas. The yacht was made most welcome and all on board invited to attend the opera. Argentina had strong trading links to Britain. Over the last thirty years, British capital invested in Argentina had increased from £2.6 to £45.6 million by 1885 but visiting yachts were still most unusual. It was, after all, a very long way to travel. Lord Porchester sent an invitation to the President to dine with him on board and received various businessmen as well.

He wrote amusing letters back to his sister and related how, when he had mentioned how much he enjoyed opera and that he could, with limitations, play the piano, he then found himself called upon to replace the opera's missing accompanist at a rehearsal. 'He admitted – for he loved telling a story against himself – that the request was never repeated' as he related that he could only accompany the artists 'according to his, rather than their notion of time'.

By December, Lord and Lady Carnarvon were at Government House in Melbourne for a series of receptions and Porchey was considering whether to sail on further to perhaps meet up with them. They were all therefore abroad when Winifred's husband Alfred Byng suddenly collapsed and died. A widow after only ten months of marriage, she was just 22 years old. She had to let his family know but asked if the burial could take place at Highclere. Her brother and parents sent wreaths and her aunts Lady Portsmouth and Lady Gwendolen met her from the train with the family rallying around.

After Buenos Aires, *Aphrodite* then went on to Cape Town and Porchey kept his sister in touch and did his best to offer her distraction with his adventures. Like many before him, he decided to engage a guide to hunt big game. Being Porchey, in his case the role of hunter and hunted were soon reversed. Accompanied by a single guide, he lay in wait for an elephant and in due course one appeared. But Porchey missed his shot and, after checking to see if there was any sight of his quarry, slid down the tree to amble back to camp. He was making his way across some flat ground to the trees on the other side when he realized that he was being stalked by the elephant. He had no time to reload but instead took to his heels with a speed he never imagined he could achieve, dropping his rifle, cartridge bag, binoculars and coat, all of which he flung to the ground as he ran for dear life with the elephant in hot pursuit. He reached the shelter of the trees again and clambered desperately up one of them, deciding there and then never again to go after another elephant.

On one occasion, after a night out, Porchey hired a boat to take him back to his yacht, which was moored some distance from the shore. He was helming whilst a couple of local fishermen plied the oars when suddenly, roughly equidistant between land and the safety of *Aphrodite*, the fishermen dropped oars and gave him a choice of paying them a large sum of money or being pitched into the water. He listened quietly and motioned to them to pass his dressing bag, which they did, presumably imagining they were going to be given the ransom money. Unfortunately for them, the situation was swiftly reversed when Porchey extracted not a well-stocked wallet but a revolver. Pointing it at the hapless pair, he sternly bade them to row on or he would shoot. Porchey thought this was a very funny story and later greatly enjoyed telling it to everybody.

He eventually returned to London in the winter of 1888, by which time he was once again quite ill with bronchitis. His father was also not well, and the family had decamped to Portofino. Porchey followed them out, but it was not a happy journey. First he was robbed en route to Belgium and then laid up in bed in Milan. His father noted, 'he reports himself better and the doctor satisfied though he cannot come on at once. I have offered to go to him and telegraphed', but his valet, Mr West, passed on the message that they were setting off for Genoa. By February 1889 both father and son were back in London, though neither was particularly well. Lord Carnarvon had had a very bad fainting fit but Margaret was being presented by Elsie and Lord Carnarvon was very proud of the two ladies as they set off – they 'looked very nice in their dresses when they went to court'.

Porchey decided to find warmer weather in Egypt, returning in May to find his father not feeling very strong. Porchey immediately offered to represent him at a funeral he had to attend. His old school friend Prince Victor was now in the Army and assigned to his regiment in Halifax, Nova Scotia, where he was not entirely enjoying himself. He was a man far more cut out for the theatres and music halls of London than a parade ground and military duties. In any case, Porchey would have made poor company for his friend as he was seriously unwell: his father thought he had 'poisoned himself with over-smoking'.

Porchey took time out to recover at Bretby and was trying to decide whether to sell it or lease it when his father suggested that they let it to a relative, Sir John Ogilvy. That settled, he spent the autumn shooting before leaving for Australia with his father's blessing to meet some of his contacts there and report back on the family investments. At that time, few sons travelled quite so extensively as Porchey, and the newspapers reported that it was largely because of his health, which had been poor for some time. He arrived at Melbourne House as the guest of the Earl and Countess of Hopetoun and attended numerous events including a grand civic lunch in Sydney before returning home via India.

Lord Carnarvon was sorry to see his son leave but that Christmas at Highclere he nevertheless noted that he felt thankful for all 'the blessings and happiness which are around me'. He had found and was busy editing unpublished letters from *Lord Chesterfield's Letters to His Son and Godson*, which he prefaced with a dedication to his own son: 'My dear Porchester . . . the great-grandson of Philip Stanhope – the godson of the great Lord Chesterfield.' He hoped to publish them early the next year, which sadly began with yet another funeral, that of the poet Robert Browning who had been a regular guest at Highclere. Lord Carnarvon was determined to attend.

In typical fashion, Porchey had left his father to deal with a summons issued against him for not having a gun licence, having forgotten to renew it in time. His father organized solicitors to represent his conveniently absent son although, in his defence, Porchey had not been seen actually shooting, although he was out with beaters and dogs. While his father was far from thrilled about the whole business, in the end the case was dismissed.

The final decade of the century began with a happy occasion as the family gathered in Brighton where Lord Carnarvon was recuperating. Lady Portsmouth noted in her diary: 'dear Winifred has engaged herself to Mr Herbert Gardner [the Liberal MP for Saffron Waldon in Essex] – worse luck – a natural son of the late Ld Gardiner, but if he cares for her and is well principled and good tempered what more can you wish – she is a sweet dear child and I wish her happy.'

Porchey was sad to miss the wedding, but he really did not feel well. Elsie helped organize it and the bride wore a beautiful peach-coloured dress embroidered with Neapolitan violets. The carriage and horses had been sent from Highclere and although it was already March, there was still snow on the ground, which Lord Carnarvon felt was 'very strange'. Winifred, however, very much desired her father to give her away and could see his health was fading. 'Dear Winifred. I trust it will be a happy marriage . . . everyone speaks well of him, and I like what I see of him' and Mr Gardner was described 'as the handsomest man in the House of Commons'. After the wedding, the couple then left by special train for Holwood House in Kent, which had been lent to them for their honeymoon by the Earl of Derby.

The remainder of the family returned to London before departing for Portofino, where Lord Carnarvon hoped he could rest and have a pleasant, quiet time in the fresh air for the next six weeks, reading and writing. He wrote that the years of this marriage 'had been eventful years to me and mine, and with some cause for anxieties and troubles, but filled up to the brim with causes for continuous thankfulness'. In that vein, he had had inscribed over the entrance to their house in Portofino 'Reddens Deo gratias et redditurus' (Giving thanks to God).

The newlyweds joined them so that Winifred could spend precious time with her father and ensure that Herbert could get to know him a little. One rather unexpected outcome of the holiday was that her husband had an attack of malarial fever, misdiagnosed in Italy and for which he had to be treated later in London. In May, Lord Carnarvon felt strong enough to return to the House of Lords and Elsie tentatively sent out cards to an 'At Home', but it was all suddenly cancelled as once more her husband became ill to the point where he even had to be carried up and down stairs.

Recognizing how ill his father was but with the optimism of youth and hoping for the best, Porchey agreed to be presented at a levee at St James's Palace by Viscount Lascelles, which he knew would please his father.

6

MY FATHER'S HOUSE

In June, Lord Carnarvon's family were gathered around him in his bedroom in his London house. Elsie had sought every medical treatment possible; no stone had been left unturned and no leading doctor had failed to be consulted. Over the last few weeks her husband had become ever more uncomfortable, unable to keep any food down, his joints aching. He had always been slim but now the skin on his hands seemed paper-thin and it was painful for him to be touched.

His brother Dr Alan Herbert, who was in attendance, was aware that his brother's body was simply shutting down and there was nothing that could be done. As a leading political figure, the state of his health was reported on most days throughout the country and in Ireland as well as in newspapers further afield. 'The latest information as to Lord Carnarvon's condition shows, we regret to say, that his lordship is sinking.' It was 'some sort of neuralgic gout combined with an influenza'. Lord Carnarvon died at 5 p.m. on Saturday 28 June at the age of 59, surrounded by his beloved wife Elsie, his children and his brothers and sister. Later, Lady Portsmouth thought she must have dreamed hearing that his last words were 'very happy'. Knowing much of the Bible so well, his family knew he left in peace, trusting in God as Jesus said, 'in my Father's house there are many rooms . . . I will not leave you. . . come to me'. His faith had upheld him in the most difficult times: he had chosen for Evelyn's monument an adaptation of words from Psalm 21, striking in its acceptance of the life to come as being life in all its blessings: 'We asked life of thee and thou gavest her a long life even for ever and ever.'

He had been a good man and a successful one. 'He was intensely popular among his tenants and the poor; and in the adjacent town of Newbury, he was idolised. No statesman acted from higher motives and was more entirely devoted to his country's good. He was the pleasantest of hosts, and had an immense knowledge of the inner life of the political.' He understood his son's passion for travel and he had himself travelled widely as a young man, publishing an edition of his own father's travel journals from Greece and Lebanon which were very much sought after when they first appeared. He was also a very fine classical scholar.

Both the Queen and the Prince of Wales were immediately informed and sent messages of condolence to his widow and family, along with many others. The Empress Frederick, who had stayed with them at Portofino several times, was prompt to leave her calling card, as did a host of ambassadors. The body was transferred to Highclere where the coffin was placed in the Library so that the local dignitaries could also pay their respects.

The funeral took place on 3 July. At 10.15 a.m., a special train left Paddington with Col. the Hon. H. Byng representing the Queen, Lord Sheffield representing the Prince of Wales and Lord Lathom (the Lord Chamberlain) representing the Grand Lodge of English Freemasons. In addition, the train stopped at Slough to pick up the Prime Minister, the Marquess of Salisbury.

Given that the Queen and other members of the royal family wished to express their condolences, and the social stature of many of the other guests, the order of service had been carefully put together with the help of Lord C's brothers along with Elsie's brother. Winifred was not at all well and Porchey missed her acutely but found the calm demeanour of his uncle Alan immensely reassuring.

Elsie was just 34 years old and overborne with grief. She was escorted by her brother Stafford Howard of Greystoke Castle as well as her mother and sister. The party gathered in the great central saloon of the Castle before the procession set off, the coffin covered in a purple cloth but with so many wreaths that it could not be seen. The wreath from the Queen read, 'A mark of regard from Victoria RI', and the congregation was an extraordinary mixture of clergy, peers, farm workers, gardeners, local representatives, agents from Lord Carnarvon's estates and house staff. Lord Salisbury led the mourners on foot as the procession slowly made its way to the cemetery. Elsie had arranged for white flowers to be distributed to everyone who followed, which were afterwards laid on the coffin. The hymns began with 'When the day of toil is done, When the race of life is run, Father, grant Thy wearied one, Rest for evermore', a tune so familiar that, while only a few of the mourners could fit inside the chapel itself, everyone waiting outside joined in the singing. The service was followed by luncheon in the Castle after which the Prime Minister and the others who had travelled down from London returned, again by special train, to town. Porchey was exhausted: it was only a week after his twenty-fourth birthday and he felt white with the effort of presenting a dignified appearance.

Elsie had also arranged for a commemorative service to be held at Chapel Royal of the Savoy at one o'clock on the same day as the funeral. This was also entirely full: Mr and Mrs Gladstone attended as did Lord and Lady Derby and many other members of the House of Lords, the House of Commons and the Freemasons.

The death of Lord Carnarvon left a huge gap in every way, from his experience of handling a multitude of roles to his academic achievements. By common consent, 'his family, the neighbourhood, and the country had sustained [a great loss] by the death of Lord Carnarvon'. From early scholarly distinction, the 4th Earl had acquired both an enormous number and hugely diverse collection of roles, which included High Steward at Oxford University, High Steward at Newbury, Pro-Grand Master of Freemasons, President of the British Archeological Association, President of the Society of Antiquaries, Constable of Carnarvon Castle, patron of many churches and livings, Lord Lieutenant of Ireland, Lord Lieutenant of Hampshire, politician and member of innumerable charitable boards, all of which he managed with calm and unfailing courtesy. The eulogies spoke of a chivalrous man, for whom the word courteous summed up a character marked by 'a kind, gentle manner, and entire banishment of pride, or any semblance of superiority in mixing with others, whether high or low'.

He was a traveller in the truest sense. In reality he journeyed widely due in part to inclination and in part to the exigencies of his responsibilities, but he was also a wide and eclectic reader, always studying new subjects. East or west, from architecture to modern political machinations, it all appealed to him. He was also a spiritual man and his faith never failed him: 'there lies the City of God'. Ultimately, he was one of the great Victorian statesmen upon which the British Empire was built and sustained: intelligent and articulate, well educated, intellectually curious, humble in the face of his position and sure of the responsibility of his role in bettering the lives of his fellow man, whether they wanted to be improved or not.

In modern parlance, it was an almost impossible act to follow and there was much curiosity about the new Earl of Carnarvon. He was credited with having set the fashion (odious in the eyes of many) of wearing brown shoes but, given his youthfulness, it was hoped that he would have many years ahead of him in which to associate his honoured name with something more than just an unconventional fashion dictum.

The new Earl also needed space for his own grief and he found the company of his uncle immensely comforting. There was little that Dr Alan Herbert had not seen from his experiences of living through the Siege of Paris in 1871, where every day he was out in the streets simply helping those in need, working at the hospital and serving his local community in Paris. Close to his nephew, he was a loving support and together they went up to Bretby for a week before returning to Highclere and then going on to London and Paris respectively.

Almost Porchey's first task as the new Earl was to draw up his own will, dated 28 July 1890. He asked Winifred's husband to be one of the executors as well as the Hon. John Scott Montagu, later Lord Montagu, and Lord Moreton. It ensured that, in the event of his demise, his sisters were looked after and he included legacies to some of the staff (£100 to the butler Albert Streatfield, £100 to his valet George Fearnside, £100 to the agent James Augustus Rutherford along with one of his cigarette cases) as well as £500 to his friend Prince Victor Duleep Singh – presumably to have a riotous party in his memory.

Porchey wished both to do as he ought and yet still be free to travel. Racing at Trouville beckoned over the summer and, since Winifred was now happily married, his younger sister Margaret became a regular companion. He was made very welcome everywhere he went. With estates bringing in £40,000 a year, many society mamas were easily persuaded that their daughters just needed the opportunity to meet such an eligible young man.

In the autumn he went up to Bretby with his all sisters and from there they travelled to Greystoke Castle to meet up with Elsie for the formal reading of their father's will. As might be expected from a thoughtful husband, father, brother and friend, all were remembered and looked after. Elsie remained at Greystoke for the time being, but Porchey suggested that she might like to take up residence at Pixton in Devon with her two boys, Aubrey, now 10, and Mervyn, who was 8, along with Porchey's sisters Vera and Margaret. Aubrey was desolate at the loss of his father and Elsie thought she and the children would be happy at Pixton. It was also situated near her sister-in-law, Lady Portsmouth, who would stop sometimes with her en route to Eggesford ('went to Pixton, darling Elsie met me at the station . . . the children are bright and happy').

Afterwards, Winifred and her husband went back to Highclere with her brother and continued to act as his hostess, quietly stepping in as needed and forming a bridge between the house steward, the housekeeper and the cooks.

Along with the burden of the emotional loss, the young man, now Earl of Carnarvon, also felt the weight of the administrative detail and ongoing management of Highclere and the other estates. One of the key figures in his father's life was the agent Mr Rutherford, who lived with his family at White Oak, a house within the Highclere parkland just past the cricket ground. The young lord appreciated that much of estate life was about continuity and thus was most anxious that Rutherford would stay on and remain his right-hand man. It was also partly a recognition that he would rather not be held back by the detail of the day-to-day life if Rutherford were happy to continue with it.

Winifred was more than able to help with the household details while her brother preferred to concern himself with shooting, racing and travelling. Prince Victor had given up the Army, committed neither to its structure nor its lifestyle, and both he and his brother were frequent shooting guests. One of the new Earl's first acts was to set about building a large shoot, as was the fashion in this new era of competitive game shoots. Prince Victor's father had been very much the exponent of large, extravagant bags and had developed a much-admired shoot when he was at Elveden, and it had been the fashion on the Continent for years.

Carnarvon possessed the landscape, trees, coverts, history and acreage that were needed and so set out to create one of the most outstanding shoots. It also suited his bonhomie to acquire friends from all his travels and be able to invite them back to Highclere to shoot. Furthermore, it involved the whole rural community from boys working for pocket money to loaders, beaters and picker-uppers, all earning wages and needing to be fed.

Much of the future success of these plans could be put down to Carnarvon luring Henry Maber away from the Duke of Grafton's shoot to be the new head keeper at Highclere. A true countryman covering the estate on a stout cob, his salty language and experience enabled him to manage the large teams of men and boys working under him.

Shooting in the winter was followed by tennis, cricket and racing in the summer, all of which brought a continuous stream of friends, both new and old, to Highclere. One such new friend, who was both a great sportsman and a good shot (pigeon shooting), was René de Knyff. De Knyff was a keen automobile entrepreneur who earlier that year had been privileged to see the first car produced by Panhard et Levassor. Porchey was fascinated and wanted to know when he could try one.

In some ways, de Knyff was as unconventional and bohemian as the new Earl. During the next decade, he would become the standard-bearer for French motorists, investing some 5,000,000 francs in the car company after the death of its founder Émile Levassor, who was fatally injured in a crash while trying to avoid a dog. De Knyff became a pioneer of car racing and, later on in life, a president of Commission Sportive Internationale, now known as FIA. Between 1897 and 1903 he took part in eighteen car races, five of which he won. He always drove a Panhard et Levassor, wore a captain's cap, which he inevitably lost right after the start, and was famous for both his gentlemanly manners and his sportsmanship.

A year after his father's death, Carnarvon decided to sell the house in Portman Square and buy one in Berkeley Square instead. Irrespective of his family's constant admonitions to take more care of himself, Porchey's health was never good. He never did ease up on his shocking smoking habit which, combined with regular bouts of bronchitis and what we would probably recognize today as asthma, meant that his sisters were often extremely worried about him. His brother-in-law Herbert Gardner was also ill that summer with what was probably a resurgence of his earlier malaria but, in any case, they all went down to stay with Elsie at Pixton. Carnarvon was fond of his little brothers and Aubrey resembled him not just in looks but also in character in terms of his curiosity, his thirst for travel and his propensity to leap into the next project. Elsie was glad that Porchey seemed to have such a devoted valet in Fearnside and a useful secretary, James McCraw, to assist him in life, but the latest bout of illness really laid him low and sent him to the seaside to recuperate.

Of all the family, Elsie was the most serious-minded, managing her affairs and investments and those of the children. She was looking forward to returning to Portofino, a place which offered much solace and pleasure, but was slightly concerned as she had heard that 'The Queen does not care to pay another visit to Grasse, and she will not go to Cannes. M. Doane was instructed to make inquiries along the coast between Genoa and Spezia.' She had heard about the Carnarvons' house in Portofino and had expressed a desire to visit. Her daughter, Empress Frederick, had often spoken of her delightful visits to her mother but, to Elsie's relief, the house was not large enough for the Queen and all her entourage.

At Highclere, Rutherford had proposed that the reservoir on Siddown Hill to the south of the Castle should be renewed. A new one holding 135,000 gallons of water would not only supply the Castle and surrounding buildings with water but also a fire main circuit. This would be laid around the exterior of the Castle with a fire main running up through the building and fire hydrants on each floor. Carnarvon found it very interesting and liked the practicality of it.

Otherwise, he very much relied on Winifred to keep things ticking over and, at the drop of a hat, disappeared to Egypt in the winter months or to Monte Carlo for shooting with de Grey until January 1893, when he was brought up short by the sudden death of his cousin Claire, only 19 years old, who passed away while staying in Portofino with her father Auberon and other sisters.

Winifred reminded him that his younger sisters wanted to go to parties in London and that if he too went as a guest to a few weddings, he might find some of his dance partners rather charming.

Aubrey was now at Eton, having a mixed experience, much like his elder brother. His tutors complained he had too much money which he seemed to spend on a surfeit of sweets. Carnarvon sent him hampers on a regular basis and he wrote to his mother, 'when you see Porchey will you thank him so much for me. I ate the partridge and the pheasant Friday night.' Just like his half-brother, he kept pets but, instead of a snake, he kept a jackdaw, a squirrel and a white mouse.

7

TIME WILL TELL

THE FUTURE OF any girl of a certain class was, perhaps somewhat unfairly to modern eyes, decided in her first season. Anyone who failed to secure a proposal within a year of their coming-out ball could only wait for her second season with somewhat lowered hopes. After that, India might be a possibility.

On 9 May 1893, Lady Julia Wombwell presented her 17-year-old niece at court. Dressed in a simple but exquisite white dress, Almina walked carefully through the tall, gilded doors into the Throne Room of Buckingham Palace. Concentrating on keeping her head high and looking straight ahead, she performed a deep curtsey in front of the Queen. As one of five hundred debutantes presented that year, she attended a ball at Buckingham Palace two months later along with a myriad of other parties. Her cousin Miss Mabel Wombwell was now 30 years old and still attended some society events, which allowed for a certain amount of 'smudging' of society records of entrees.

Sir George and Lady Julia Wombwell were from a notable Yorkshire family who lived at Newburgh Priory, an old house famous for supposedly containing the remains of the seventeenth-century Protector of England, Oliver Cromwell. Sir George's younger brother Frederick had joined the Army and married Maria, a beautiful half-French, half-Spanish lady. Their only son (also Frederick) was born a year later but Captain Wombwell soon abandoned his role as husband and father for the delights of drinking and gambling, and it was the former that led to his death in 1889.

Meanwhile, his wife Marie had quietly met Mr Alfred de Rothschild and adored by him, now lived discreetly in a most elegant house in Bruton Street, Mayfair, dividing her time between London and Paris. Some eight years later, in 1876, a daughter was born. Marie, always known as Mina, named her child Almina (Wombwell) with Alfred nominally standing as godfather.

Given that Sir George and Lady Julia Wombwell had already skilfully guided three daughters through London society and that she was not able to move, without comment, in the same circles, Marie asked them if they would help their niece. Alfred did so by inviting Sir George to stay with him at Halton House from 1884 where, of course, Marie Wombwell was often a guest, especially if the soprano Adelina Patti was also staying. All the guests felt very privileged to be listening to her dazzling lyrical voice in impromptu pieces after dinner.

Alfred had met young Lord Carnarvon and they shared a love of opera. He had first asked the young man to stay at his house in the country in December 1892 but invited him back in August the following year when Marie Wombwell and her daughter Almina were staying. Alfred thought that the wayward, charming young man had a bit of spark and Lord Carnarvon in his turn enjoyed the conversation and music, amusing Almina with tales of the high seas, lucky escapes and careless bravery. He was entirely relaxed, much used to the company of his sisters at Highclere and enjoyed the admiration of a very pretty girl. Almina was petite and always beautifully dressed, so much so that later she was referred to as a 'Dresden doll' for her perfection of face and figure. She was well-read, loved music and obviously was fluent in French.

He could not help but confide to his sister Winifred in the hope that she might have come across Miss Wombwell with her aunt, Lady Julia. Fortuitously, Lady Julia's second daughter, Cecilia, was a contemporary of Winifred and had come out at the same time. In turn, Winifred related the story to her husband Herbert. Many of her and her brother's friends were getting married at this time, but it had been a while since she had heard her brother so enthusiastic about any girl, describing her as both beautiful and engaging. She certainly seems to have flattered the young Earl as he praised her as 'a wonderful listener'.

The 27-year-old Earl divided the summer of 1893 between London and various race meetings, before being invited once more to stay at Halton by Alfred de Rothschild, who had curated a small house party which included Mrs Marie Wombwell and Almina. Nothing came of their meeting, however, and, as was his habit, Carnarvon then dashed off to explore new climes, in this case Sweden, before returning for an autumn of shoots at his various estates. Prince Victor, meanwhile, was the guest of Elsie Carnarvon at Pixton and had agreed to take part in an amateur theatrical, *Time Will Tell*, a play in three acts written by Winifred's husband Herbert. Prince Victor was much admired for his role as Clodworth, before returning to join Carnarvon for various shooting expeditions along with de Grey, Ashburton and Alexander McDonnell at the beginning of October.

Shooting weekends were an excellent opportunity to return hospitality and Carnarvon invited a mixture of those whom he had met on his various travels along with more traditional English friends. The parties were invariably successful and the English admired the dress and vivacity of friends such as Bertha, Princess de Wagram, an ardent Anglophile who divided her time between her house on Avenue d'Alma in Paris and the Château de Grosbois. Born a Rothschild, she was much admired, managing even to charm Marcel Proust, and had married a prince, which meant she hosted the best of salons. Lord Carnarvon would always find an 'At home' awaiting him at his hotel whenever he was in Paris.

Halfway through the shooting season, Carnarvon suddenly took off for Berlin. There was a new bath chair type of motor car and a new opera: irresistible! But he was taken ill once again and forced to rest. Meanwhile, Princes Victor and Frederick had had to return to Paris to their father's bedside: an unhappy and forlorn man, the Maharajah Duleep Singh kept changing his mind about where he would spend the winter. Prince Frederick duly set off to London to find a house and, gathering that Lord Carnarvon was ill in Berlin, Prince Victor caught the train to join his friend.

Berlin was not to be enjoyed, however. On 21 October, having gone to the theatre, which was thriving in Berlin (Oskar Blumenthal had written a series of hits, including one in the English language), both men had enjoyed a late supper before retiring to their hotel. Prince Victor tended to leave the light on when he slept and, waking suddenly in the small hours, he found himself staring up at his father, who was gazing at him intently seemingly out of the picture frame on the wall of his room, rather like a hologram. Naturally somewhat startled, Victor got up and walking across the room, found, of course, that it was in fact just a painting of a girl holding a rose. He returned to bed and the next morning related the strange events to Lord Carnarvon over breakfast.

Shortly thereafter a telegram arrived. His father the Maharajah had suffered a seizure late on the Saturday evening and never recovered, dying on Sunday 22 October at the Hôtel de la Tremoille in Paris. Prince Victor felt wracked with guilt that he had not been there with him and, wholly distressed, immediately wanted to rush back. Carnarvon quietly helped him make the practical plans to return to Paris.

Queen Victoria and the Prince of Wales had been informed of the sad occasion by the Ambassador in Paris, Lord Dufferin, even before Prince Victor had heard the news.

'My dear Victor Duleep Singh, it is with sincere concern that I heard of the death of your father . . . Pray accept the expression of my warmest sympathy in your heavy loss . . . I shall always take the deepest interest in the welfare and happiness of yourself and your brother and sisters – always your affectionate friend and Godmother Victoria RI.'

The Maharajah's body was brought back to England and buried in a vault in the church at Elveden, in Norfolk. The coffin was covered in flowers and wreaths, including one of immortelles from Queen Victoria, while the Prince of Wales's wreath said simply, 'For auld lang syne'.

Lord Carnarvon stepped in to offer Bretby as a haven for Prince Victor and all his family for as long as they wished, and the Prince's stepmother, brother and all his sisters joined him there following the funeral. The agent arranged the house and undertook to make the Duleep Singh family comfortable for as long as they wished.

Later in the month, Carnarvon and his sisters persuaded Prince Victor to stay at Highclere, and then to be part of their family group at Pixton with Elise and his sisters, before they all returned in December to spend Christmas together at Highclere. It was very much a distraction as the New Year began with a servants' ball for eighty. It was chaired by both Mrs Powell, the housekeeper, and Mr Streatfield, the house steward, while the coachman, Mr Brickell, was vice-chair. All the house party, including Prince Victor, joined in the early dances enthusiastically, for which a Winchester band played tirelessly.

Elsie and the family stayed on at Highclere until they left for Paris, then went on to Rome before sailing for Cairo in Sir John Pender's yacht. Sir John was a Scottish-born cable pioneer and now MP and it was a huge treat as it was such a comfortable yacht. Afterwards, they all returned to stay in Portofino. Meanwhile, Winifred, her husband and Carnarvon had left directly for a short yachting cruise in the Mediterranean before arriving at Monte Carlo for the shooting competition, the Grand Prix du Casino.

Winifred was delighted that her husband, already on the Board of Agriculture and not merely handsome but noted as one of the best-dressed men in the House of Commons, had now been offered a peerage. In deference to the Carnarvon family, he took the title of Lord Burghclere, named for a local parish near the Castle.

Prince Victor and Frederick Duleep Singh had stayed behind in England as they were dealing with the remains of their father's estate and the somewhat depressing ensuing correspondence with the India Office. Naturally, they were still highlighted in all society newspaper columns as, following the death of the Maharajah, Queen Victoria had decided that Prince Victor was to be accorded the precedence of being after the royal dukes but before the Archbishop of Canterbury and his Grace the Duke of Norfolk. All agreed with Her Majesty that 'Prince Victor is said to be a most charming young man'. In between times both brothers attended a lovely wedding in London where Victor could not help but notice one of the bridesmaids, a tall, slim, dark-haired girl some 20 years old: Lady Anne Coventry.

Lord Carnarvon returned to Highclere in early summer, a beautiful time of year with the gardens ablaze with the showy azaleas that had been planted en masse and the promise of sunshine and longer light-filled days. He wanted to rid the lake of some of the large pike which were so destructive to broods of duck and restock it with trout, and he had heard of a novel way of doing so which both amused and amazed his friends. He decided to submerge dynamite charges at a depth of several feet which he then set off. Quite a number of the pike were indeed killed, but so was everything else and the mess was considerable. It was, moreover, a very large lake and the pike remained an issue.

As usual, much of June was spent in London and Carnarvon was there for the presentation at court of his youngest sister Vera. She was much admired at the Buckingham Palace State Ball and noted in all the papers as goddaughter to Her Majesty the Queen. Following the season, Vera left for Switzerland with her sister while Carnarvon, feeling exhausted, left for Aix-les-Bains. Whether it was the air pollution or the constant smell of ammonia due to the inordinate amount of horse manure on the streets, Carnarvon always found the air in London affected him quite badly, encouraging bronchitis to reappear even in summer. At Aix-les-Bains there were a number of excellent hotels, a good crowd, casinos, cards and racing.

The autumn began predictably with shooting at Highclere and Bingham. However, acceding to the path that many of his contemporaries were following, in October his life changed. To the chagrin of many mamas, all the papers excitedly announced the engagement of the Earl of Carnarvon to Miss Wombwell. Many of those reports were not quite right, stating that Miss Wombwell was the daughter of Sir George and Lady Wombwell. These were later corrected to acknowledge that she was their niece, with 'a very fair complexion and fair hair rather elaborately dressed' although often seen at the opera in the company of Mr Alfred de Rothschild.

8

'A YOUNG MAN IN POSSESSION OF A GOOD FORTUNE'

THE ENGAGEMENT CREATED enormous interest as the Earl was an exceedingly eligible bachelor with a large income, a number of excellent properties and a good name. He was even quite young. Other papers mentioned that Mrs Frederick Wombwell had a connection to the Rothschild family and that Alfred, whose liberalness was proverbial, had expressed his intention of settling a dowry as a marriage portion of £300,000 on Miss Wombwell.

Mr Alfred de Rothschild kindly invited all parties to stay with him at his 'humble' country retreat.

In November 1894 Lord Carnarvon and Prince Victor Duleep Singh arrived at Halton in time for tea. Immaculate liveried staff hurried towards the carriage that had conveyed them from the railway station and helped the guests descend from under the portico and step quickly out of the cold, dark afternoon. It was the first time Prince Victor had been invited and, as the gentlemen shook off their coats, they stood looking up and around at the brightly lit grandeur of the huge hall: it was immense, rising two storeys with a large glass dome and enormous chandeliers.

The house was spectacular. Completed in 1884 and built in the French style, it was situated west of London near the other great Rothschild family mansions, such as Waddesdon, Mentmore Towers and Ascott House. A Rothschild cousin described it as 'looking like a giant wedding cake'. The first guest had naturally been His Royal Highness the Prince of Wales, for whom 'Mr Alfred' organized a truly memorable weekend with his orchestra, a dance, floodlit fountains and gardens and, of course, exquisite food served in various sumptuous rooms.

The central saloon was flanked by four dramatic, stunning rooms with smaller, more intimate spaces providing a linking enfilade in between. A staircase ascended from one end, with palms and lights anchoring it as it swept up and divided towards the gallery bedrooms.

Throughout the chateau, the doors, friezes and woodwork were gilded in the elaborate eighteenth-century style, the decorations of swags, and the Rothschild arrows competed with monograms woven into woodwork and his possessions, such as his writing case. French silk tapestries, huge Chinese vases and classical statuary abounded and the house immediately felt incredibly luxurious, warm and comfortable. Even the lighting had been carefully considered in the planning, and allowance had been made to power the central heating, which required large coal bunkers hidden under the house. The fireplaces were well stocked with wood as well as coal and, since the temperature was dropping outside, it was all very welcome.

Lord Carnarvon had already stayed several times at Halton, but Prince Victor was delighted by the invitation. The two young men were shown across the Great Hall and into the South Drawing Room, where tea was to be served and a welcome fire was already blazing. The house party was organized with Rothschild's usual care and thus Miss Almina Wombwell was already seated there with her mother and her face lit up when Lord Carnarvon entered. He went straight across, smiling, to bow and kiss her hand. Mr Alfred entered, bidding them all to sit down and enquiring after Carnarvon's and Victor's journey.

Alfred de Rothschild, often known as 'Mr Alfred', was not a tall man but he was always immaculate. Despite his lavish hospitality, his slim figure reflected his abstemious nature and the careful dietary advice of his doctors. Fastidious about his dress, he was equally meticulous about every detail which would ensure perfect comfort and elegance for each guest. Tea was offered on the prettiest of china, enquiries made, of course, as to whether each guest would prefer tea from Ceylon, China or India, whether milk or lemon was preferred, before considering the tempting tiny cakes on offer.

After tea, Mr Alfred asked if his guests would like to see some of his favourite paintings, saying he had some new acquisitions to show Almina's betrothed. Lady Dorothy Nevill, a frequent guest at Highclere and a stalwart of the social scene, considered Mr Alfred 'the finest amateur judge of French 18th century art in England'. He was both a connoisseur and an aesthete, delighting in living with his art and sharing it with friends. Whether it was a painting by Boucher, Lancret or Watteau, each was of the highest quality: beautiful arcadian tableaux which in some ways reflected the beautiful scenes created in reality at Halton. The Winter Garden in particular was famous. Classical marble pillars led you into the Orangery, built in quatrefoil shape under a large glass dome with symmetrical wide stone steps leading from each side. Full of exotic plants, palm trees and orchids, it gave Mr Alfred as well as his guests much pleasure.

It was this love of collecting that Mr Alfred had in common with Carnarvon. From a young boy, Carnarvon had taken much pleasure in collecting, from stamps to blue and white porcelain. He felt there was an intrinsic joy in holding and looking at something made in centuries past, and if it was rare it was even more interesting. The rooms at Highclere likewise bore witness to centuries of collecting by his own family, of choices made for beauty or rarity.

Almina and her mother had left to rest and change for dinner. Almina had decided she was completely in love and her mother could not have been happier.

Dinner was laid in the Bampfylde Room, dominated by and named for the Joshua Reynolds painting of Lady Bampfylde. Nothing was too much trouble; the French chefs provided outstanding food and the best Rothschild wines were served. The evenings would often be enlivened by a performance by Mr Alfred's own private orchestra which he would himself conduct with a diamond-encrusted baton. He even insisted that every member of the orchestra looked equally smart with the same neatly trimmed moustaches. After dinner, just as at Highclere, there was a well-appointed billiard room decorated with an outstanding painting by Jacob Jordaens. A Flemish painter, draughtsman and tapestry designer, after Reubens and Van Dyck he was considered the leading Flemish Baroque painter of the day. Carnarvon would soon have realized that he was looking at an outstanding collection and, even at this stage of his life, his interest in collecting would be piqued.

The shoot the next day was equally well orchestrated, with Mr Alfred preferring to ensure all was well rather than shoot himself. He was, of course, perfectly dressed for the occasion and, just in case anything went wrong, Mr Alfred's doctor with his medical bag accompanied the guns as well.

He was, however, equally solicitous to those who were working – Sir Algernon West recorded in his diary that 'in the cold bitterness of winter mornings he [Alfred] sent a cart round every morning with hot coffee and bread and butter to every labourer on his estate'.

Sunday was a day less for church and spiritual observance than for amusement and exploration of the grounds. Mr Alfred was very concerned about fire breaking out at Halton so he kept his own fire brigade permanently on standby and Lord Carnarvon wanted to show Prince Victor the splendid horse-drawn fire engine.

The visit also offered the opportunity to discuss the date of the wedding, the guests, church and entertainment. Lord Carnarvon had asked Prince Victor to be his best man and Mr Alfred indicated that it would be his pleasure to offer his help in all aspects of the wedding.

The subject of the dowry had already been broached, as had some help with the young bridegroom's outstanding debts of some £150,000 (£21 million in 2022). Mr Alfred was most obliging and hoped that the young man would take best advantage of his advice in the future.

The marriage settlement, dated 25 June 1866, was between three people: Alfred de Rothschild, Miss Almina Wombwell and the Earl of Carnarvon. Beautifully written on vellum, Alfred set out that he was making provision for Almina and that, once the marriage was solemnized, the first payment of £12,000 would be made and thereafter half yearly (about £1.5 million today). The capital sum was set out as £500,000 and the settlement also set out the stock and debentures in which it could be invested. Security was key. Equally, Alfred insisted that, where he was able to, the 5th Earl offered up Highclere and Pixton House and estate as security so that Alfred could help contain any borrowings.

Returning to London by special train provisioned by baskets of treats from Mr Alfred's chef, Lord Carnarvon hurried off to Paris. Staying at the Ritz Hotel, he had noticed a shop open just opposite on a sunny corner at 26 Place Vendôme. The jeweller Frédéric Boucheron had established his business in this new 'maison' just a year earlier, in 1893. Already appreciated for his beautiful creations and gem cutting, Boucheron had also had the innovative idea of combining pearls with diamond rondelles. Lord Carnarvon asked him to help him design a tiara and necklace for his bride-to-be as well as purchasing some diamond and pearl necklaces.

Returning to Highclere to shoot, the following weekend he welcomed his fiancée and her mother to Highclere. On Saturday 15 December Carnarvon asked his sister Winifred to join them for supper and to help him ensure that it was all a great success. Winifred later said of Almina that she was 'very pretty, with an immaculate figure and tiny waist'.

Winifred had asked her husband what he thought. 'P is not the sort of person to marry merely for money . . . he likes the girl and that being so, the rest will follow'. Herbert had seen Porchey with Mr Alfred at Seamore Place and told her: 'It is practically settled about Almina. You will hear from him yourself no doubt and from the others so I will not enlarge on the topic but I think you may ease your mind on the subject and hope for the very best.'

While looking forwards to his wedding, and feeling rather prosperous, Carnarvon decided that this was the moment to charter a yacht and sail towards South America, very happy to leave the wedding arrangements to his bride-to-be and her mother.

He chose the steam yacht *Catarina* (531 tonnes) from Mr Rattray and was busy fitting her out at Gosport to make ready, asking Prince Victor to accompany him. Crossing the Atlantic would take three weeks, perhaps closer to four, and they would then sail south, although they knew they would have to return by late April as Prince Victor's younger sisters were to be presented at court. Almina wanted to go with him, so excited at being engaged to be married.

Winifred read her husband's letter from London: 'I have seen Elsie, who is very good and a dear about Porch – and A. who seems to live there. I do not think [she] can keep it secret any time – she was literally bursting with it . . . she seems to be head over ears in love and says why can't we be married and go on the yachting cruise.' Rather fortunately, in those days, of course, she could not just sail off with a young man to whom she was not yet married and the cruise was more adventurous than expected, with bad weather anticipated.

Arriving in Lisbon in December 1894, Carnarvon bought a beautiful logbook bound in marbled paper and red leather in which he planned to record the voyage. The first few days were diligently written up with a description of the voyage first to Madeira and then onto Tenerife, where they experienced some atrocious weather and were forced to linger for a week. Carnarvon got in some shooting and complained that his valet was unwell and running a temperature of 104.

Prince Victor, a far less experienced sailor, turned to prayer to keep his spirits up and wondered if he had made the right decision. From Tenerife, they set sail as soon as they could to catch the easier trade winds across the Atlantic, crossing the equator on 19 January and reprovisioning in Cape Verde. The logbook entries become fewer and less descriptive, but Carnarvon loved the sound of the waves, the groans and creaks of the yacht and watching as the weather ebbed and flowed, ensuring a taut rope was lashed to the wheel in bigger seas. They sailed as far as the Falkland Islands, reaching Port Stanley on 11 February, and, after two weeks' exploration, set off home again.

One of the prerequisites of his later career as an excavator in Egypt would be stoicism in the face of the heat and dust and, with most days, very little to show for it. Perhaps in the loneliness and silence of ocean sailing Carnarvon developed the quiet inner peace to help cope with the pursuits and challenges that were to come later in his life.

9

WEDDING INVITATIONS WERE prepared and the church was booked. Mr Alfred adored arranging parties and was studiously flamboyant himself. He had, for example, achieved some notoriety as, in place of the lion cub that he could be seen with a year earlier, he had now acquired two zebras in his stables who would pull his carriage.

Meanwhile, early in 1895 Almina and her mother had visited Worth in Paris. Mr Alfred was delighted to provide the wedding trousseau, although Almina confided to a friend that she was exhausted after standing for hours on end while the dresses were fitted. She was now 19 and a bridesmaid herself at several London weddings in April and May. She much enjoyed them and gained some knowledge of the music which she would like. One magazine with a rather waspish bent noted that she was being gifted a number of beautiful jewels and commented that, given she was so petite, there would soon be more jewels than countess.

Prince Victor rented a smart house at 18 Park Lane, Mayfair, for his sisters' season. In due course, and as a favour to her brother's best friend, Lady Winifred Gardner was pleased to present the Princesses Bamba, Sophie and Catherine Duleep Singh at a drawing room at Buckingham Palace, not merely in the presence of Her Majesty the Queen but also of the Prince and Princess of Wales and other members of the royal family. They looked very distinguished in their court gowns of white and silver. Prince Victor and Frederick, as well their sisters, were later included in a State Ball followed by a State Concert to encourage other leading ladies to follow the royal example and include them in their parties, too. In addition, Prince Victor had promised to give them all a dance in June with a magnificent oriental theme.

In 1894, the two princes had bought Hockwold Hall, in Norfolk, as their family base and readily took on their local responsibilities, from distributing presents at Christmas to planning a dinner for those who had worked on the new extension to the Hall later in the summer.

The Earl of Carnarvon, immaculately dressed, with a perfectly starched collar and a carnation buttonhole provided by the Rothschild carnation house, stood next to his best man, Prince Victor, by the entrance to the chancel of the ancient parish church of St Margaret's Westminster. The church could seat 750 but seemed modest compared to its next-door neighbour, Westminster Abbey. It was the bridegroom's twenty-ninth birthday and, being superstitious, he thought it was lucky that they coincided. Winifred and her husband, as well as Elsie, Aubrey, various Howard cousins, the Earl of Pembroke and the Earl and Countess of Portsmouth, were seated in the rows behind him. They all felt it was such an entirely happy day for Porchey, for whom they wished nothing but the best. Predictably, he had chosen an unexpected bride but his journey in life had already taken many innovative turns and each generation sailed its own course.

More guests arrived to fill the church, among them the Earl and Countess of Bathurst, the Cadogans, shooting and school friends from Lord Ashburton to Lord de Grey, the Marquis and Marchioness of Bristol. The Duchesses of Marlborough and Devonshire were in attendance, as were Lord and Lady Charteris and the greater part of London society. Lord Rosebery, the former Prime Minister, was also a guest. He had travelled to Windsor Castle just four days earlier to offer his resignation to the Queen, who then asked Lord Salisbury to form a government. Queen Victoria, at 76 years old, sent greetings to the young couple.

Behind the bride's mother and brother, Alfred, were the Wombwell cousins and many friends and relations of Alfred de Rothschild. Baron and Baroness de Worms, Baron Ferdinand de Rothschild, Baron Adolphe de Rothschild, Lady de Rothschild, Mr Reuben Sassoon, four other Sassoon cousins, Mr Wertheimer, Mr and Mrs Ephrusi, Baron and Baroness de Hirsch. Both Marie and Sir Alfred had a great many friends in the theatre and the celebrated prima donna Adelina Patti, now Madame Ernesto Nicolini, was also a guest.

St Margaret's was beautifully decorated with tall palms, exquisite white lilies, orchids, peonies, carnations and hundreds of roses. The bridegroom had persuaded the Rev. John Troutbeck, who had been chaplain to his father, as well as the Rev. Hugh Rycroft, rector of Highclere, to assist the rector of St Margaret's, the Rev. Herbert Moore. St Margaret's could not have been a more fitting choice for the wedding, as it had just been refurbished by Sir George Gilbert Scott, the celebrated Victorian architect, who had completed the commission of the new Highclere church just twenty years earlier.

As the sun poured through the new stained-glass windows that depicted English heroes across the centuries, at 2 p.m. Mr Baines, the organist, struck up the opening chords of the hymn 'The voice that breathed o'er Eden' and Almina, on the arm of her uncle Sir George Wombwell, stood framed in the light of the door before walking nervously down the aisle.

She wore a small wreath of orange blossom under a veil of fine silk tulle. Her dress was by Charles Worth, the most fashionable couturier of the age and known for his use of lavish fabrics and trimmings. Almina's dress was made of the richest *duchesse* satin, with a full court train and draped in a veil of lace caught up on one shoulder. The skirts were threaded with real orange flowers and Almina was wearing a gift from the bridegroom: a piece of very old and extremely rare French lace that had been incorporated into the dress.

Eight bridesmaids and two pages followed Almina: she had, of course, asked Porchey's two sisters, Lady Margaret and Lady Victoria Herbert, to be her bridesmaids, as well as Prince Victor's sisters Princess Kathleen Singh and Princess Sophie Singh and also some of her friends from her last two years in London – Lady Kathleen Cuffe, Miss Evelyn Jenkins, Miss Wombwell and Miss Davies. The bridesmaids were dressed after a design in a picture by eighteenth-century artist George Romney in cream silk muslin over white satin skirts trimmed with pale blue ribbons. Large cream straw hats also trimmed with silk muslin, feathers and ribbons completed a charming picture. In addition, each had a beautiful ruby and diamond brooch decorated with the initials of the bride and bridegroom and carried loosely arranged bouquets of Rothschild carnations, both gifts from Lord Carnarvon. The two pages, the Hon. Mervyn Herbert and Lord Arthur Hay followed, dressed in Louis XV court costumes of white and silver, with hats to match.

The couple left the church to Wagner's 'Bridal March' from *Lohengrin*, recalling Elsie's wedding at Greystoke on Boxing Day 1878. They were now 5th Earl and Countess of Carnarvon. A new life lay ahead of them.

Elsie, the 5th Earl's stepmother, had been delicately trying to liaise

THE DISCOVERY OF TUTANKHAMEN'S TOMB.

The Man to Whom the World Owes the Discovery

Special Sphere picture by Lewis J. Steele

LORD CARNARVON LEAVES HIGHCLERE CASTLE ON AN ARCHÆOLOGICAL EXPEDITION

It is owing to the persistence of Lord Carnarvon and his able chief of staff, Mr. Howard Carter, through seventeen years of labour, that the world owes the great discovery of King Tutankhamen's tomb. Lord Carnarvon is a man of many attainments; he is well known, amongst other things, as an archæologist and amateur photographer. He is the fifth earl, the first being the Hon. Henry Herbert, later Baron Porchester, and Earl of Carnarvon in 1793. In the above picture he is seen setting off from Highclere on an archæological expedition with a camera tucked under his arm

The Sphere's front-page report of the 5th Earl and the discovery of the tomb of Tutankhamun, February 1923.

The Drawing Room, Highclere Castle c.1895.

Highclere Castle c.1900.

A shooting party outside the castle. (Left to right) Lord Ashburton, Lord Carnarvon,
Prince Frederick Duleep Singh, Prince Victor Duleep Singh, J. Rutherford esq.

A shooting party including the Prince of Wales, December 1895, outside of the Grotto Lodge.

Family photos. (Clockwise from top left) George's mother, the 4th Countess of Carnarvon (*née* Lady Evelyn Stanhope); George's father, the 4th Earl, Henry Carnarvon; his wife, Almina, the 5th Countess of Carnarvon with their son, later the 6th Earl; George's half-brother, the Honourable Colonel Aubrey Herbert; and his elder sister, Lady Winifred Herbert.

The inauguration of the Highclere Golf course.

Lord Carnarvon makes the cover of *The Tatler*, March 1909.

The first flight by Geoffrey de Havilland, September 1910.

Geoffrey de Havilland sitting in his aerial motor, 1910.

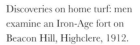

Discoveries on home turf: men examine an Iron-Age fort on Beacon Hill, Highclere, 1912.

Driving through the Valley of the Kings, February 1923. Lord Carnarvon is seated back right in the Ford Motor.

Lord Carnarvon with his daughter Evelyn (left) and Howard Carter (below), February 1923.

An early selfie of Lord Carnarvon, with Susie the dog encroaching.

with her stepson and Almina and Almina's mother to plan the wedding reception. She wrote to the Countess of Portsmouth, the Earl's devoted aunt, 'We have a family difficulty. We have neither called upon her [Mrs Wombwell] nor received her, though Almina of course has been with us constantly.' Elsie felt responsible for the younger sisters and did not want to compromise any propriety, and so she asked the advice of family friends such as Lord and Lady Stanhope as to what would be an appropriate venue for the wedding breakfast. Her stepson was wholly uninterested in such social niceties, which was awkward, but fortunately Mr Astor offered the loan of Lansdowne House, on the south side of Berkeley Square, and Almina's mother, Marie, agreed that this would be most acceptable. It was a most impressive London house.

Alfred de Rothschild immediately orchestrated the reception with Almina's mother. Lansdowne House was designed by Robert Adam with many elegant reception rooms. Every room was filled with flowers from hydrangeas to palms and ferns, 'gloxinias of rich and varying hue were used for one room's decoration, red and pink roses with wreaths of smilax for another, and tall white lilies for other'. Through the courtesy of Mr Alfred, Gottlieb's famous orchestra was there to play the latest fashionable music. Refreshments were served in one of the rooms, while in another there was a wedding breakfast, a high three-tier bride's cake adorning the centre table. Near the bride and groom sat Prince Edward of Saxe-Weimar, Elizabeth Countess of Carnarvon and Mrs Wombwell. Elsie was handsomely attired in a toilette of silver-grey *duchesse* satin, adorned with a Marie Antoinette fiche of antique Brussels lace, while Mrs Wombwell wore a very dark purple-shot silk dress, veiled with black silk embroidered muslin, and a bonnet to correspond trimmed with black and white fancy ribbon and little soft ostrich tips.

The wedding was without doubt a society 'crush'. The presents were displayed in the rooms and ranged from gifts from the staff at

Highclere and Bretby, which Lord Carnarvon thought so kind, to Louis XVI vases, enamel tables, silver boxes, brooches, and, of course, Lord Carnarvon's present to his bride: a high diamond crown, an emerald and diamond tiara, a rare pearl and diamond necklace, a long row of pearls, a diamond and sapphire bracelet, ruby and diamond bangles, dress ornaments and some carefully chosen rings. The bride gave her husband some beautiful gifts, selected with the help of Mr Alfred, including two aquarelles by the Chevalier de Lespinasse. They depicted charming Parisian scenes and her husband was delighted.

After the reception, the bride changed into a travelling dress of very fine pink gauze, printed with a design of shaded roses, a collar of delicate rose-pink velvet, wrought with pearls and finely blended colours.

Leaving their guests, the newly married couple were driven by Henry Brickell, Lord Carnarvon's head coachman, from Mayfair to Paddington, where Mr Alfred had arranged a special train to take the young couple to Highclere. From Highclere station, the under-coachman, Arthur Hayter, drove them through the London Lodge entrance and into the park. From this point, Mr Alfred's organization ceased and Mr Rutherford, Highclere's agent, took over. Highclere's park was in full leafy beauty and the entrance gate, the first point of welcome, was adorned with a 'Welcome Home' sign. At the crossroads in the centre of the park two outer towers had been constructed, standing tall and wide with an archway composed of 'foliage of conifers, brightly relieved with sprays of the golden yew'. Blue letters on a white ground proclaimed 'Health and Happiness'. Lord C stopped the coach at this point and the horses were removed from the traces while the bridegroom took the opportunity to shrug off his long formal coat and swap it for a favourite, much-darned blue jacket and a straw hat, both of which had been left in the landau for him.

The couple then climbed back into the carriage and ropes were attached by Bowsher, the farm foreman, and Scott, the forester foreman. The two men and eighteen other volunteers then pulled the landau under the archway and up the hill to the main door of the Castle, accompanied by a lively march from the Newbury town band, which had been paid seven guineas for its services.

The staff were thrilled that the couple had decided to spend their honeymoon at Highclere and some of the estate tenants were still in the gardens to watch proceedings. They had all been entertained in a marquee by the band and there had also been a tea party given for 330 of the local children. The whole event had been threatened by thunderstorms but luckily the weather had cleared in time for both the tea party and the arrival of the bride and groom. It was almost the longest day of the year, and the light was still good.

The front of the Castle had been decorated and there to greet the couple were Mr Streatfield, the house steward (a most superior butler), and Mr Rutherford and his wife. Wedding festivities at Highclere continued for the next two days for all employed there, as well as at Lord Carnarvon's Somerset and Devon estates.

Lord Carnarvon was familiar with the drives, the park fields, the woodland and downland from all his childhood rides with his sister. He knew without thinking where to walk or ride, what everything was called and where to find it, and quite often forgot how new and vast it must sometimes have seemed to his bride. Beyond the park were the neighbouring villages, local families and scattered throughout a community of 250 families who worked for different departments in the house and estate. Attending Highclere church for morning service on the Sunday after they were married involved Lord Carnarvon greeting everyone cheerily and assuming Almina would remember not only their names but how they fitted in.

In early July they attended a formal address in Newbury to which Lord Carnarvon replied, 'Mr. Mayor and gentlemen, on behalf of Lady Carnarvon and myself, I thank you most heartily for the good wishes which you, in your address, have expressed for us and for our future.'

The couple then left for France, first to Paris and then on to Aix-les-Bains. Lord Carnarvon very much liked this small town, in its heyday a mecca for high society, and it was great fun to introduce his young wife to its delights. He had taken rooms at the Hôtel Splendide, high on the surrounding hill with an excellent view across the glassy green lake. Almina had seen nothing like it. Queen Victoria had often visited it and theoretically stayed incognito as the Countess of Balmoral. Famous for its thermal baths as well as the calm of the Lac du Bourget, the town offered a wealth of entertainment from opera to dancing and music, including, of course, the casino. The casino included billiard rooms, cafés, salons for music and dancing, tables de jeux – the 'jeu' in this case being baccarat – as well as a most charming garden, in which guests could smoke and read. There was also a brand-new golf club. Given that Alfred de Rothschild had kindly discharged all the bridegroom's debts, Aix-les-Bains suited both of them very well.

The later part of the year was naturally spent shooting, beginning with two weeks on the grouse moors in Scotland where the Earl had taken one of Sir Charles Forbes' celebrated shoots in Aberdeenshire. The Delnadamph moor had by reputation yielded the heaviest bag of grouse on record – 3,279 brace in four weeks. Prince Victor and his sister Princess Sophie were part of the party, as were Mr and Mrs Rutherford from the Highclere estate and the Hon. Alexander McDonnell. Fortunately for the ladies they could attend the Lonach gathering later in the month. Lord Carnarvon then brought his bride to Bretby for a few days' partridge shooting, in which he was again to have the help of that crack shot Prince Victor Duleep Singh, along with Lord de Grey.

10

THE ROYAL VISIT

LORD CARNARVON THEREFORE spent much of the first six months of married life on a moor, in a shooting field or on the edge of a wood and, in the first haze of married life, Almina stood devotedly with him in all weathers. Mr Alfred had let them know that he had arranged a royal visit which would thus put the seal of approval on the wedding of the Earl and his new Countess. There was not much time to arrange everything for the visit but it was, of course, planned around a shoot in mid-December. HRH the Prince of Wales accepted the invitation from the Earl of Carnarvon and Mr Alfred had also written a note of grateful thanks to the Prince.

In many ways, the large driven shoots so prevalent at the time had developed because shooting was the passion of the Prince of Wales. His physique was not perhaps best suited to the hunting field, but the tradition and rhythm of a partridge and pheasant shoot entertained him throughout his life. Such shoots were a huge enterprise and formidably expensive. They had certainly in no small part contributed to the ruination of Prince Victor's father, for example.

Luckily, Lord Carnarvon's shoot held the record for the largest bag. He took it seriously and shot in a competitive spirit with de Grey, Ashburton and Lord Ripon, so much so that Lord Ashburton, an excellent shot, delighted in teasing Carnarvon that his keeper had not managed the beaters' line well enough, that the guns were not properly placed and so on. Carnarvon was an outstanding shot, and it had been something he had enjoyed so much with his father, who was also a good shot. He had passed on his calm and accurate approach. When Carnarvon succeeded his father, the annual bag was only about 2,000 pheasants and 500 partridges, but in the season 1895–6, Carnarvon and his friends killed nearly 11,000 in three days while the total bag was 32,000. Carnarvon described it as 'the most wonderful show of birds I have ever seen anywhere. The total of pheasants I believe beats anything previously shot.' In those days, of course, all the game was given away to the local community and nothing was ever wasted.

The head keeper could only run such a shoot with considerable help. There were some twenty-five under-keepers and, during the season, an army of beaters and picker-uppers with their dogs, while each gun needed three loaders and usually a boy as well. Highclere's undulating, wooded countryside and steep downland was a naturally beautiful backdrop and provided some excellent and challenging drives. The Prince of Wales was therefore rightly anticipating some fine sport.

Lord Carnarvon's planning for the royal visit concentrated almost solely on the shooting field and he was confident of a successful day, with interesting drives and well-stocked game. Almina had a far greater job with very little time left for planning between the invitation being accepted and the date of the royal visit. She had observed her mother's domestic management and, although well trained, she was still extremely young. Luckily, she had both the expertise and resources of Mr Alfred to draw upon and his organizational skills were second to none. With his guidance, she refurbished one of the large east-facing bedrooms which had a view of the temple across the lawns. She commissioned new hangings in royal red damask silk and a new matching red carpet, acquired a silver mirror, an exquisite clock, inlaid furniture and a huge new bed. He also offered help with the menus, wine and flowers, provided Gottlieb's Orchestra to play one evening and professional billiards players, as well a juggler, a conjurer and a very up-to-date Parisian singer on another. There were so many indoor amusements that, however unfavourable the weather, HRH could not have been bored.

Meanwhile, Streatfield, the house steward, and Mrs Bridgeland, the housekeeper, had to house and make arrangements for all the additional guests in the Castle, or at local pubs for the men. Mr Alfred engaged no fewer than nine chefs.

Below stairs at Highclere required significant management skills and appreciation of its own hierarchy. Mr Streatfield employed a senior butler and an under-butler, and fourteen footman, all of whom would be required to wear powdered wigs as well as their immaculate navy livery when serving at dinner. There was also a steward's room boy and a hall boy. Allied to his team but distinct from them was Fearnside, the valet. For her part Mrs Bridgeland liaised with the cook who might well be supplemented by a French chef as well as the usual pastry chefs and then, of course, the kitchen maids. Mrs Bridgeland was directly responsible, however, for all the housemaids, who might number eight, and liaising with the ladies' maids, who were invariably rather grand. There were further 'departments' such as the stables, maintenance, gardens and general help bringing in the logs for the fires or the oilman lighting the lamps every evening.

On 18 December His Royal Highness, travelling by special train on the Great Western Railway, arrived at Highclere station at 7 p.m.

where he was received by his host. 'The Prince was attended by Captain the Hon. Seymour Fortesque and the party invited by the Earl and Countess of Carnarvon to meet the Heir Apparent included Lord and Lady Westmoreland, Lord and Lady Chelsea, Lord and Lady Howe, Lady Dorothy Neville, Lady De Trafford, the Hon. Mrs Lowther, Sir Edward and Lady Colebrooke, the Russian First Secretary, and the Brazilian Minister.'

The Russian diplomat Mr Boulatzell, a great friend of the Prince of Wales, was a capital shot and a great linguist, wit and conversationalist and thus an important part of the house party. It was still the era of lese-majesty and for all his charm the Prince of Wales was a stickler for protocol. Almina and her guests worked hard to ensure they all did the right things and kept the Prince entertained. Mr Alfred also reminded his son-in-law to arrange to take a photograph to mark the occasion, for which the party lined up in front of Grotto Lodge during the shoot.

The first night Lady Carnarvon wore pink with diamonds and pearls; the second night she was in white with emeralds and diamonds but on neither night did she wear a tiara. Lady Dorothy Neville, such a wonderful old friend of the family, was the life and soul of the party, always ready to share amusing gossip.

Upstairs and downstairs were exhausted with the effort, but it was most successful. Happily for the staff at Highclere, Lord and Lady Carnarvon spent Christmas at Halton, with Mr Alfred's splendid hospitality and amusing evenings of cards or music. Carnarvon learned that his host loved to compose songs in the French spirit, but for all his love of entertainment, Mr Alfred always balanced it with practical support of those who were less well off. Every Christmas the Rothschild brothers would distribute a brace of pheasant to most of London's bus and taxi drivers.

Mr Alfred was an excellent host, but he was also a banker. He had worked for the family bank all his life although rarely arrived much before lunch. He became director of the Bank of England at the age of 26, a post he then held for twenty years. He was part of a select delegation of five financiers sent in 1892 by the British Government to an International Monetary Conference in Brussels, but he was also the only financier to arrive with four valets and quite so much luggage. He adored Almina but did gently suggest that Carnarvon would need to become more responsible given he was now married and would hopefully welcome children and heirs into his life. Alas, his advice was rarely taken.

If Carnarvon loved to travel, Almina adored a project, and from being entirely spoilt with life at Halton, she decided to electrify Highclere Castle. While the happy couple spent spring in Paris, followed by visits to Monte Carlo and Cannes, extensive improvements were carried out at Highclere. The house and even the stables were all now lit by electricity and a considerable portion of the interior of the Castle redecorated.

In June of that year, the Dowager Countess of Carnarvon presented Almina, Countess of Carnarvon, at Her Royal Highness the Princess of Wales' Drawing Room, which was all a great success. Elsie still preferred to wear mourning clothes on formal occasions, but the Queen rather approved of this. That done, and having enjoyed a Garden Party to celebrate the proposed wedding of Princess Maud to Prince Charles of Denmark, Carnarvon needed to be off again and hired Sir Donal Currie's steam yacht, *Iolanthe*, to cruise in home waters. In her imagination Almina had wanted to sail round the world with her handsome husband. Sadly, in reality, she found she did not like sailing at all.

It was welcome news when, having given birth to a third daughter, Carnarvon's sister Winifred asked Almina if she would be willing to stand as one of the baby's godparents and if she might allow Almina to be one of the child's christening names.

In September, Elsie's eldest son Aubrey, who had always been troubled with poor eyesight, left with Elsie and Vera for Dr

Pagenstecker's clinic in Wiesbaden, Germany, where, without anaesthetic, he underwent a small operation which then had to be repeated again in October. It must have taken enormous courage, but the eventual success of the procedure fundamentally changed his life. It meant he was no longer effectively blind and could see distances and shoot and at least distinguish figures if not faces. Benson, his Eton housemaster, kept in touch with Aubrey while they stayed in Wiesbaden for a few months, and a tutor was engaged to help continue his education.

Much like his stepbrother, Aubrey never really enjoyed Eton but, equally, his housemaster never really understood the extraordinary untidy, brilliant young man he had in his care. Thus, like his brother, he too left the school early but, unlike Carnarvon, Aubrey was academic and went up to Balliol, Oxford, to join his cousin Bron (Auberon Herbert), where he read history. While their father the 4th Earl had been most conventional and neat in his dress, his second son was, like his eldest, also unconventional in his dress. Taller than his brother but just as slim, he never seemed very coordinated, with often wildly gesticulating hands. Oxford suited him very well: he wrote to his brother that 'there were any number of awfully nice people here'.

Carnarvon and Almina only had two children. Their son, Henry George Herbert (Porchey, like his father before him, after his honorific title Lord Porchester) had been born in November 1898. Then, in August 1901, Almina gave birth to a daughter, Lady Evelyn Leonora Almina Herbert. As was typical in that era, neither birth particularly impacted their parents' lifestyles and their social diary and travels continued almost uninterrupted.

Elsie, the Dowager Lady Carnarvon, was a dedicated letter writer, unlike the young couple: she noted with some asperity, 'as you know they both have a curious incapacity for writing letters'. However, the new Lady Carnarvon was in all the magazines and newspapers, commended for her style, beautiful clothes and outstanding jewellery, the latter of which was itemized on a regular basis. It is perhaps not surprising, then, that they were the victims of their own great train robbery. Somewhere between France and London, Lady Carnarvon's jewels mysteriously disappeared. Her jewellery case apparently contained some £20,000 to £30,000 (perhaps £25 million in 2022) worth of gems but only the top layer seemed to have been taken: two watches set with diamonds and turquoises, earrings, diamond bangles, rings and a gold chain with a tiny miniature of Lord Carnarvon. The Earl immediately communicated with Scotland Yard and a Detective Inspector Drew was placed in charge of the case. However, it remained a mystery: the valuables were never recovered, nor was the thief ever apprehended. The valet Fearnside and the lady's maid were both interviewed but, despite numerous investigations, no information was gleaned.

Lord and Lady Carnarvon left it all behind them and took a White Star liner for New York. Almina had never been to America and White Star's *Oceanic* was one of the biggest and most luxurious in the world, with a domed dining room, large spacious cabins, plus a smoking room (essential for Lord Carnarvon). The ship was late arriving in New York, which the American press put down to the sheer weight of 'titled foreigners' aboard.

The Carnarvons stayed at the Waldorf Astoria and Carnarvon paid a visit to all the racecourses in the environs of New York as well as visiting Mr J. E. Keene's perfectly equipped stables. Meanwhile, Almina had been asked to a number of luncheons and balls, including one given by Mrs Stuyvesant Fish, renowned for her irreverent tongue and mad antics. She was, however, a notable leader of high society and Almina's fashion sense created a flutter of admiration. The couple travelled west by train so that Lord Carnarvon could (allegedly) take part in a hunting trip, but this was not quite the whole truth: Mr Alfred had given them an introduction to William Alvord, a banker and industrialist from San Francisco. Carnarvon was also the guest of Richard McCreary, who was deeply involved in bloodstock and who would later become a regular visitor at Highclere.

I I

HORSEPOWER

I N August 1897, the Carnarvons decamped to Deauville, just across the Channel in northwest France. With its wide sandy beaches stretching for miles and pretty timber-framed houses, it had become a popular holiday destination for both the French and the English. The sea breezes made for a temperate climate and there were casinos and golf courses to occupy the time, as well as sailing. The grand hotels catered to the most discerning visitors and a brand-new railway line made it very convenient.

In just three years of marriage, Almina had already had experience of visiting quite a number of casinos but the one at Deauville was most elegant, with a dusky pink marble staircase greeting the guests as they entered. She always liked to dress for the occasion and in any case everyone was required to wear formal attire within the casino. The *Gentlewoman* magazine noted: 'At Deauville . . . Lady Carnarvon's dresses are the admiration of everybody here.' Christabel writes from Deauville to *Truth*: 'I send you a description of a few of

97

the pretty dresses worn here at the races. Lady Carnarvon had on one day a skirt of striped pearl-grey gauze, with five flounces of the same, edged with fringed out gauze; the bodice was porcelain blue gauze, very much trimmed with white lace; white straw toque hat with fluted brim, ornamented with Maréchal Niel roses.'

That year also saw Carnarvon's first foray into the world of horse racing in France, albeit quite modestly. He registered his first colours as a variation on those of his grandfather, Lord Chesterfield, the papers commenting, 'Lord Carnarvon's colours are new to racegoers – scarlet, blue sleeves, scarlet cap, black and white cross belts'.

The spring edition of the *Illustrated Sporting and Dramatic News* had the following to say: 'Racing on this side of the Channel has of late been of more interest from the social than the sporting standpoint. We had two "big" days at Auteuil and Longchamps on Easter Sunday and Monday, the President of the Republic attending the Auteuil Meeting to witness the race which bears his name, and here, as at Longchamps, twenty-four hours later, were to be seen a host of English people including Lord and Lady Carnarvon, who are settled in Paris for some time, Lord Ilchester, Sir Horace and Lady Farquhar, Sir Blundell and Lady Maple and Lady Gosford. It seems that Lord Carnarvon and Lord Ilchester intend to take an active part in French racing, as each purchased one of Mr. Ridgeway's two-year-olds . . . Lord Ilchester gave £840 for a two-year-old by Guise Leda, while Lord Carnarvon purchased for £320 a two-year-old named Maronne, by Puchero Maud. These two-year-olds have been sent to Chantilly to be trained for their engagements, and it will be a pleasant revival of old times to see an English nobleman's colours in French races other than the Grand Prix.'

In his first season, Carnarvon had four horses trained at Chantilly in France and, later on, another five with George Chaloner at Chetwynd House, Newmarket. None of the horses were very successful but he thoroughly enjoyed himself.

'Nothing could possibly be more delightful than the weather which has so far favoured the pleasant meeting at Deauville, and if it lasts over the Grand Prix next Sunday a very great success will have been secured from the social point of view. There have not for many years been so many people spending the month of August upon the Norman coast, and it is not too much to say that the twin towns of Trouville and Deauville have been specially favoured in regard to both the quality and the number of their visitors. Deauville, which, in the current slang of the day, is the "smarter" of the two places, is certainly made very attractive by the great variety of sport provided for visitors, as, in addition to the racing, which extends over eight afternoons, two being reserved for hurdle racing and steeplechasing, there are such attractions as pigeon shooting, golf, and polo. The pigeon shooting goes on much as usual, the competitors being pretty much the same year after year; but the golf is a comparatively recent introduction and seems likely to draw more visitors to Deauville. The course is a very good one, and M. H. Ridgeway, who is president of the club, may be counted upon to induce many of his Pau friends to come and play here. The polo ground, which was so well laid out in the centre of the racecourse, is in excellent playing order . . .'

Deauville became their headquarters during the race week but, given there was also a regatta, Carnarvon also decided to cruise along the Normandy coast with his sister. Almina stayed in Deauville. Their stay was brief, though, as the shooting moors of Scotland beckoned. Carnarvon also hoped to see his horse Buckbread win the Zetland Stakes on the opening day of the York meeting on Tuesday 23 August.

Carnarvon's sister Margaret, at 21, was the middle child, neither as academic as her eldest sister Winifred nor possessed of her younger sister Vera's wayward charm. She was, however, very kind, affectionate and sensible and much beloved by her younger brothers Aubrey and Mervyn. Since Winifred was now married, Margaret spent more time with her brother Porchey and with Almina who was, after all, the same age.

Margaret sometimes wondered whether it was his illness and bronchitis that drove her brother to fill every minute of every day or if the restlessness stemmed from the loss of their mama all those years ago. In any case, most of the time Almina seemed very happy to pack and repack for the next adventure, although the entourage of servants who travelled with them ensured this was not so very onerous for her personally and that their leisure time was not much disturbed. Almina had travelled less that summer: to the young couple's delight she was pregnant.

The Carnarvon's London address was number 13 Berkeley Square. As both of them were rather superstitious about the number thirteen, Almina wondered whether she should instead rent a friend's house for the birth. In the end, they still had not quite decided when Henry George Alfred Marius Victor Francis was born on 7 November 1899.

Christmas was for once a small, cosy affair at Highclere before the family returned to London once again for the christening, which took place in the Chapel Royal, St James's Palace. The Rev. Edgar Sheppard officiated, using water brought from the River Jordan itself. The baby was named in honour of both his grandfather, the 4th Earl, still often referred to in the newspapers as an eminent statesman because of his work in Ireland and Canada, and of his father, comments about whom, in contrast, were almost solely about his racing or his somewhat esoteric collection of hats. The godparents were Mr Alfred de Rothschild, Mrs (Marie) Wombwell, Prince Victor Duleep Singh, Lord (Francis) Ashburton and the baby's aunt, Lady Burghclere.

As was traditional at Highclere, Carnarvon ordered a special cask of 300 gallons of beer to be made by Mr Sam Walter of Newbury. The cask was made of well-seasoned oak, grown on the Highclere estate, banded with massive brass hoops, and bearing a coronet and the inscription 'May Highclere flourish'. In addition, Carnarvon planted an extension to the avenue of lime trees originated by his ancestors towards Beacon Hill to mark the happy event.

At first Almina stayed at Highclere with her mother while Carnarvon visited Newmarket to see his horses and then Bretby to shoot. Once the shooting season was over, though, both parents left for Paris, followed by Rome and Egypt, leaving their three-month-old son in the care of his nanny and nurses.

By this point an annual visit to the warmer climes of Egypt was becoming something of a fixture in the Carnarvon diary. At this time, his interest in Egypt was little more than that of a tourist: Egypt had a wonderful dry, warm climate in winter and was very much the place to be at what was otherwise a rather wet and dreary time of year in England.

Travel was by steamer to Alexandria and thence a hot and dusty train journey to Cairo, even when travelling first class. The most famous hotel in Cairo was Shepheard's: its terrace was the place to see and be seen. It was a magnificent building in the French style, with symmetrical facades, an immense frontage and set back from the tree-lined street. A broad flight of steps led up between the terraces while large pots of palms marked the visitor's arrival into the opulent entrance hall, which was guarded by two small stone sphinxes, originally, it was said, from a temple at Memphis. The famous terrace was framed by an intricate wrought-iron balustrade and tiled with blue, green and orange motifs, upon which were scattered rugs with rattan chairs and tables, any of which offered a fine view of the latest arrivals as well as the never-ending, colourful activity in the street and the shops opposite. Tall alabaster pillars supporting the ceiling rose out of the entrance hall, decorated with lotus flowers, and on the walls were paintings and sketches of ancient temples and agricultural scenes. An elegant double staircase led to the bedrooms on the next floor.

Although the hotel was in the middle of Cairo, it had beautiful gardens and terraces behind it. Very much the centre for English travellers, there was a drawing room with carefully placed conversation-piece sofas and the inevitable small palm trees, a music room, a well-equipped reading room and a quiet room in which to write. The dining room was high-ceilinged with Moorish arches and screens and had a cool elegance perhaps due to the fountain set to one side in the room. The service was renowned for its excellence, with the waiters dressed in white kaftans with wide red cummerbunds and a red fez and slippers. Almina enjoyed the colour and the chance to wear the latest fashions and preferred an audience, but there was a private dining room which Carnarvon hired for them as well.

Wealthy tourists flocked to Egypt for little more than four months of the year and the season was at its height in January and February, as had been the case for the last five decades. The English novelist and Egyptologist Amelia Edwards wrote: 'As a diversified amusement nothing quite takes the place of the "Terrace" at Shepheard's in the height of season, say about February, when the chairs before the little wicker tea tables under the gay Oriental hangings are all taken, and a crowd, clothed in all colours, and of all degrees of celebrity and brilliance, is gathered to hear the band play, gossip and watch the multi-coloured population of this most cosmopolitan of Oriental cities drift ceaselessly past.'

The Carnarvons returned to Highclere in time to entertain a large party for Easter before leaving for London and the season. Lord Carnarvon was very proud of both his wife and his son but, as was usual for the times, the baby was left behind at Highclere with the staff while the parents followed their own interests, sometimes together, sometimes separately. Almina was much admired for her sense of style, dress and figure despite having given birth only six months earlier, and she enjoyed being at the centre of

London's fashionable life. Meanwhile, her husband began to develop his love of racing into something of a more serious business.

He had undoubtedly inherited his passion for the turf and racing from his mother's family. As a gambler he was obviously interested in what gave the horse the best advantage, but he was also becoming more and more seriously interested in the whole business of breeding and training racehorses. To that end he had struck up a partnership with the top American jockey Tod Sloan, who had moved to France with a view to setting up as an owner and consultant and who was renowned as an excellent judge of horseflesh. This led to the purchase of a number of horses for Carnarvon among others and the engagement of 'Boots' Durnell as their trainer, based at Maisons-Laffitte.

Charles 'Boots' Durnell first appeared on the racecourses of France in the spring of 1901. Encouraged by Sloan, he rode and trained horses belonging to Fernand Charron and Baron Léonino, as well as Lord Carnarvon and Sloan himself. 'As a rider, Durnell was popular with the patrons of the courses, and as a trainer he apparently left nothing to be desired. In both capacities, as trainer and as jockey, his services were in constant demand. Brief as was his stay here, it was said that he made much money. Success seemed to attend him on every hand. Go where he would his services as a rider were eagerly sought for, and he had all the horses that any one man could care to train if not more than any one man could properly attend to.'

Unfortunately, his career on the French turf was a brief one. In the autumn of the same year, he made a hurried and unwilling exit, propelled by an edict of the Société d'encouragement pour l'industrie nationale ruling him off. He was piloting one of Carnarvon's horses, Londres, who was favourite for the Prix de Marly le Roy at St Cloud on 28 October, but they failed to start. The ruling shut Durnell out of all weighing rooms, debarred him from all training grounds and forbade him from entering, running or riding any horse on racecourses ruled by the Code des Courses. It was left to Tod Sloan to take on the role of looking after the horses for their autumn engagements. On the surface this seems a rather harsh measure for what happens with some frequency today when horses refuse to go into the stalls. Perhaps he was doing just a bit too well for the local trainers and jockeys so the infringement on Londres was enough to get him banned in France.

With Charles Durnell gone, Tod Sloan was appointed Lord C's trainer. Sloan had arrived in England in 1897 and completely changed the way horses were ridden. English jockeys still used long leathers and long reins, but Tod Sloan had short stirrups, crouched low in the saddle and used short reins. Initially mocked as 'a mere monkey on a stick', it soon became apparent that his method was superior and that he was often so far out in front of his rivals that he was 'on his tod' (Cockney rhyming slang: 'Tod Sloan', 'on his own').

Carnarvon's most successful racehorse in France was Mauvezin. Bred by M. E. Blanc in France, Mauvezin was a small, black horse, standing just 15 hands, 3 inches. He was purchased as a 5-year-old out of a selling race, on Tod Sloan's advice, for just 11,000 francs. (By value this is perhaps one million pounds today). The vendor explained that he had rheumatism and that that was their reason for letting him go, but Sloan didn't believe it. They turned him out to let his hooves recover and regain his strength, after which he won six races on the trot. Sent to England to join Carnarvon's other horses at George Chaloner's yard in Newmarket, the strength of his feet collapsed once more whereupon this handsome horse was sent up to Bretby where he was nursed back to health by a talented stud groom, Charlie Whincup. He had one excellent race, which he won at very good odds (40-1), delighting Lord Carnarvon, who had placed a rather large bet on him, but then, after a few less successful runs, he was retired to stud.

Carnarvon also extended his racing interest in England. He sent his horses to a trainer whom he considered had an innate knowledge of racing through not only riding as a successful jockey himself but by being the son of a jockey as well. George Chaloner trained two good horses for Carnarvon. Simonside, who at 2,000 guineas was an expensive purchase, looked like justifying his high price tag by winning, on his debut, the prestigious Forty-First Biennial at Ascot (June 1898). But perhaps it was the other Chaloner-trained horse, Baldur, who could really be described as Carnarvon's first good horse. Named for the heroic son of Odin in Norse mythology, Baldur did indeed become something of a hero for Carnarvon, for whom he won five races between 1899 and 1902, including a prestigious race at Ascot. 'I think Lord Carnarvon has to thank (Tod) Sloan for the victory of Baldur over Osbech, as the American jockey rode one of the best races of his life on the winner.' Sloan received £500 from Lord Carnarvon for his efforts but afterwards Baldur had to be retired. The 'well-known American owner-breeder Mr J. S. McDonald enquired about what Lord Carnarvon was going to do with Baldur. The next day Lord Carnarvon appeared at Mr McDonald's hotel with the deed of gift (despite having been offered 1,500 guineas for him). He very much hoped that the horse will be used for breeding purposes in America.'

Almina, meanwhile, was attracting all the prizes at Ascot for her sense of dress: 'There were a great many of the young married women present, among whom none looked better than Lady Carnarvon, in deep royal blue foulard, spotted with white, while her wide picture hat was wreathed with black tulle and black velvet.'

Nineteen hundred and two was a major turning point in the Earl's racing setup. Given that Durnell had been struck off in France, Carnarvon reduced the number of horses he raced there. Meanwhile, in England, he had The Solicitor, Etruscan, The Buck and six year-lings transferred from George Chaloner's yard to Whatcombe to be trained by Philip Greusel, under the management of his good friend Richard Cecil 'Dick' Dawson. The new yard was only sixteen miles from Highclere, which made much more sense as Carnarvon could more easily visit.

Additionally, he moved the brood mares, which included Grand Prix, Navaretta, Sistrum, Valenza and Minnie Dee, from Bretby to Highclere. He had first started buying a few mares five or six years earlier but now, living practically all year round at Highclere, there seemed little point in having a stud so far away. Therefore, when the Siddown Warren Farm became vacant at Michaelmas 1902, Carnarvon decided to take it in hand and create a stud farm there. The farm buildings were remodelled and converted into loose boxes and a separate yard constructed capable of enlargement to almost any extent, as circumstances required. The mares were accompanied by Charlie Whincup, who was duly appointed stud groom at the newly named Siddown Warren Stud. The stallion Mauvezin moved into his new quarters and on a clear day would now have a lovely view of Winchester Cathedral twenty miles away, if he was ever interested in such things.

Of the two hundred acres, at first only about half was converted into paddocks, nestled into a natural bowl on the chalk downland and framed by Beacon Hill and Siddown Hill. Burghclere station, from which the horses could be transported by rail, was just over a mile away.

A visitor reported: 'Whatcombe nestles snuggly in the heart of the Berkshire Downs, about three or four miles distant from Letcombe Regis where so many big winners have been trained by Morton in recent years. The establishment is not arranged on a palatial scale. It is less elaborate, for example, than some of the stables at Newmarket, but in all essential details it is well suited to its purpose. The boxes are roomy and comfortable.'

12

MOTOR CAR-NARVON

By 1897 Carnarvon was becoming a well-known spectacle, riding on top of a different sort of horsepower. He could be seen and heard in Newbury as he drove through at a spanking pace. Motor cars had moved on a little since their earliest days but were still quite loud and smelly. This particular vehicle was described as being built after the character of a hooded mail phaeton and is said to be the one that took first prize in the motor race in Paris (a Paris-Bordeaux-Paris event). It apparently cost him 700 guineas.

A list of the first 236 members of the RAC which was published in January 1898 includes the Earl of Carnarvon among other Englishmen. On the other side of the Channel, its French equivalent organized the 'Grande Course d'Automobiles de Périgueux', a race that followed a 145-kilometre (90-mile) public roads course. The winner was Georges Leys in a time of 3 hours 54 minutes, driving a Panhard et Levassor. Carnarvon had offered to buy back one of the faster cars but was refused, so then he had 'to find a very speedy auto-car, for which he paid considerably more than £1,000'. In 1901, just after the race from Paris to Berlin, Lord Carnarvon bought the Panhard racer which had been driven by Georges Leys.

Soon nicknamed 'Motor Car-narvon', he undoubtedly, if only on the roads, bore a certain similarity to A. A. Milne's later fictional character Toad of Toad Hall: 'Here today, up and off to somewhere else tomorrow! Travel, change, interest, excitement! The whole world before you, and a horizon that's always changing!' He had immediately grasped all the advantages of cars as a mode of travel as well as the excitement of driving them, and he threw himself into researching and learning about which were the best cars and how to drive them. In this field, the French were very much leading the world, so inevitably Carnarvon's first driving licence was also French.

This new type of motor 'horse-powered' mode of transport was still very rare throughout much of the Continent and legislation was entirely on the side of the real horsepower with four legs which above all must not be frightened. A car driver was required to alert other road users in a neighbourly fashion and a special Act of Parliament, 'The Motor Car Act', only allowed motor cars in 1896 as long as each car was preceded by a man walking ahead and waving a red flag. As only the third owner of a car in England, Carnarvon naturally also became one of the first to incur speeding tickets and on 17 September 1898 he was summonsed for driving at more than 12mph in Newbury. The complainant claimed his horse was much frightened and that, furthermore, Lord Carnarvon did not stop. The magistrate, noting that since his car, a Panhard et Levassor, had four gears, it may have allowed a speed of up to 13mph and promptly fined Carnarvon £5.

After that, a certain pattern was formed and every summer Carnarvon seemed to be summoned to a different court. Fined in 1900 for furiously driving a motor car in Woodford, Essex, the local comment was that he had the reputation of being 'sumaat of a scorcher'.

Nearer to home in the parish of East Woodhay, a police officer in plain clothes riding his bicycle reported Carnarvon driving his motor car from the direction of Highclere Castle towards Woolton Hill at a very fast rate of speed well over 21mph. The progress of the car caused a big cloud of dust and calculating distance and time between two landmarks on the road paced out by the policeman allowed him to confirm that 'This gives a speed of over 28 mile an hour. There was a lady in the car, whom the defendant said was wee Lady Carnarvon'.

Two years later he was summonsed again for racing against his French mechanic, Georges Eilersgaard, at Epping while on their way to Newmarket, each driving a 40hp Panhard et Levassor. A policeman described him as coming at a terrific speed down a hill doing at least 25mph and that neither car stopped when he put his hand up. Fortunately, there was already a barrister, Mr Staple Firth, who specialized in defending motorists and who managed to keep Carnarvon on the road. (A few years later, Carnarvon's chauffeur Trotman was not so lucky and lost his licence for six months.)

Lord Carnarvon was fined £5 and costs by Kingston County magistrates for exceeding the 20mph speed limit while driving a motor car in Terrace Road, Walton-on-Thames, on a Bank Holiday. His lordship was represented by Mr G. Washington Fox, who made an amusing speech. 'I don't dispute the evidence of the police,' said Mr Fox, 'and, from what I gather from my instructions, his lordship feels too indebted to the police to challenge their statements. It appears that his lordship was running a horse at Hurst Park races on this particular day, and just at the critical moment when the horses were nearing the winning-post, a police officer on horseback got in the way of the horses and knocked over the jockey riding the winning mount, therefore leaving my client in undisputed possession of the field.'

As one report was listing a number of speeding fines, it emerged, not surprisingly, that all the defendants were on their way to the Bibury Club races. Lord Carnarvon was fined £20 and costs for driving a motor car at excessive speed on successive days while Mr Henry Cross, chauffeur to Lord Carnarvon, was fined £5 and costs. In fact, Lord Carnarvon's first meeting with his runaway Steward's Cup winner, Mauvezin, took place in a paddock at Highclere. According to the *Sporting Times*, 'the horse came open mouthed for his noble owner who had to flee for dear life'. 'Ah,' observed his lordship when the incident was finished – 'I suppose he recognised me as a habitual record-cutter in a motor car.'

Carnarvon loved the freedom cars gave him, the opportunity to explore both England and abroad. 'The poetry of motion! The real way to travel! The only way to travel! Here today – in next week tomorrow! Villages skipped, towns and cities jumped – always somebody else's horizon! O bliss! O poop-poop! O my! O my!' (*The Wind in the Willows*). On one trip reported in the press, he had driven to Folkestone with his French engineer intending to cross to the Continent. The Countess remained at Highclere as she would not, it was thought, care for the luggage restrictions given her reputation for 'elegant and charming dress', but she considered that her husband's absence would not be long as he was a 'splendid shot and Highclere is famous for its shooting'.

The old carriage houses in the mellow-bricked Castle courtyard were now used to stable motor cars. In addition, Carnarvon built garages with a mechanic's pit behind the courtyard and a separate garage in which he installed a petrol pump for his personal use and that of his guests along with a water supply to wash cars, as needed.

As Carnarvon replaced his vehicles with newer and better models, he was mindful that these were still rare by most people's standards. Thus, in 1912, he donated both the de Dion Quadricycle built in 1899 and an Endurance to the London Motor Museum, having himself bought a 38hp Belgian Métallurgique.

Mr Alfred (de Rothschild) was also an early proponent of motor vehicles, all of which were beautifully painted in his blue and yellow livery. In order to ensure his safe arrival, he always had a spare car following behind his in case of breakdown or accident, employing four chauffeurs under the head chauffeur, Mr Rolf.

The August 1898 edition of the *Automotor & Horseless Vehicle Journal* confirmed that Carnarvon had entered the Paris–Amsterdam–Paris 'city to city' motor race driving a Peugeot. It took place over seven days from 7 to 13 July and covered 1,431km in a very competitive fashion. The winner was Fernand Charron recording an astonishing average speed of 26.82mph. Fellow Panhard et Levassor driver Léonce Girardot was second and Carnarvon's friend René de Knyff was fourth.

In fact, Panhard et Levassor took all the top places and Carnarvon was to buy several of this marque. They were pre-eminent among early French car makers, establishing a reputation for fine engineering, excellent craftsmanship, superior reliability and outstanding performance. It was with a Panhard et Levassor that Charles Rolls, the noted car driver and later aviation enthusiast, chose to commence his competitive career, driving one of the French manufacturer's cars on the Thousand Mile Trial of 1900. Later that year Charles Rolls used his Panhard to give the Duke and Duchess of York, later King George V and Queen Mary, their very first ride in an automobile.

Motor racing became part of Carnarvon's life, to the extent that in 1907 he walked round the Dieppe circuit, taking photographs of the French Grand Prix. It was a challenging race, over forty-eight miles long, and was won by a Fiat. By this time, Carnarvon thought that he himself had driven some 60,000 miles at home and abroad, which was quite an achievement. In 1903, his great friend Lord Montagu had presented the Motor Vehicles Registration Bill before Parliament, sensibly introducing vehicle registration and drivers' licences and increasing the speed limit from 4mph to 14mph. Hugely popular with many enthusiasts, the ten cars on the road in 1897 grew to over 16,000 by 1907 and 150,000 by 1912.

13

A SLICE AND A HOOK

Aᶠᵗᵉʳ ᵃ ʳᵉⁱᵍⁿ of sixty-three years, Queen Victoria died at Osborne House on 22 January 1901. For a queen who had spent much of her life in mourning, she requested that her funeral should not be black to reflect this, but instead her coffin should have a white pall and that, as a soldier's daughter, it should be a military funeral. Despite her age, the unprecedented length of her reign made it hard for family, country and empire to come to terms with her death. On the whole, though, it did not really affect the Carnarvons or the measure and pace of their life, which carried on much as it always had.

Outside the world of racing, both four-legged and four-wheeled, Carnarvon's other great sporting love, cricket, had diversified some time ago to also include an enjoyment of tennis. Each summer, the gardeners would mark out tennis courts on the lawns outside the library. The ground was reasonably flat there and since the wind tended to come from the other side of the Castle, there was less excuse for missing a serve. It was excellent entertainment for a weekend and the ladies were able to enjoy it quite as much as the men. Later, Carnarvon had also taken up golf in quite a serious fashion and was even photographed demonstrating how to swing his club for *Tatler* magazine.

With a certain inevitability, Carnarvon's next project was therefore to build a nine-hole golf course. He chose a site at the foot of Beacon Hill and demolished the large old red-brick gatehouse to build instead a wooden clubhouse. Golf was quite the game of the day and in 1901 it was reported that His Majesty King Edward VII was also trying his hand at it. In 1901, the Highclere course was formally opened with an exhibition match played between James Braid, Harry Vardon and J. H. Taylor (who played at the Royal Winchester), all of whom were the leading golf celebrities and players of their day. Born in Crieff, Scotland, Braid was considered the longest 'driver' living. He would win the Open five times and become a renowned golf course architect.

The game was followed with much interest by Lord Carnarvon, Prince Victor Duleep Singh and other members of the Highclere Castle party, along with several members of the Crookham Golf Club 'as well as boys from Horris Hill School, the masters are all keen golfers'. The course was very much in its infancy, but Carnarvon came to enjoy the routine and the practice very much. He claimed it taught him humility, empathy with his friends and patience. There was something entirely relaxing about addressing a ball; it was in a beautiful setting and the game is about mental control above all else.

By now, it was increasingly obvious that they spent more time at Highclere than at any other estate. Thus in 1901 Carnarvon decided to sell Pixton to Elsie who in turn gifted it to Aubrey. Pixton was a house of much charm and happy memories, if less architectural merit than Highclere, lying in the middle of Exmoor, and Aubrey, like his brother, enjoyed the shooting, the hunting, the wildness of the moors and the beauty of the parkland trees.

Also like his brother, Aubrey welcomed endless streams of friends collected from his travels as well as from Balliol, and at this time it was a world apart from the shadow of the South African War which hung over Aubrey and his generation. His cousin Bron had gone out and returned with one of his legs amputated, which horrified all the family, although his courage and cheerfulness overcame the catastrophe. Aubrey had tried and failed to join the war due to his terrible eyesight. Hoping to lay out a role for her son, Elsie found him a position in the diplomatic service, through family connections, firstly in Japan and then in Constantinople. He was the same inveterate traveller as his brother. He was also unaware of the theory or practice of budgeting. Luckily Elsie was not.

Most fashionable newspaper articles which mentioned Carnarvon inevitably included the long list of his titles, respected ancestors, estates and acreage. Having stepped with enthusiasm into the social seasons and leisure pursuits of the last decade since the death of his father, the person upon whom he always relied to look after his inheritance was the agent for the estate, James Rutherford. Unfortunately, the agricultural revenues which supported such great houses and their families were now steadily diminishing, as it was for their tenant farmers as well. In some ways the year of Lord Carnarvon's birth was a key one: the end of the American Civil War meant an inexorable rise in wheat exports to Europe which reduced the price for home-grown wheat with a commensurate knock-on effect on estate income.

Rutherford's office was a wooden lodge built in a similar fashion to the new golf club and conveniently situated near both his house and the sawmill. His role covered many areas from supervising building projects (or golf courses), casting his eye over the budget of the farm and gardens or being a sounding board for matings at the stud. Most importantly, he was a good shot and was often asked to be one of the guns on shoot days and to liaise with the head keeper.

Lord Carnarvon's travels gave rise to several letters each week making suggestions or answering Rutherford's queries: Carnarvon said he found travel very peaceful in that it gave him thinking time. For all his restlessness and the speed at which he tackled life, some of his letters in this period begin to set out his concerns about the precariousness of his position and show an attempt to foresee where he might find equilibrium in the future.

As it had been in the past, the Castle and estate remained remarkably self-sufficient, with a huge walled kitchen garden. It did, however, need a veritable army of gardeners, led at this time by the bearded head gardener, Mr Pope. He was succeeded in 1908 by Mr Blake. Neat, long rows of vegetables with a few scarecrows standing in the midst of the beds jostled with fruit cages, while espaliered pears and apples trees were planted against warm south-facing walls. Following years of experience and, of course, crop rotation, it enabled the Castle to be successfully supplied with vegetables and fruit over a long productive period. The local community of those who lived and worked at Highclere also benefited.

Effectively, estates such as Highclere had to be managed as much as a business enterprise as a home if they were to survive. They required good management and efficient organization and, of course, money. If Lord Carnarvon had entered the racing business as an amateur, he found himself increasingly focused on developing it as a profitable enterprise.

In 1903 the stables earned £10,674 but 1904 was an extremely successful season for Carnarvon. Of his 26 horses in training at Whatcombe, 17 of them won 29 races and £12,143 10s. in prize money. Of these, Robert Le Diable topped the table by some distance, winning just short of £5,000. One of Lord Carnarvon's most successful wins was the City and Suburban Handicap at Epsom in April 1904. It was a brilliantly fine cloudless day and His Majesty, accompanied by Prince Christian, was among the spectators. 'Robert' started at 40-1, having failed ignominiously in 1903. However, as the field rounded Tattenham Corner and came into the straight Robert Le Diable hit the front, winning very easily by five lengths, Lord Carnarvon cheering and shouting from the stands. He was duly retired to stand alongside Mauvezin at the recently created Highclere Stud. He was 'devilishly good looking but angelic of temperament', but it's more likely he was named for a popular opera as that was a passion of both Lord and Lady Carnarvon.

Lord Carnarvon also changed his racing colours to scarlet, blue collar and white cap 'which were becoming most recognised, and the partnership with Philip Greusel [who] was a very clever and careful trainer [at] the Whatcombe stable has been doing very well over the past couple of seasons. He was, I believe, an excellent stable-man.' Greusel acted as the much-liked Irishman Dick Dawson's right-hand man but sadly died of consumption in 1905.

Rutherford became ever more versed at horse breeding and fortunately for his employer he and his family were also very interested in motor cars. He had six sons and one of them, E. J. Y. Rutherford, had built the Rutherford steam car. With Lord Carnarvon's help he went into business, forming the Highclere Motor Car Syndicate Ltd. This motor car had a Serpollet-type flash boiler and a 3-cylinder single-acting engine rated at 30/40hp and went into production as the EJYR tourer, later the 'Rutherford', from 1907 to 1912. Sadly, it did not compare favourably with the 38hp Métallurgique that Carnarvon then bought for himself.

14

CEYLON

IT HAD BEEN an exhausting and busy Christmas with many friends and family staying but, following tradition, on Monday 9 January 1905, Lord and Lady Carnarvon had arranged for a servants' ball to be held at Highclere which would also include the local tradesmen. The fires were lit, and all the housemaids and kitchen staff were beyond excited and arrayed in their best frocks. They had been practising their dance steps in the evening in the stone-flagged staff dining room, with the old stand-up piano providing accompaniment.

The evening was held in the state dining room and began with dancing. Mr H. Walch's band provided the music and were seated close to the far window so that as many as possible could take to the floor. Lord Carnarvon opened the ball by leading Mrs Bridgeland, the housekeeper, onto the dance floor while Lady Carnarvon danced with Mr Streatfield, the house steward. Supper was provided by Staples of Newbury and the band, well sustained with beer throughout, played until four o'clock on the Tuesday morning.

Almost one hundred guests were present, and Mr Streatfield proposed the toast to the Earl and Countess with the deepest appreciation and respect and 'the choicest of blessings'. Lady Carnarvon replied with a pretty, graceful speech and thanked Mr Pope and his team from the gardens for his decoration of the supper room.

Two weeks later, the Carnarvons were on board the P & O steamer *Marmora*, sailing towards Marseilles from where it took a further two weeks to reach Ceylon. Launched in 1903, *Marmora* was the last word in comfort with a smoking room as well as an ornately panelled dining room and lavish turned wooden staircase.

They had planned a winter tour with Prince and Princess Victor Duleep Singh, who had set off slightly ahead of them and were already in Colombo indefatigably playing golf, their new interest, before leaving for the hills of Kandy as guests of the Governor and Lady Blake. It was the first trip to the tropics for both Lord and Lady Carnarvon: the humidity, the heat and glare of the sun, the brassbound rickshaws, the silks, spices, sapphires and curios – all were new to them. After a few days' relaxation and sightseeing in the capital, they boarded the train that wound its way from the humid plain with its gleaming rivers, paddy fields and coconut groves to the cooler air inland, passing rubber plantations before finally reaching the gentle, vivid green terraces of tea that lay in the centre of Ceylon. Almina hugely enjoyed the journey: the very different air, the deep colours and size of the leaves and flowers captivated her. Her husband had taken his camera and they would thus return with some wonderful photographs to show the children and nieces.

Kandy may have been thousands of miles from London, but it was entirely structured for an expatriate way of life. It lay around a tranquil lake welcoming a perpetual stream of tourists from Colombo, all of whom stayed, if they could, at the Queen's Hotel. Set into the surrounding hills were tea estates, one of which belonged to the famous tea entrepreneur Sir Thomas Lipton. Born in a tenement in

Glasgow, Scotland, by this point Lipton had built a business distributing his teas throughout Europe and the USA and had become a friend of both King Edward VII and his son George V.

There was much for the Carnarvons and Duleep Singhs to explore, from riding along hillsides to visiting the tea plantations and temples and finding enchanting hidden villages. Silver oaks and other trees acted as windbreaks for the tea through which the pickers walked every ten days to carefully collect the leaves. It was all so different, a magical world with lazy afternoons spent in a painted boat on the lake and evenings in which they sat dazed and entranced by hundreds of fireflies.

Almina wrote letters to her children, albeit for Nanny to read out – they were only 6 and 4 years old – describing the diverse, deeply lush landscapes, the vivid emerald greens and the tumbling waterfalls which interrupted every journey. The misty morning views were perhaps somewhat familiar to Highclere, but the warm, humid scents were a world apart. Carnarvon experimented with photography, looking to express not just a visual record but to achieve a more painterly effect.

Tennis was much enjoyed and, of course, there was a 'Club', the centre of life for bridge, billiards and cocktail parties. Princess Victor was a noted bridge player and had decided to write a book in French on the game. It was a very social place and both couples played cards although, given the opportunity, the men would play for far higher stakes than their wives.

Neither Almina nor her husband had travelled beyond the Middle East before and they enjoyed the landscapes and pageantry of the East Indies. When the visit was over, the Carnarvons resumed their sea voyage, travelling on to India while the Duleep Singhs returned to Monaco as the British Government considered it politically undesirable for them to return to their homeland.

By mid-April, both couples were back in England for the races at Newmarket and some glorious English spring weather. Almina, a less avid racegoer than her husband, took the opportunity to spend some time with her children at Bretby and left her husband to his horses.

The London season brought everyone back to London. As usual, it was a mixture of family soirées and bigger events. Almina had a wide circle of friends and relations through marriage and both her parents, who adored her children, were still alive. As the *Illustrated Sporting and Dramatic News* (February 1905) wrote: 'Lady Carnarvon does not share her husband's taste for racing and is seldom seen at a meeting whereas his tall grey hat is usually to be found, with its owner underneath it, in the vicinity of the paddock. She is more often at the Opera and at smart assemblies in town and is always charmingly turned out, after a dainty and rather French fashion.'

Married for a decade now, Almina chose what she attended, but was, of course, at her sister-in-law Winifred's house when she gave a charming children's party at Charles Street, where Porchey and Evelyn behaved very well, and Almina gave an elegant dinner in Berkeley Square with each of the round supper tables beautifully decorated with flowers to celebrate her husband's fortieth birthday and their tenth wedding anniversary.

Above all else, as a couple, the Carnarvons loved the opera: the music and the spectacle. On 8 June they set off from Seamore Place with Mr Alfred to attend a gala night at Covent Garden in honour of the state visit by a genial young King Alfonso of Spain. Mr Alfred de Rothschild's box afforded a spectacular view not only of the stage but of the fifty thousand red and yellow roses reflecting the colours of the Spanish flag which decorated the horseshoe-shaped auditorium. King Alfonso arrived in a striking white and gold uniform in the company of King Edward VII, who in turn wore the uniform of a Spanish admiral, while Queen Alexandra, in a black silk dress with a magnificent diamond collar and a massive tiara, led in the other members of the royal family. The audience was dressed and bejewelled with as many baubles and insignia as there were garlands and festoons around the theatre and stage. After the national anthems, the performance began with the balcony scenes from Gounod's *Roméo et Juliette* followed by the third act from *La Bohème*. It was a dazzling evening and a special moment in what had already become a challenging year with an attempted revolution in Russia and war in the Far East.

One of the highlights of the season each year was the Royal Meeting at Ascot which took place, as it still does, in mid-June. Lord Carnarvon, as an avid enthusiast and racehorse breeder, was always to be found in the Royal Enclosure, although not always following the strict social protocols of the time. While Lady Carnarvon was much admired for her style, figure and jewels, her husband's dress sense was a little more unconventional.

As the *Sporting Times* noted pointedly: 'Fashion is always at its foremost at Ascot, and sumptuary rules are very religiously observed. King Edward, Bohemian in his way, was a martinet for sartorial etiquette. On one occasion he sent a message to Lord Carnarvon that he should remove himself from the enclosure until he was suitably dressed. The offender was wearing white shoes.'

Lord Carnarvon duly left the enclosure for the paddock, where he was more than happy.

This lack of convention on Lord Carnarvon's part continued for much of his life. In 1920, the *Sporting Times* once again drew attention to it as part of a more general complaint: 'We were discussing the other day a certain lord, and, in response to my query of an old-timer, why the chap with a new tag to his name was not a member of the Jockey Club, I received the following answer in all seriousness: "Because he will still persist in smoking a cigar with the band on." I happened to repeat this story to a well-known editor, and he remarked that a famous member of the diplomatic corps did likewise. I suppose you can afford to be eccentric if you have Norman blood in your veins but dare not chance things if the lineage is of the Stratford-atte-Bow variety. Of course, the racehorse owner might have done worse; he might still have kept the gold foil on his weed! Lord Chaplin can wear baggy blue trousers and a frock coat, and Lord Carnarvon can display beach slippers at Ascot, but you and I dare not do these things.'

Nor did Carnarvon confine his eccentricities of dress to Ascot.

'Lord Durham and one or two sticklers for precedent make that long pilgrimage to the paddock, but I noticed that the majority of Turf bosses preferred to be personalities elsewhere at Epsom, and I do not blame them. Lord Chaplin, still hale and hearty and wearing like a two-year-old, seems to prefer the pitch which we always used to associate with the late Mr. Leopold de Rothschild. He and his son-in-law, Lord Londonderry (with a very clean-shaven face you would inevitably associate with the clever diplomat or the barrister) seem particularly proud of each other. Lord Derby has smartened considerably since he went to Paris and is certainly thinner. Sir Robert Jardine is one of several who still favour the round-cut tailcoat – I must ask for a job next on the "Tailor and Cutter" – and, as for Lord Carnarvon, he never did care how he flaunted the conventional.'

However, it wasn't so much a general unconcern with the sartorial rules but more the impatience of the sporting man with impractical or uncomfortable garments. As the *Sporting Times* continued: 'To Lord Carnarvon was given the credit of introducing tanned leather shoes. He was, before his marriage, greatly devoted to yachting, and gave several yachting parties, at which it was a rule that only tan or white shoes were to be worn.' Soon they came into general use, and now '. . . tan boots and shoes are undoubtedly more suitable for country wear than black'.

Nearer to home, Lord Carnarvon was instrumental in establishing Newbury racecourse some six miles from Highclere. He excitedly scrawled 'First Newbury Meeting' in Highclere's guest book and entered no fewer than nine horses into races over the two-day meeting, winning three of them and blithely ignoring any possible conflict of interest by acting as steward as well. The *Daily Mirror* commented:

'Only one thing was wanted to make the opening of the Newbury racecourse one of the most brilliant events of the present season, and that was a thing beyond the power of mankind to command. I allude to the absence of sunshine, which was wanting to make the scene one of the prettiest to be found anywhere in the country. Millions of pounds are invested in racing pursuits in England, and the latest venture, Newbury, inaugurated this afternoon, involves a sum probably not less than a quarter of a million. It has made a brilliant start, and the thousands of persons visiting the beautiful course were loud in its praises. It seemed fitting that to Lord Carnarvon, a local magnate, and one of the chief supporters of the meeting, should fall the honour of winning the chief prize, the Inaugural Handicap of 1,600 sovs., with Missovaja, a filly whose name, however, had hitherto been linked with ill-success. No fewer than 15,000 persons paid for admission today. The number of club members is about 600, and – from this source an income of some £4,000 a year is secured. Newbury is beyond all question the prettiest club course in England. The mere track is one of the best, with its straight mile, slightly undulating, and the longer courses sweeping round with gentle Curves, the whole circuit well within view of the spectators on the stands.'

Carnarvon was devoting an increasing amount of time to his breeding campaigns for the next year. His useful but accident-prone filly Missovaja, winner of three races to the value of £2,400, including the Prince of Wales Nursery Handicap at Doncaster, had injured herself just before the prestigious Cesarewitch Handicap. He decided she might make an excellent brood mare and duly had her transported to his stud at Highclere where he now stood two stallions,

Mauvezin and Robert Le Diable. A great deal of interest was being shown in both. The *Sporting Times* opined: '. . . Another cheap horse worth a trial is the black Mauvezin, by Reuil out of Modest Martha. Mauvezin's Stewards' Cup victory at Goodwood was very easily obtained, but in France he won many races under substantial weights and over all distances up to mile and a quarter. He has some very promising foals, having had a full subscription list previously, but in the coming season he will serve mares at 9 guineas only. He stands at the Highclere Stud, near Newbury, where the lord of the harem, Robert le Diable, is full for the season, and nominations are being booked for 1907.' Indeed, 'Robert' was proving extremely popular and a bit of a superstar. His fee, by contrast, was 66 guineas plus a 21*s*. groom's fee.

The following winter took the Carnarvons again to Egypt and Ceylon and on to the Strait of Malacca. Lord Carnarvon was considering investing in a rubber plantation as, from his own knowledge of car production, he thought the associated demand for rubber might explode. In the end, though, he decided not to go through with it as it was too remote in every way from his areas of expertise.

Instead, he returned to England for the racing season accompanied by a curry chef from Ceylon whom he had managed to persuade to come to Highclere. Lord Carnarvon really enjoyed curries and tried to procure the relevant spices as well, but the new chef was not wholly approved of. The kitchen staff at Highclere were not happy that he had also brought his monkey with him who would sit on his shoulder as he cooked.

Strategically, on this trip Lord Carnarvon had also made the acquaintance of the British engineer Sir William Garstin, who led the Ministry of Public Works in Cairo within which sat the Department of Antiquities. Lord Carnarvon had become increasingly fascinated by Egyptology, which was regularly reported on in the London papers and which he had seen first-hand watching the treasure-hunting escapades of the American millionaire Mr Theodore Davis. As a result, he had gradually come to the conclusion that, rather than simply visit Egypt as a tourist, he might see whether he could apply for a concession to excavate in Egypt. Garstin was thus an excellent and influential contact as well as a fellow enthusiast who had led the campaign to fund and build the Cairo Museum, which was constructed by an Italian engineering firm with a French architect, Marcel Dourgnon.

15

THE MUMMIFIED CAT

A GREY, WET autumn unfolded into an unusually cold winter with snow enveloping the Castle and gardens in December. As usual, a large party of family and friends filled Highclere with laughter and well-stoked fires, but it was not a good Christmas for Lord Carnarvon. He could not shake off a cold, refused to give up smoking and suffered from the predictable January flu. Exhausted and running a temperature, the only remedy was to rest and stay warm, reading by the fire in his sitting room and absorbing as much information as he could about ancient Egypt from the library. He had also bought three beautiful illustrated books by Auguste Mariette, the illustrious scholar who had founded the Egyptian Department of Antiquities and who became known as the father of Egyptian archaeology. Mariette had excavated more than thirty sites and dreamed of building a museum to bring together all his finds.

Carnarvon's illness delayed their departure for Egypt, but they finally set off via Paris, staying briefly at the Chatham Hotel and visiting Lord Carnarvon's uncle, Alan Herbert, who was still practising as a doctor. Eventually, by late February, the Carnarvons were ensconced in the Savoy Hotel in Cairo where Lord Cromer gave Lord Carnarvon an introduction to the current Director of Antiquities, a Frenchman, Professor Gaston Maspero, from whom Carnarvon hoped to get a concession to excavate at Thebes.

Convention dictated that the Director of Antiquities in Egypt was always a Frenchman, reflecting France's idea of their special relationship with Egypt since the time of Napoleon. Germany, on the other hand, through Émile Brugsch, held the office in charge of the Cairo Museum and additionally had Ludwig Borchardt curating the catalogue. Outside the world of archaeology, the British were ascendant both politically and economically and effectively dictated all communication be made through the High Commissioner, Lord Cromer.

It was a delicate and at times uncomfortable balance. Nominally, the Egyptian Khedive was a subject of the Ottoman Empire but Lord Cromer, to all intents and purposes, supervised all government policy and the British led the Army. On the plus side, the British invested long term in Egyptian agricultural resources and improved the Nile's irrigation through multiple engineering projects such as the construction of the original Aswan Dam in 1902 and the Nile Barrage, but this was as much for their own benefit as that of the Egyptians'. The British financier Sir Ernest Cassel created the Bank of Egypt in 1898, of which he owned 50 per cent, while in the previous century the Rothschild family had famously provided the finance to the British Prime Minister Benjamin Disraeli to purchase the Khedive of Egypt's shares in the Suez Canal. Thus, the British could also control the trade routes through to India.

All the practical ministries were under the remit of Lord Cromer, including the Ministry of Public Works led, of course, by Garstin, who thus had some sway over Professor Maspero at the Department of Antiquities.

It was a short walk from the Savoy hotel to the new museum near Tahrir Square, which was now more or less finished. Soft, rose-coloured stone facing created an imposing building with an inner central dome from which a large, central galleried hall created an airy interior with smaller galleries leading from either side and behind. Outside, the building was guarded by statues of sphinxes while inside the sheer size and number of statues and works of art from Predynastic times through to the Greek and Roman eras was almost overwhelming.

Maspero had been a professor of Egyptology in France since 1869 when Lord Carnarvon would have been just 3 years old. He had had an eminent career and was responsible for one of the greatest 'discoveries' of recent times in Egypt. The physical preservation of the deceased was the essential tenet of Egyptian beliefs and religious practices and, in order to preserve the mummies of the pharaohs and wealthy elite, they were sometimes moved by faithful acolytes out of their original burial sites and into secret caches. The most famous of these was the Royal Cache of Deir el-Bahri, just outside the Valley of the Kings. Ironically, it was not so much Maspero's archaeological skills but those of detection that won the day. In 1878, it had begun to dawn on him that the increasing volume of ancient funerary objects and important papyri for sale among the Luxor antiquity dealers, many of which bore royal names but not from any licensed excavation, meant that someone, somewhere, had discovered something important.

The trail led back to the village of Qurna, and a particularly enterprising family of tomb robbers called Abd el-Rassul. After interrogation, including infighting among various family members, Maspero got what he wanted. Down a 15-foot shaft, through a narrow 10-foot-long corridor which then changed direction and shape for another 100 yards, was a gallery of untold riches. More than fifty mummies, including some of the greatest pharaohs of the 17th–20th

Dynasties, along with over 6,000 antiquities, mostly shabtis and papyri, were discovered, packed up and moved by steamboat from Luxor back to Cairo.

Perhaps charmed by the enthusiasm of a British lord who happened to speak excellent French, Maspero reluctantly agreed to let Carnarvon have a small concession where he could do no harm although, in reality, he would have found it hard to refuse given it was entirely about who you knew at that time.

Unlike Maspero, who was at heart a scholar, at this time the main 'excavator' in Luxor was an American banker and lawyer called Theodore Davis who was a treasure hunter, impatient of any historical or archaeological care and interested only in the prize. The newspapers were full of the latest dazzling treasures he had discovered, the most recent of which was his firm belief that he had uncovered the tomb of the legendary Queen Tiye. Without any firm evidence, Davis declaimed ecstatically, 'It is quite impossible to describe the surprise and joy of finding the tomb of the great queen', enthusing how drawn he felt to a commoner who, through beauty and brains, had become so powerful.

However, the tomb was in a chaotic state and Davis's methodology more akin to vandalism to modern eyes. Exposure to air made much of the gold disintegrate as soon as it was revealed, nothing was accurately recorded, unimportant artefacts flung aside, and photography left until after the tomb was thoroughly searched for any prizes. Genuine details of the treasures emerged only in later years, from the 'magical bricks' inscribed with spells for the dead to the gold foil ribbons encircling the mummy with the name Akhenaten. Later on, it also became apparent that the skeleton discovered was most definitely male, not female, and therefore could never have been Queen Tiye. Davis was furious and never really believed it, regarding it instead as an envious slur on his greatest discovery.

All this, however, was from a later perspective and Carnarvon had read of Davis's discoveries with great interest. It was therefore with keen anticipation that he arranged a train from Cairo down to Luxor and arrived at the Luxor Hotel. The first person to be introduced was the new Chief Inspector of Antiquities for Upper Egypt, Arthur Weigall, before going on to the practicalities of setting up his dig.

At only 25, Weigall was unusually young and inexperienced in his administrative role in Luxor. From a prominent family of Victorian artists, he had become fascinated by Egypt at an early age and had worked with Flinders Petrie at Abydos before joining the German Egyptologist Friedrich Wilhelm von Bissing. He replaced James Quibell, an experienced and respected Egyptologist whose brief tenure had been abruptly brought to an end when he was suddenly transferred to become Chief Inspector at Saqqara in place of Howard Carter.

It was an impossible job in some ways given the size of the territory it covered, but Weigall was young and full of the energy required, and felt very strongly about the need to conserve and protect the artefacts and monuments that were gradually being stripped from Egypt. He enmeshed himself in the archaeological and bureaucratic life of Luxor and Cairo until his career was sadly cut short by a personal breakdown and the start of the First World War.

Advised by Weigall, Carnarvon proceeded to appoint a reis (foreman) and a local team to work on his site. Carnarvon was aware of his inexperience, noting: 'I may say that at this period I knew nothing about excavating so I suppose with the idea of keeping me out of mischief as well as keeping me employed, I was allotted a site at the top of Sheikh Abdel Gurna.'

Most of the experienced workmen came from the notorious village of Gurneh. It stood as an untidy mass of huts among the tombs of the Theban Necropolis at the heart of one of the world's largest concentrations of archaeological treasures. Amateur tomb robbers to a man, the village played a pivotal supporting role in the work of most of the official Egyptologists as well, though their honesty was continually questioned. Later on, the same villagers were to provide the bulk of the labour for Carnarvon and Carter's extraordinary discovery of Tutankhamun's tomb in 1922. Today, many of them are still involved in dig sites.

Carnarvon set off to his concession with undiminished enthusiasm every day. Sometimes Almina accompanied him, sitting under a canopy enclosed by a tent of fly nets, immaculately dressed and with a large sun hat to provide extra shade and protect her complexion. The American artist Joseph Lindon Smith and his wife Corinna sometimes shared a sandwich lunch with them, thoroughly enjoying their company, and Corinna remarked that she was full of admiration for Almina's resolution in being there. The site was just on the edge of the Tombs of the Nobles and barely ten minutes' walk across the pale hot shale and sand to the Temple of Hatshepsut. Joe Lindon Smith, originally a portrait artist from Boston, made his name painting Egyptian scenes under the patronage of the Hearst family. Although he is best known for his work with the American archaeologist George Reisner, he was a fixture at many of the most important digs during the first part of the twentieth century and later on would visit Tutankhamun's tomb with Howard Carter.

With beginner's luck Carnarvon did find something, though not the riches he may have dreamed of: 'I had scarce been operating for 24 hours when we struck what seemed an untouched burial pit.' He continued, 'Now, this gave rise to much excitement in the Antiquities Department which soon simmered down when the pit was found to be unfinished. There, for six weeks enveloped in clouds of dust, I stuck to it day in and day out. Beyond finding a large, mummified cat in its case which now graces the Cairo Museum, nothing whatsoever rewarded my strenuous and very dusty endeavours. This utter failure however instead of disheartening me had the effect of making me keener than ever.'

Determined to continue with his new career as an excavator, Carnarvon learned all he could about the various sites and kept an eye on the politics and manoeuvrings of his fellow archaeologists. Taking short walks from his excavation work to escape the wretched clouds of flies, he took the time to explore and walk the ground around Luxor, asking his reis for advice and, as ever, was generous with his thanks. Over his favourite thick, black Turkish coffee and the inevitable cigarette, he gathered that there might be a hidden tomb near the old village mosque at Gurneh. He walked around the area and could see the challenges – dwellings had been built around the proposed excavation site – and quietly planned his campaign to get the necessary permissions.

Before they left Lord Carnarvon hired a dahabiya, a shallow-bottomed boat, for the day so that he could float past the reed villages and enjoy the bird life along the edges of the Nile. Almina very much enjoyed this, and felt reassured that the clear, dry air suited her husband since there was no humidity, with cool evenings and swift sunrises and sunsets.

16

HOWARD CARTER

HOWARD CARTER WAS born in Kensington, southwest London, in March 1874, the youngest of eleven children. A sickly child, he spent much of his youth with two maiden aunts, Kate and Fanny Carter, in the village of Swaffham in Norfolk, where his family came from. His father was the artist Samuel John Carter, a member of the Royal Academy, a successful animal painter and an excellent draughtsman. Two of his brothers worked at the Royal Academy, his sister Amy was a painter and another brother was a talented clock cabinetmaker.

Depending on his health, Howard intermittently attended various local village schools. Luckily, he had inherited his father's skills as a draughtsman and combined his natural talent with hard work and an organized, detailed mind.

Close to Swaffham was the estate of Lord and Lady Amherst, both of them amateur Egyptologists, which contained one of the most important private collections of Egyptian art and papyrus in

England. Lady Amherst published a sketchbook of Egyptian history in 1904.

Carter's father had accomplished various commissions already for the Amhersts so in 1891, when their friend the Egyptologist Percy Newberry needed a draughtsman for his excavations, Howard's name was put forward.

Duly appointed, Carter was sent on a training course at the British Museum in London to prepare him for the job before arriving in Egypt in October 1891 as assistant draughtsman. Newberry was one of the great Egyptologists of the time and had begun work at Beni Hassan in 1890. Later, he become a professor of Egyptology at Liverpool University and professor of ancient history and archaeology at Cairo University. Four short months later, Carter was thrown in the deep end when he was sent by Newberry to assist fellow British archaeologist Flinders Petrie at Tel el-Amarna in Middle Egypt, working on the temple and palaces of Akhenaten, the heretic pharaoh and father of Tutankhamun, who had founded his new city there. This was an extraordinary period in the pharaonic history of Egypt, leading to some beautiful works of art, although the city appears only to have been inhabited for a few years before being abandoned almost immediately after Akhenaten's death.

The ruins of the ancient city of Akhet-aten emerge from the Eastern Desert sand, covering the area from north to south across the modern villages of El-Till, El-Hagg Qandil, El-Amariya and El-Hawata. The existence of these ancient remains had been known since the beginning of the eighteenth century, but it was not until 1891 that the Egypt Exploration Fund – the forerunner of the Egypt Exploration Society – commenced excavations. Petrie carried out several test trench excavations in selected parts of the city area which enabled him to identify not only the most important palace and temple structures but also the expanded residential areas, workshops and adjoining refuse dumps.

Howard Carter had found his calling. Working with Flinders Petrie provided him with the most thorough training, knowledge and experience available at that time. Considered one of the fathers of modern scientific archaeology, Petrie became the Edwards Professor of Egyptian Archaeology & Anthology at University College London before being knighted for services to archaeology in 1923. He was a difficult and meticulous taskmaster but a matchless mentor who taught Carter about observation and the importance of detail, of paying attention to facts to make sense of even seemingly irrelevant trifles.

Over the next few years, Carter held a number of different jobs with the Egypt Exploration Society working under the aegis of the Swiss academic Henri Naville. One of his first tasks was to record the paintings and inscriptions of Queen Hatshepsut's temple at Deir el-Bahri where he worked from 1893 to 1899. Despite his almost mechanical precision, Carter's notes record a quote from the art historian John Ruskin, 'in true art the hand the head and the heart of man go together', and he believed that while he should intelligently reproduce Egyptian art, it should also be with a feeling for the essence of the piece as well. Carter was fascinated and enthralled by ancient Egyptian civilization and its art and his feeling and empathy for his subject are clearly visible in his drawings and watercolours.

His free time was often spent drawing the local wildlife, especially the birds, and his notebooks and diaries not only record his detective work as he explored the area around Deir el-Bahri but also show how relaxed he was, wandering alone and drawing the desolate, craggy cliffs.

Eighteen ninety-nine was a turning point in Carter's life and career when Maspero appointed him Chief Inspector of Monuments in Upper Egypt and Nubia with headquarters at Luxor. The appointment was a tremendous recognition of Carter's qualities and the trust that Maspero was prepared to invest in him, and, in turn, Carter's notebooks record his admiration and appreciation of Maspero and his determination to work hard to justify his elevation.

Carter's first project was to document and map the necropolis on the west bank of the Nile so that it could be better controlled and protected. This included Dra Abu el-Naga, the Eastern Valley of the Kings, the Western Valley of the Kings and the Valley of Queens. This was long overdue and took Carter four years to complete. He also organized the laying of thousands of feet of electric cable in and around the tombs and the Valley of the Kings, an extraordinary feat which allowed for far better observation and recording of each tomb and helped deter the more opportunistic thieves. Furthermore, he put in place gates for the more important tombs and cleared mounds of debris. Naturally, funds were always short and Carter was grateful for donations from visitors or philanthropists. Nevertheless, it was an impossible area to police and Carter sensibly suggested to Maspero that significant items should be removed to the Cairo Museum.

Then, in 1905, it all went disastrously wrong. A somewhat prickly character, conscious of his own lack of social standing but full of self-belief, overworked and stressed, Carter had a calamitous run-in with a party of aristocratic French. Blown out of all proportion as it was by politics and the press, and despite all efforts to salvage the situation, Carter, feeling he had no other choice, resigned, and walked away from his salary, house, reputation and any role in an excavation. At the age of 33, having worked in Egypt since the age of 17 but with few personal resources and no connections, he spent the next few years in a precarious situation until his life became famously intertwined with Lord Carnarvon's sometime later.

After his resignation, Carter moved back to Luxor where he was offered lodgings by a guard who had much respect for his old boss and took up painting. Theodore Davis offered him work as a freelance draughtsman, which Carter found galling but had had to accept, confiding to Percy Newberry that 'Davis has behaved like a bear to me of late'.

He had good reason to feel irked and humiliated by Davis. A few years earlier, Carter had recorded in his diary: 'Davis often told me that he would like to have some active interest during his sojourns in Upper Egypt. Thus . . . I put the following proposition to him. The Egyptian Government would be willing, when my duties permitted, for me to carry out the researches in the Valley of the tombs of the Kings on his behalf, if he would cover the costs thereof, that the Egyptian Government in return for his generosity would be pleased, whenever it was possible, to give him duplicate antiquities resulting from these researches. At the same time, I told him of my conjecture regarding the possibility of discovering the tomb of Tuthmosis IV . . .' Davis agreed and began his sponsorship. In return, he expected an annual 'discovery' which in 1902 was the reused tomb of the nobleman Userhat.

Since 1889, Davis had spent every winter sailing up and down the Nile on his dahabiya *Bedawin*, with his companion, Mrs Emma Andrews. It was a beautiful boat, the living quarters in the centre, shaded by awnings, a huge sail at the front and a smaller one at the rear. Davis was a millionaire who enjoyed collecting and had built a mansion in Newport, Rhode Island, in order to display his works of art. In fact, a fair amount of his fortune had been obtained at the height of America's Gilded Age by virtue of his being a lawyer presiding over the liquidation of bankrupt banks but helping himself to some of their prize assets on the way. Of medium height he could be distinguished by his bullish stance in his riding jodhpurs flaring at the hip, polished boots, elaborate moustache and whiskers. He was also impatient, headstrong and was rarely denied anything he wanted.

Davis was happy for Carter and Maspero to continue to suggest sites for him to work in and, in January 1903, they found the tomb of the 18th Dynasty pharaoh Tuthmosis IV. Despite initial excitement at the sight of the painted marking in the first corridor, the tomb proved to be a disorderly mess and, as they feared, they found it had indeed been thoroughly ransacked and robbed. The sarcophagus was empty, but they did find some extraordinary remains, for example, part of a chariot and, nearby, one of the King's gauntlets.

In the same year, Carter began to clear the rock-hard fill and debris in the corridor of what is recorded as KV20. It had already been explored in earlier centuries but perhaps not entirely and, due to the discovery of foundation deposits bearing the cartouche of the fabled Queen Hatshepsut, Mr Davis was most encouraged for Hatshepsut was one of his 'particular favourites'.

It is an extraordinary tomb, descending and bending around in a clockwise direction far under the outer entrance. Working through a series of rubbish-filled corridors, past the first pillared chamber, it took Carter weeks to clear. At the end, the roof had collapsed into the final low burial chamber which took further months to empty before they found the three smaller ones leading off it. Carter wrote: 'It was one of the most irksome pieces of work I ever supervised.'

Only early the following year, when Mr Davis returned from America, could Howard Carter lead him down to the empty red sandstone sarcophagus belonging to Queen Hatshepsut. Nearby was an empty one belonging to her father Tuthmosis I. Professor Maspero believed it might be the oldest one in the Valley of the Kings and the theory is that the tomb was built first for Tuthmosis I and later adapted and extended further and deeper by his daughter.

By 1907, therefore, Carter was very much the outsider, dismissed by Weigall as 'ill tempered, knowing nothing of archaeology' if, in the past, a 'magnificent organiser and policeman'. Neither was probably entirely correct. At the time, Weigall had been dazzled by Carter, who enjoyed the shows of ceremony and flourishes he put on as a leading official in Egyptian antiquities but at other times was exasperated by him. Carter had, however, always got on very well with Maspero who liked him very much, so Weigall's antipathy was not always wise. Weigall wrote, 'I admire Carter immensely as an official though I rather dislike him as a man' yet later on he would also comment, 'I forget to do anything but like him very much.'

Weigall for his own part was given to melancholic fits, at this point in time madly in love with a lovely dark-haired, graceful girl called Hortense whom he was to marry six months later. Throughout their life, he was perpetually worrying about money and his letters reflect his strong swings of mood and opinion.

Feeling important in his new role, Weigall took Lord and Lady Carnarvon to have tea with Theodore Davis. It was always a privilege to be invited on board *Bedawin* and the Carnarvons duly admired the boat, but Mrs Andrews immediately had reservations about the unconventional couple and described them in her diary as rather 'wild'. Theodore Davis was full of bonhomie as he thought he had just discovered the tomb of the mythical Queen Tiye and had brought some of the treasures back to his dahabiya. With flagrant disregard for the ethics of excavation, he had given the exquisite crown to Mrs Andrews 'to keep in the closet at the head of her bed'.

Aware both of Weigall's feelings and of the politics of excavation, Lord Carnarvon deftly danced around both by cultivating Professor Maspero in particular. He charmed the other academic experts, listening and talking long into the evenings with the French archaeologist Georges Legrain, immaculately dressed with starched high collars, as well as Percy Newberry.

In addition to attending her husband's daily excavations, Almina organized elegant dinners in a private dining room in the hotel, with chefs and delicacies brought in from afar. The best Rothschild wines would be served with some excellent ports, Madeiras and brandies, as their guests preferred. The Carnarvons enjoyed Luxor and from

Almina's point of view, since Luxor was a haunt of the beau monde, she had many pleasant companions for tea or walks as the sun dropped towards the amber-tinged cliffs on the opposite banks.

On 9 March 1907, however, Lord Carnarvon received a telegram forwarded to Luxor from the Savoy Hotel in Cairo informing him that his uncle Alan Herbert had died the day before in Paris at the age of 76. A much-loved figure, Carnarvon had continued to rely on him both for medical reassurance and friendship. So many wonderful stories emerged following his death. Many people had almost forgotten the grim Siege of Paris forty years earlier when Prussian forces closed around the city. Alan had established a soup kitchen aided by Richard Wallace (who later left a legacy in the shape of the Wallace Collection in London), as a result of which he was decorated as Chevalier de la Légion d'honneur for his service to the poor and as a medical doctor. Renowned for his charity, he was a man of singular personal charm and made many friends.

Lord and Lady Carnarvon returned to Cairo and prepared to go back to Europe but stayed longer than expected as Carnarvon felt rather seedy once again with a bad bout of flu. Almina was convinced it was partly the sadness of losing his uncle which had settled too heavily in his spirit. Alan's death had followed on closely that of his aunt Eveline Portsmouth in October 1906 and of his uncle Auberon Herbert in November the same year. Carnarvon was most anxious about his aunt Gwendolen and wrote to Winifred asking her to take care of her when he was not at home.

Before leaving Egypt, his enthusiasm for excavating far from diminished, Carnarvon met with Maspero and asked for the licence to excavate alongside the village in the Valley of the Nobles and, if possible, the slopes beyond.

Politically, the world of antiquities and excavations was something of a minefield. Appointments in the Antiquities Service and collaboration with wealthy excavators or professional institutions such as museums were minutely scrutinised and the subject of much gossip and jealousy. Carnarvon earnestly explained that he knew he could count on the informal help of both Professor Newberry and Georges Legrain, who had kindly spent some time showing him around the work he was undertaking at the Temple of Karnak, and Maspero agreed that he could have the concession.

Georges Legrain had been working at Karnak since 1895, when the site was more or less covered in rubble and farmed. The same age as Lord Carnarvon, Legrain was a member of the French Institute before being appointed by Jacques de Morgan as director of the works at Karnak in 1895. It had been an immense project and involved considerable restoration as well as recording as some of the pillars collapsed due to rotting foundations.

In September 1903, Legrain had discovered a famous cachette of nearly eight hundred statues when he commenced work in a northern area of the temple. His letter to Maspero records how he was still making finds 15 or 16 metres below the original ground surface, pulling statues out of the mud, describing how each statuette was pulled up and cleaned so the features of 'a smiling face would appear', allowing him to make the acquaintance of 'kings, princes, high priests of Amun . . .'. Many of these now reside in the Cairo Museum, some were bought by museums in other cities while others found their way to the antique dealers' shops. It was impossible for Legrain to keep an eye on everything. Then, in 1907, he photographed a stela some 2½ metres by 1½ metres which, although smashed and defaced, still reflected the artistic beauty of the time of Amenophis III as well as Tel el-Amarna influences. It was undoubtedly a king wearing a royal headdress called Tutankhamun.

17

THE TOMB OF TETAKY

Lord Carnarvon returned to Egypt in January 1908. Both he and Lady Carnarvon liked the Winter Palace Hotel. An elegant pink-coloured building, it was perhaps 30 feet from the Nile, offering unsurpassed views towards the rocky escarpments and temples of the west bank. The large, high rooms were designed and built by the French with fine carpets strewn over parquet floors. The wide entrance led into a large, grand marble salon with an imposing staircase sweeping upwards lit by fine large chandeliers at night. Comfortable desks and sofas were scattered through wide corridors and rooms. The pale walls were decorated with framed aquarelles of Egypt's temples and mortuary sites, lit by tasselled silk lampshades over Chinese vases. The windows were shaded by angled white blinds by day and the high panelled doors and lofty rooms help to provide a sense of coolness during the heat of the day. The piano bar was lined with books and created a convivial atmosphere for guests to enjoy at the end of the day.

Lord Carnarvon was full of anticipation and armed with his latest camera as well. This time he employed three head reises: Mansur Mohammed el Hashash, Mohammed Abd el Ghaffer and Ali Hussein, and, to begin with, a smallish team of up to seventy-five men and boys. Each day Carnarvon would cross the Nile from his hotel, hire a donkey and jog over to the site to begin work. After two weeks of shifting rock and debris, the shape of a courtyard tomb became apparent.

Overall, it was not an easy site to excavate: areas of the courtyard tomb were blocked by masses of broken rock and, because it was on the edge of an existing village, there were mounds of dust and rock debris not far from outlined walls on which the villagers' homes sprawled. Their inhabitants and predecessors had over centuries taken anything of immediate interest simply by dropping down into the tombs. Two of the passages from the courtyard tomb led under houses in the village so, while it was not possible to excavate there, presumably there was nothing left anyway.

Predictably, the tomb was indeed a robbed sepulchre, but of great interest to Carnarvon was the discovery that its owner had been a king's son named Tetaky who had been a mayor of Thebes at the beginning of the 18th Dynasty. Tetaky's coffin was nowhere to be found, but there were beautiful coloured wall-paintings. It was clear that it was a walled mortuary chapel with a vaulted chamber within the courtyard but no obvious rock-cut tomb. There were also two tiny, vaulted chambers and some interesting wall alcoves with small shabti in them. Presumably in lieu of greater riches, the earlier tomb robbers had left some very early shabtis and model coffins, as well as a few larger wooden coffins to add to the find.

Appreciated for his generosity, Carnarvon was soon nicknamed 'Lordy' by the locals and between his basic Arabic and their English they managed passably well.

Despite the absence of gold or more obvious treasure, Lord Carnarvon found the depiction of everyday life painted in yellows, reds and blacks on the walls a fascinating insight into ancient Egyptian life. He could stand and stare into the face of this man Tetaky with his short, curled beard who had lived here 3,500 years ago and clearly discern the eternal scenes of this man's life, his wife and members of a household assisting in the act of worship and remembrance. On one wall a figure is gathering grapes, a woman is sitting next to a harp, a man drives a donkey while other figures lay more offerings. And so began the careful excavation of what proved to be a large courtyard temple and far more interesting than Lord Carnarvon might have anticipated.

In the deepest part of the tomb, he found a very fine, heavy limestone offering table as well as a fragment of a limestone seated figure of the official Tetaky. The limestone fragment was inscribed 'Mayor of the Southern city [i.e. Thebes] Tetaky Justified'. Lord Carnarvon duly presented the offering table and fragment of the figure as a gift to the British Museum.

While satisfied with his own small progress, there had been a much more exciting discovery and ensuing scandal in the Valley of the Kings by Theodore Davis and his team led by the British archaeologist Edward Ayrton. Just before Christmas 1907, on a deserted part of the hillside some 100 feet up the southern side of the valley from the tomb of Ramesses VI, they had found a pit about 7 foot square and 6 foot deep filled with sealed white jars. On closer inspection there were a dozen or more large, plain, pale red jars, filled to the brim, sealed, whitewashed, and placed in regular rows. Furthermore, in early January, Ayrton then struck a new shaft near the entry to the tomb of Ramesses VI where, 20 foot down, they found the door to a tomb which had been flooded. Chipping away to clear it, Ayrton found a piece of glittering gold and later a cache of jewellery of exquisitely beautiful workmanship. The gold tomb as it was named (now KV56) was possibly a cache moved when Tawosret's (final pharaoh of the 19th Dynasty) tomb was usurped.

Davis's enjoyment of his discoveries was interrupted by the new Consul General Sir Eldon and Lady Gorst who telegraphed with the instructions that 'as he intended to be in the Valley of the Kings in a few days, could all discoveries be postponed until his arrival'. Sir Eldon wanted to see a discovery for himself and therefore there were not to be any until he reached the site about a week later. Inconvenient, but he was the British Consul, ultimately the most powerful man in Egypt, and Davis was flattered and wished to impress him.

He was not sure what he could produce on demand, but he thought that the jars from the pit (later referenced as KV54) might prove sufficiently exciting. They had been brought back to Davis's excavation house where he had watched as they broke open the first one to find a little gold mask. Assuming this was a good portent, the remainder were left until Sir Eldon's arrival. A dozen huge white pots were neatly lined up and others carefully laid on their sides.

Theodore Davis reserved the honour of hosting the Consul General to himself – thus Herbert Winlock, working for the Metropolitan Museum's team at the site, was not part of the welcome party and went off to have lunch with Howard Carter. Returning to Davis's house that evening, he heard from Edward Ayrton how the afternoon had gone.

Pots were now strewn broken and empty over the ground, linens and papyri pulled out and left in a tumbled mess. Davis had shouted at Ayrton, feeling he had been made to look a fool by the lack of gold while Gorst had left having complimented Davis on his cook and not much else. Emma Andrews, meanwhile, recorded in her diary that she 'like[d] Sir Eldon very much – Lady G exceedingly pretty and chic'.

Later, Winlock gathered that Davis had shown his guests the resilience of the papyri by trying to tear them apart. By 1908, Ayrton had been replaced by Harold Jones who persuaded Davis to send the remains to Maspero for examination. Winlock then asked if it could be offered to the New York Metropolitan Museum of Art where it was later carefully catalogued. Within the pit they had found fragments of gold leaf, a floral collar, pottery dishes, linen and various knobs from pieces of furniture.

Winlock returned to the house in Medinet Habu where Carter was staying and over supper related the story of the afternoon. No one had at this time spoken to Maspero or Ayrton but, as seasoned Egyptologists mulling over the large jars and bundles of natron and linen, over the next few weeks they came to think that the large pots in the pit tomb did not denote a pharaoh's tomb.

Meanwhile, Davis's luck continued. On 29 February he and Ayrton dragged and pulled themselves through the mouth of a tomb which might belong to the great pharaoh and general Horemheb. News travelled fast and it was soon related how they had laid ladders across a well that was to take away any water before continuing another 180 feet along a corridor which was covered in paintings. The largest room at the end contained a beautiful granite sarcophagus, and a few small objects dropped in haste from earlier robberies.

Maspero arrived in Luxor to view the latest tomb and wrote: 'Our first impression on entering these rooms is one of unmitigated admiration. The colours are still so fresh, and the play of tones so harmonious though so bright, the arrangement of the figures on the walls is so well balanced that we can feel nothing but pleasure and satisfaction.'

Lady Carnarvon asked Weigall if he could kindly show her the tomb and Joe Lindon Smith went as well. Ironically, Weigall tended to complain about other people wasting time with visitors but was easily flattered and charmed by Lady Carnarvon. In turn, she proved very game, clambering down into the tomb even if access was some-what improved from the initial challenges. She found the vivid colours of the wall-paintings quite extraordinary and viewing them an enthralling experience.

Human remains were also found in the side chambers, possibly of two women and a man, while the sarcophagus itself contained the bones of a single person, though far less care was taken with these compared to the interest in the treasures.

Maspero was staying on the dahabiya *Miriam* which was tied up at the Winter Palace Hotel mooring. Apart from congratulating Theodore Davis, he also wished to see Carnarvon and accepted his invitation to join him in the gardens of the Winter Palace. Despite his own far more modest success, Carnarvon claimed that he had never enjoyed anything quite as much and would very much like to apply and return next year to complete the recording of the tomb of Tetaky. He would also like to look to establish a further concession and would willingly take Maspero's advice.

Sitting back in a comfortable high-backed rattan chair, looking out over the gardens and the immaculately swept paths framed by tall palms, Maspero contemplated the English Earl seated next to him dressed in a rather creased pale suit with his sparkling pale blue eyes and ready sense of humour. Perhaps it was his experience with Davis or perhaps he was just charmed by Carnarvon, but one of Egyptology's greatest discoveries, Tutankhamun, had its roots in that evening's meeting.

With the exchange taking place in French, and based on Carnarvon's notes, we may imagine the conversation went something like the this:

Maspero: 'May I propose, Lord Carnarvon, that you employ another Englishman, a man called Mr Howard Carter, to act as your aide-de-camp and help organize your future endeavours?'

Carnarvon: 'Thank you for the suggestion – I have in fact met him but do you think he would be interested?'

Maspero: 'Lord Carnarvon, as you know Mr Howard Carter is experienced, he trained with Flinders Petrie and Newberry, and he is an excellent draughtsman. Given he was Inspector of Antiquities here in Luxor he is most familiar with the landscape.

I like him, I have always liked him. He is a proud man, not sociable, and he crossed into the politics of visitors and Anglo-French relations. I warn you now, diplomacy is not part of his make-up! He is utterly devoted to Egyptology and has no regular employment. You could offer him a job extending to the next season and consider matters thereafter.'

'I suggest you have lunch with him – he is living in the old Antiquities service house at Medinet Habu for the time being.'

Following the lunch, Lord Carnarvon offered Howard Carter a salary of £400 per annum payable quarterly. Carter was thrilled, and Carnarvon had his 'learned man'.

In return, Maspero was able to note that Carnarvon 'has entrusted the supervision of his working site to our former inspector Mr Howard Carter whom we have been very happy to see return to archaeology at least for a time', and which justified his decision as Director of Antiquities to grant Carnarvon a concession to extend his excavation work into the Valley of Deir el-Bahri.

In celebration, Lord and Lady Carnarvon gave a dinner party in the Temple of Karnak. Neither was worried about money, and, like her father Alfred de Rothschild, Almina loved organizing every little detail to make it an entirely magical evening.

The Carnarvons greeted their guests at the Ramesses III temple to the right of the forecourt and by the entrance to the dinner. Practically all the staff from the Winter Palace Hotel were there, immaculately dressed in costume and standing in front of what probably looked like a set for the opera *Aida* rather than an English dinner party held between the immense pillars of the temple.

All the great and the good, from Professor and Mrs Maspero to the teams working at the Metropolitan Museum and, of course, Howard Carter, were invited. The full moon cast a surreal light on the scene, set as it was with beautiful tableware and candles. Maspero, sitting to the right of Lady Carnarvon, led the conversation which centred mainly on Karnak and Legrain's finds there. It must have been extraordinary to be seated at a banquet in a place which had probably last seen such grand entertainment some 3,000 years earlier. Enough to stir the imagination and lead to talk of a possibly lost boy pharaoh whose stela had been found there.

Lord Carnarvon continued with his own work at Tetaky's tomb and was also permitted to clear a nearby tomb which was later numbered 9 in the sequence of records. He found a huge quantity of pottery and two poorly preserved mummies as well as two tablets, each of which was covered with a white gesso plaster on which was hieratic script. Having no experience of reading hieratic, Carnarvon decided it was best to leave them, along with some further pottery, on Weigall's desk although he wasn't there at that time. As it was the end of the season, and they were about to leave for home, Carnarvon just left a short note with the pieces. In turn, Weigall logged in his accounts for the year that Carnarvon was simply 'conducting some small excavations' and was unhappy with the cursory note and the tablets left on his desk.

In fact, these two damaged writing boards created great interest and are still known today as Carnarvon Tablets 1 and 2. A little later Lord Carnarvon devoted time to finding an expert to help with the translations and historical context. Hieratic is the name given to the Egyptian cursive writing which was used from its development in the third millennium BC until it was superseded by demotic in the mid–first millennium BC. It was generally written in ink with a reed pen on papyrus. That it could be translated was primarily down to the work of the French linguist and Egyptologist Jean-François Champollion (1790–1832) who identified hieratic as being based on hieroglyphic script, the difference being that while hieroglyphs were used on stone, hieratic was used exclusively on papyrus. He also worked out that demotic was the writing used by the people – the administrators and bureaucrats.

The first tablet related to the expulsion of the Hyksos from Egypt during the reign of Kamose, a pharaoh from the 17th Dynasty, c.1555 BC, and created a certain amount of scholarly excitement and controversy as to whether it was an accurate historical account or a later fictional narrative. The most persuasive argument was proposed sometime later, in an article in 1916, by Alan Gardiner who suggested that it was indeed of historical importance, later confirmed by a large stela found forty-six years later in Karnak.

Weigall's often ungenerous comments around Lord Carnarvon reflected his own firm belief that excavation should only be undertaken by professionals; he also felt that he had been outmanoeuvred by Carnarvon. He had no time for wealthy amateurs and dismissed Carnarvon with the comment 'his labours were fruitless'. He also thought that Carter would have only a temporary reprieve in employment as Carnarvon would soon become bored and Carter's luck would run out – again.

18

MARVELLOUS MEN IN THEIR FLYING MACHINES

L ORD AND LADY Carnarvon left for England and the English
spring, only to be snowed in for a week just when they arrived,
by one of the heaviest late April snowfalls recorded. Once the snow
had gone, however, the end of the month brought the swallows back
to Highclere, nesting under the soffits in the courtyard behind the
Castle. With them came the French aviation pioneer Charles Voisin
and his wife, who arrived in the company of the English engineer
and enthusiast Geoffrey Moore-Brabazon. Carnarvon had witnessed
some of their early flights in France and photographed these incred-
ible square flying contraptions. With his usual geniality, he had asked
the pioneers to stay at Highclere. As well as signing the visitors'
book, Voisin drew a little plane by his name.

Like the Wright brothers in the New World, the two brothers
Charles and Gabriel Voisin, along with their compatriot Louis
Blériot, were celebrated in France for their courage and
success. These two early aviation pioneers made their first powered

flight on 16 March 1907 when Charles flew for 10 metres. Moore-Brabazon decided that it was essential for him to be in France where aviation was making such rapid progress and made his first flight there, mastering the intricacies of the Voisin biplane and making his first solo flight in November 1908.

Inspired by French entrepreneurship, Moore-Brabazon's idea was to build a flying machine at the foot of Beacon Hill in the middle of the Highclere estate which could then run down the shoulder of the ancient, grassed hillside to launch itself. Lord Carnarvon agreed that he could build twin metal hangars at Seven Barrows, beneath the downland slopes of Beacon Hill, in which Moore-Brabazon could house his Voisin biplane, *Bird of Passage*. He had brought it back to England in March 1909 to exhibit at the Olympia Aero Show where it was the only aircraft on display that had actually flown. When asked by a reporter from the *Evening Standard* about his future plans, Moore-Brabazon replied airily: 'I may go to Lord Carnarvon's place at Highclere, or I may go to the Aero Club's new flying ground on the Isle of Sheppey.'

In a later interview, Moore-Brabazon commented that lately, most of his attempts at long-distance flying had been made at Highclere, where Lord Carnarvon had given him sanctuary. 'Patience is essential,' he said. 'Sometimes you wait for a fortnight for a favourable hour or two to try your machine. You have got to be on the ground all the time, for you can never tell when the favourable hour may come, and when it does come something in the machine invariably breaks. The trials one undergoes are enough to drive one perfectly silly.' Moore-Brabazon was entirely innovative, he had the same confidence and lack of fear of experimenting as his host and in the newspapers Moore-Brabazon was described as an 'amiable lunatic.'

Lord Carnarvon, fascinated by this new mode of transport, decided to undertake a driving tour of France and to be on hand to watch the Wright brothers win acclaim for their demonstration of their advance in aeroplane control. They had made the world's first powered flight on 17 December 1903, from a spit of land between the sea and Albemarle Sound in North Carolina. Perhaps most extraordinary was the fact that it barely made the US press, which remained particularly unreceptive to the claims of two unknown bicycle makers from Ohio.

A subsequent British visitor, Colonel J. Capper (later superintendent of the Royal Balloon Factory) was, however, very impressed and he returned home to Hampshire to share his stories and observations with his friend Charles Rolls. Charles Rolls was fascinated and became the second Briton to go up in an aeroplane piloted by Wilbur Wright on 8 October 1908 from Camp d'Auvours, 11 kilometres east of Le Mans. He then bought one of the Wright Flyers, eventually making more than two hundred of the aircraft.

Moore-Brabazon, conversely, turned to the Isle of Sheppey where the Short brothers were building their second aeroplane, designed and constructed on similar lines to the one used by the Wright brothers. Finding the Short machine much nicer to handle, he eventually decided to conduct his flying experiments at Sheppey rather than Highclere. He sold the Voisin *Bird of Passage* to Mr A. E. George, from whom it was bought by Cecil Grace, another rising member of the Aero Club and the sheds at Seven Barrows, Highclere, were no longer needed. To foster competition, the *Daily Mail* offered a £1,000 prize for the first British-built aeroplane to fly a circular route of one mile.

Meanwhile, Lord Carnarvon was relieved that his wife seemed in better spirits – earlier in the year he had been concerned for her health, but she had spent a few weeks at Margate, followed by Woodhall Spa in the Lincolnshire Wolds to rest, and was feeling much better. By November 1908 they were watching a golf match and once more hosting a shooting party before Christmas followed by a return to Egypt. Both Carnarvons felt grateful that they had their health, their children, a large number of friends and their different pursuits, and thus they toasted the New Year 1909.

19

THE CARNARVON AND CARTER PARTNERSHIP

Lord and Lady Carnarvon returned to Egypt and Luxor in January 1909 and Carnarvon began to work with Howard Carter with planning, diligence and great anticipation. Their first project was to complete the recording and photography of the tomb of Tetaky and thence to begin to excavate in the Valley of Deir el-Bahri. Lordy's team of men and boys was hugely expanded to some 275 over the next few years and, as they worked, so Lord Carnarvon took photographs of the sites, the dust, the scale and depth of activity.

Carnarvon took much pleasure in his photography, recording local endeavour and colour. His knowledge of Arabic was still minimal, but he had some phrases which sounded like 'tel a beth', 'stand still', and was able to use some of the local boys to give scale and perspective to his photographs, although he tended to leave the more detailed photographs of the inscriptions to Carter.

The inscriptions on the walls required the help of an expert and Legrain happily obliged, interpreting the paintings in detail, although some were very disfigured. Particularly curious was the placement of model funerary statues in small alcoves on each side of the tomb. Seemingly inscribed with the names of members of his family, Carter and Carnarvon assumed that perhaps they were there to protect Tetaky. Lord Carnarvon was fascinated that one of the painted scenes was a portrait of the Queen Ahmose (mother of the famous Queen Hatshepsut) who later became the patron goddess of the necropolis here.

Lord Carnarvon immediately moved on with an expanded team of men and boys to the site in the Birabi. In order to make good progress, Carnarvon would sometimes have well over three hundred men and boys working for him. They began by clearing back what was obviously a well-built brick wall near tomb number 9, which they had found the previous season. About 40 metres were cleared, including a doorway, which suggested it had been an outside wall. Later they found two names, Pu-am-ra, Queen Hatshepsut's master builder, and Senmut, her famous architect, suggesting that this wall must have belonged to a building from her reign, probably a valley temple corresponding to an axis leading to the pillared terraced masterpiece, the holy of holies, the mortuary temple of Queen Hatshepsut.

At the end of the season, though, Weigall claimed Tetaky's tomb was being robbed again and sealed it with brand new gates, allowing neither Carnarvon nor Carter further access. Weigall justified it by saying he was in any case installing gates throughout the area known as the tombs of the nobles with the help of the English benefactor and sponsor Robert Mond.

The inspector was passionate, obsessed, perhaps, with Gurneh and Luxor and wrote, 'I have always felt that the work of an inspector is to inspect and safeguard, and not to excavate'. However, he possibly craved the recognition of an excavator, and, despite his well-researched papers, he felt ignored, his moods swinging from depression to frustration. Venting his anger in letters to

Alan Gardiner, he describes nearly boiling over when the eminent German Egyptologist Wilhelm Spiegelberg actually 'patted me on the back and said he was surprised and glad to find such views held by me'. The condescension was hard to bear.

Most of Weigall's time was occupied with the latest discoveries of Theodore Davis, who was once again garnering all the acclaim. This time it was a shaft, some 25 foot deep, which led to a single undecorated chamber (tomb KV58). It took time to clear as it was 'filled almost to the top with dried mud' which had to be laboriously cleared by hand into buckets lifted up the shaft. They eventually found crumpled gold sheets stamped with the cartouches of Tutankhamun and Ay along with an exquisite alabaster statue.

So yet again the elusive pharaoh's name Tutankhamun had come up. It seemed possible that they had finally found the remains of a tomb such as it was. Subsequently, in 1912, Maspero published a paper jointly with Davis concluding that they had indeed found what remained of the burial and tomb of Tutankhamun, commenting that little was known about this pharaoh and that it was likely that 'his mummy and its furniture were taken to a hiding place . . . And there Davis found what remained of it after so many plunders.' Given Tutankhamun's challenging religious heritage, Maspero concluded that, over time, the location of the pharaoh's body and tomb furniture would probably have been continually changed to ever more obscure hiding places. He also mentioned a blue-glaze vase which had also been found earlier under a rock a short distance from this larger cache. The final sentence of the paper read: 'But this is also a mere hypothesis, the truth of which we have no means of proving or disproving yet.'

Three years earlier Ayrton had found for Davis a spectacular blue faience cup that bore the cartouche of Tutankhamun and which Davis had concluded had been dropped by robbers. It was a portent of what was to come years later in November 1922, but at this stage no one had made the link between what in effect was the final priestly ceremony of sealing Tutankhamun's tomb; so maybe his actual tomb was nearby. Herbert Winlock had written to Carter that this cartouche might be of significance with regard to the lost pharaoh Tutankhamun, giving him encouragement in the quest, but it would be fifteen years from that find before the great triumph that would link the two pieces of excavation together.

Lord Carnarvon could recite the 18th Dynasty section of Manetho's list of pharaohs by heart just as well as Howard Carter. Manetho was a Ptolemaic historian who wrote the *History of Egypt*, and, apparently, Champollion held a copy of Manetho's lists in one hand as he attempted to decipher the hieroglyphs from the Rosetta Stone using as his 'code' the cartouches enclosing the names of the pharaohs. Any detail about the obscure Amarna pharaoh Smenkhkare who had succeeded the 'heretic' pharaoh Akhenaten was entirely lacking, but there had clearly been a reign of a pharaoh called Tutankhamun who had had to propitiate the gods after the demise of the heretic Akhenaten. Slowly, this obscure pharaoh was coming into the light.

Very little was known about the life and reign of Tutankhamun but there was a reference inscribed to him on the red granite lions mentioning Amenophis III as his father. The linen wrapping found by Davis confirmed that his reign must have lasted at least six years, and it seemed from the few clues that he may have grown up in Tel el-Amarna. Maspero's theory was that Tutankhamun had moved back to Thebes from Tel el-Amarna and restored the supremacy of Amon at Thebes, and it was possible that the great colonnade at Luxor and part of the temple of Ptah might be attributed to him.

If Egypt occupied Lord Carnarvon for the first part of 1909, the latter part was spent immersed in the racing season. He was quietly excited by the prospects of his colt Valens, who had made his appearance as a two-year-old running five times, being placed, and winning once. He was home-bred, being by Laveno, son of the famous Bend Or, from the mare Valenza who won the Coronation Cup at Epsom. During 1908, Lord Carnarvon had received a fairly useful return from racing with winnings amounting to over £10,000 guineas. By such a reckoning, this made him one of the top half-dozen leading owners in the country, yet he had not won any of the great classic races.

This year, though, Carnarvon thought Valens might be a contender for the Derby. As preparation, in April he was entered for the Greenham Stakes at Newbury where he came a short-neck second. Dick Dawson, the trainer, stayed at Highclere for the race along with Almina's mother, Marie Wombwell, and Alfred de Rothschild. Valens had not been the favourite – this was Minoru, owned by His Majesty King Edward VII – but had done very well nonetheless.

There is nothing more exciting for a racehorse owner than the chance for a tilt at the Derby, one of the great classic races. It was a spectacular sunny day set amid the picturesque downs and couples sauntered through the paddocks in all their summer finery. The race for the post was watched in breathless excitement and, as at Newbury a month or two earlier, Minoru won by a head. The King walked down onto the course and led his colt through the mobbing crowd to the winner's enclosure, but Valens ran a good race and came a respectable fourth.

Meanwhile, Howard Carter was absolutely delighted to be invited to Highclere for Whitsun. He joined a house party which included Sir William Garstin as well as the trainer Dick Dawson and the Lanesboroughs (John was a school friend from Eton who had just been appointed Governor-General of Canada). There is often a moment in a person's life when they feel, almost nervously, that things are, at long last, beginning to go their way again. Following his earlier disasters, this may well have been such a moment for Carter as he was shown into a beautiful bedroom on the top floor, looking high over the greenest lawns to a tree-covered hillside. He had been assigned a junior footman in case he needed any help with his attire and was warmly welcomed. Lady Carnarvon even asked him to take her into supper one evening. In fact, both Carnarvon and Carter felt as if the stars were starting to align.

Lord Carnarvon also asked Joseph and Corinna Lindon Smith to stay, and two weeks later, in a further effort to woo Arthur Weigall, Carnarvon invited him and his wife for the weekend. Howard Carter, feeling more relaxed, returned for his second summer visit and Harold Jones arrived as well. Lord Carnarvon was keen to gather all possible information from those who had far more knowledge and experience than he did.

Harold Jones stayed on at Highclere for three weeks. He had gone to Egypt because he suffered from tuberculosis and the drier climate seemed to help. Returning to England, quite exhausted from all his endeavours working for Davis, he felt very tired and suffered from constant headaches. Lady Carnarvon insisted he stay and try to gain a little weight and better health before setting off once more. Carnarvon took the opportunity to discuss the previous excavation season with him at some length and, while Davis made it clear he thought they had discovered the tomb of Tutankhamun, Carnarvon wanted to know what Jones thought.

By the end of June 1909, Carnarvon and Carter had made a plan for the following year: they would apply for concessions in a more unfashionable part of Thebes, the area in front of the great temple of Queen Hatshepsut extending eastwards towards the area known as Dra Abu el-Naga. They would properly begin the clearance of the large area the next season, beginning in early 1910. Carter's prospects were now entirely changed: he had a generous salary paid quarterly in advance, a dedicated patron with the ability to act on a large scale and an introduction to the great and the good. It was the most wonderful reversal of fortune. Lord Carnarvon felt equally blessed, though Weigall was probably not quite so enamoured.

20

BAD SCHWALBACH

In early August, Lord Carnarvon drove noisily down the drive away from the Castle, settling into the car as he changed down a gear to make the turn at the crossroads past the redwood tree his father had planted. He was at the wheel of his latest and fastest car, wrapped up in a favourite thick coat, his lucky hat pulled firmly down about his ears, luggage strapped onto the back of the car. His devoted chauffeur Edward Trotman was sitting beside him as he turned right out of the park towards Southampton. His destination was Constantinople.

June and July at Highclere had been rainy and thoroughly un-favourable, which never agreed with Lord Carnarvon's bronchitis and lungs. Travel, he had decided, was the answer and he would follow in his brother Aubrey's footsteps and go east. He was always looking for the next adventure, a different horizon, and he whole-heartedly agreed with Edith Wharton that 'the motor car has restored the romance of travel', although in his case he enjoyed the glorious speed, the noisy roar and complete independence.

Normally, Carnarvon favoured Panhard et Levassors, the French car manufacturer which eventually became part of Renault, and found them most reliable. Today, though, he was driving a Belgian marque, a Métallurgique, a very sporting car. The firm had a showroom in Regent Street, London, which had proved irresistible to Carnarvon. He always travelled with Trotman, who was rarely required to drive but was a skilled mechanic should his services be needed.

It would undoubtedly be an adventure as, just a year earlier, in July 1908, the Young Turk Revolution had taken place in Constantinople, which violently shook the status quo and sought to dismantle Sultan Abdul Hamid's autocratic regime and reintroduce a constitution.

Curiously, the fighting and revolution had been sparked even further away: a summit in Russia between King Edward VII of Great Britain and the Emperor Nicholas II of Russia had taken place and popular rumour suggested there was a secret Anglo-Russian deal to partition the Ottoman Empire – which was not true. While the Young Turk Revolution had promised organizational improvement, once instituted the government proved itself rather disorganized and only won sixty of the 275 seats in the Chamber of Deputies. Carnarvon's brother Aubrey Herbert had been in Constantinople to witness the elections and described the procession, celebrated with endless carriages pulled by excitable horses, the mullahs, Armenian priests and imams, a cacophony of ridden horses and regiments in colourful dress. In the middle of the procession lay boxes of white voting papers.

The following year Abdul Hamid attempted to seize back power. The Young Turks once more gathered an armed force, among them Mustafa Kemal (Atatürk), and this time, on 24 April 1909, the Sultan was finally deposed in favour of his brother Mehmed V. Aubrey Herbert was excited and supportive of the efforts of the Young

Turks and stayed in Constantinople for several months, fleetingly leaving for Portofino to stay with Lady de Vesci and her daughter Mary, before briefly revisiting Constantinople on his way to Albania.

As a result of the political unrest, although the Orient Express now offered a non-stop train service to Constantinople, tourists were much reduced in number and it was not an entirely safe place. There were nevertheless still a number of excellent hotels, from the Bristol to the Pera Palace, to look after any intrepid enough to visit.

Carnarvon did not consider it safe for his wife to travel as far as Turkey and instead proposed that they meet in a fashionable spa town in Germany in three weeks' time. Thus Carnarvon had packed his camera and a minimal wardrobe, with Trotman the chauffeur acting as valet as well as engineer. In contrast, Lady Carnarvon followed her father Alfred de Rothschild's example and was never known to be under-provided with luggage. Departing later, with her own lady's maid, she would also be accompanied by Fearnside, her husband's valet, with additional luggage for her husband.

Travel by motor car was an adventure, with imperfect roads and few other cars to be seen. Their first port of call was Reims where Carnarvon attended the 'Sustained Flight' Aeroplane trials on 26 August 1909. He fell into conversation with the Special Correspondent for the *Morning Post* who reported: 'During the day I had a long chat with Lord Carnarvon, who is particularly keen on aviation and who, some time ago invited Mr. Moore-Brabazon to use Highclere Park, near Newbury, for his trials. He tells me that he intends shortly to purchase an aeroplane for his own use but cannot decide upon which type of machine to select though he at present has a distinct leaning towards the Farman biplane.'

After Reims, Carnarvon motored steadily on through Germany, Italy, the Balkans and Bulgaria before eventually reaching the hot, wooded roads with the strong summer scent of pine, marked by cypresses and wizened oaks which were so much smaller than at home due to the lack of water. Bumping along the narrow cobbled streets, the car was soon surrounded as an object of wonder. Most travellers made their way by train or boat and steamer, and horse-power was still of the four-legged variety. Having found the hotel and left the car safely parked behind gates, Carnarvon gladly retired, grateful for the shuttered cool of his bedroom and sitting room.

Although Carnarvon had visited Constantinople before, he didn't know it as well as his brother. Aubrey had originally been stationed there with the embassy some four years earlier and even their sister Margaret had come out and stayed for two or three months, regaling her oldest brother on her return with stories of leisurely afternoon picnics in thyme-covered hills and the winding arcades of the Grand Bazaar.

The old city had not changed much in over a thousand years. Built on a promontory jutting out into the Sea of Marmara and the Golden Horn, it was surrounded on three sides by glittering blue water and on the fourth by a dilapidated antique Roman wall, studded with decaying watch towers. An assortment of new towns such as Pera had sprung up on the hillsides around.

Bridging the civilizations of East and West, even in these polit-ically troubled times Constantinople nevertheless lived up to its name as the most sublime city in the world. Lord Carnarvon presented his compliments to the new British Ambassador. Sadly, Sir Nicholas O'Conor, who had been much liked by Aubrey, had died six months earlier.

As the sun's strength passed, Constantinople became a city of a hundred sounds punctuated by the haunting cries of the muezzins against a skyline of mosques and minarets. One hazy, warm August evening, Carnarvon took both Trotman and a local guide into the old city, crossing the Galata Bridge and sinking into a different world, a turbulent contrast of colours and smells.

Avoiding formal invitations where he could, over the first few days Carnarvon simply relaxed and warmed himself in the soft heat which, thanks to the sea, never seemed too intense. The scene was idyllic, the sea glittering and intensely blue, the mosaic of colours, wooden-framed houses blistered by the sun and low hills dotted with wooded gardens. He found tiny Armenian restaurants with French proprietors in the old Porte and Aubrey's suggestion of the Tokatlian restaurant in the Grande Rue de Péra proved a great success. French was more useful than English, although both were insufficient in the bazaars.

A morning was spent in the Blue Mosque and the Hagia Sophia; another late afternoon, Carnarvon took a boat from under the Galata Bridge, the captain resplendent in robes with a fine bristling moustache. They kept close to the shore, looking back at the marbled waterfront palaces, a coastline that conjured stories and heroes from antiquity.

Dr Wallis Budge from the British Museum had given Carnarvon a letter of introduction to Osman Hamdi Bey, the founder of the Istanbul Archaeology Museum, an artist and intellectual whom Lord Carnarvon felt fortunate to meet. Once more, French was the preferred language of conversation.

For all the architectural grandeur surrounding him, Carnarvon was equally happy wandering through the mosaic of shops, bidden by all to step inside, where winding, covered areas merged into old courts, each full of different sorts of merchandise, the play of light from partly tented roof coverings falling on brightly coloured rugs and textiles. The scent of unfamiliar spices heaped in sacks overlay the less sanitary smells of overcrowded conditions. He very much liked the Turkish cigarettes and carved holders and remembered to buy some rose-flavoured Turkish delight for Almina from Haci Bekir.

Rested and restored, Carnarvon and Trotman set off once more, taking a route north through Bulgaria and to the eastern side of the

Swiss Alps. He was looking forward to meeting his wife in Bad Schwalbach, a popular spa in Hesse, western Germany. It was a destination for many travellers, royalty and literati, renowned for its famous fountains and excellent mineral waters. There was even an English church. He had promised Almina to spend a week there taking the waters as well as exploring some of the historic buildings along with the less historic (but more amusing) gambling dens. Meanwhile, Lady Carnarvon planned to travel by train via Paris.

Three days into his journey, Lord Carnarvon was in excellent spirits. The car had been a great success and he was, with confidence and easy familiarity, driving at some speed along the empty, sunny roads. The road was fringed by endless thick, dark forests occasionally broken up by pockets of scattered, low-lying fields. There were more cars in Germany than in England, but not many more, and they were not especially popular in rural regions – the engines had no mufflers, so they announced their arrival well in advance and the occupants never looked back as they hastened on to new destinations.

They were now not far from Bad Schwalbach, tired, and grateful for the thick tweed coats and hats which offered some protection against the wind as they bowled along. There was no windscreen, after all. Carnarvon guessed the unusually straight road might have been laid by the Romans two thousand years earlier but, as they crested a rise, they were confronted firstly by an unexpected dip in the road and then, spread out and blocking the road entirely, were two bullock carts.

Reacting swiftly, Carnarvon drove the car onto the grass verge but hit a pile of stones. Two tyres burst and the car somersaulted, landing upside down. Mercifully, Trotman was flung clear and later said he believed his thick coat had shielded his fall.

Carnarvon, however, was trapped upside down by the steering wheel although luckily was hanging over a ditch, which probably saved his life. Trotman managed to crawl underneath to find his employer unconscious and covered in mud. Summoning help from some farm workers in a nearby field, they managed to push the car up enough for Trotman to crawl under and pull Carnarvon out, splashing water over his face until Carnarvon spluttered weakly.

Trotman then borrowed one of the wagons on which to lay Lord Carnarvon and made careful haste the last two miles to Bad Schwalbach. Lady Carnarvon was ensconced in the Am Alleesaal hotel and, hearing the furore, hurried out as the wagon arrived. Managing briefly to ask Trotman if he had killed anyone, Carnarvon passed out again when he was assured he had not.

Looking at her husband's battered, swollen and filthy face, Almina had him carried up to their rooms and summoned the doctors. Carnarvon's clothes were so caked in mud and dirt that it took some time to discover his legs were burned, he had hurt his knee and broken his wrist. In addition, he was severely concussed, his eyesight compromised and his palate and jaw badly injured. Fearnside was at Almina's side as they began to cut off his clothes and clean the patient. Trotman appeared but Lady Carnarvon walked him out of the room to find one of the doctors who sat him down quietly and checked him over.

Carnarvon drifted in and out of consciousness. Later he would describe it as being caught between darkness and a peaceful lightness where a feeling of calm and the most perfect tranquillity succeeded an almost tumultuous sensation. His mind raced and he felt as if he had some sort of panoramic view of his body and all the activity around him.

The more obvious breakages were set, and his burns were treated with topical creams. But this was 1909 and facilities and options were limited. The trauma to his head was troubling and there was no certainty that his eyesight would be entirely restored, but there was also no way to test it either at that time. As he began to emerge after the accident, Carnarvon continued to be confused and disorientated, the headaches made him feel breathless and regaining consciousness jarred his body as well as his head.

Almina had telegraphed both her father and her husband's friend Prince Victor Duleep Singh who, grasping the seriousness of the situation, on 28 August immediately took the train from Paris to come and support Carnarvon. *The Times* and other newspapers had reported news of the car crash and Almina spent the afternoons writing letters to his sisters, keeping them updated.

The biggest challenge was that Carnarvon needed an operation before he could be moved. At that time, any surgical procedure had to deal with the triple challenge of the anaesthetic (considerably less developed than it is now, of course), the operation itself and the subsequent risk of sepsis. As before with the Crimean War, the experience of dealing with injuries sustained during the Boer War in the 1890s had advanced medical knowledge, and surgeons now practised a combination of light anaesthesia and quick surgery to increase their chances of success.

Almina had developed a great interest in the latest medical practices, having visited Sister Agnes's Hospital set up by the Keyser sisters, firstly in their home during the war and then in a purpose-built hospital renamed the King Edward VII's Hospital for Officers. The list of the hospital's honorary medical staff issued by Buckingham Palace in 1904 was headed by Sir Frederick Treves, who had performed the successful operation at the Palace on HM King Edward VII in 1902, preceding his coronation. Dr Frederic W. Hewitt had administered a chloroform-ether mixture to relieve pain while Treves performed the operation, and Sir Thomas Smith assisted.

Carnarvon bore the operations with courage, never complaining but often silent for long periods thereafter and the newspaper bulletin on 1 September was at last more encouraging for all concerned.

The Am Alleesaal hotel resonated with Almina's instructions and plans. Victor sat with his friend to cheer him up. Carnarvon even quipped that their evenings of drinking and playing cards had not been nearly strenuous enough to prepare for the current headache. Victor replied that he had offered to be on feeding duty next, but Fearnside had taken that as an affront. Lord Carnarvon found it hard to swallow and was becoming increasingly thin. Almina instructed the hotel kitchens in the art of making chicken broth and creamed vegetables. She always believed in the efficacy of little glasses of sweet wine and was focused on her beloved husband regaining sufficient strength to make the journey home.

Propped up on the softest pillows, he carefully put his head on one side and said to Almina, 'I do not think I have lost my nerves.' This fast-living man, only 43 years old, who had enjoyed life to the full and followed his impulses wherever they took him, was now facing a very different life; it would be another three weeks before Carnarvon was able to be lifted onto a train to make the journey home. Slowing down with much noise and jolting, the long train pulled into the Gard du Nord, Paris, where the party rested up for a few days day before continuing on to London. Elsie went to see him and wrote to her brother, 'he is getting over his accident but is still rather crippled by it. It was a frightful one and it is the greatest mercy he was not more injured . . .'

Once back at Highclere, Dr Johnnie, their family doctor, became a full-time member of the household. The main challenge was to help deal with the terrible migraines which confined Lord Carnarvon to bed in a darkened room with cold compresses as varied as cucumber and chamomile, or warm footbaths to see if they might offer some relief, as well as tisanes of basil.

In September, Valens had been entered for the St Leger, and in normal circumstances Lord Carnarvon would have been there. Had he been present, he would have been disappointed. Rounding the corner half a mile from home, Valens took the lead. It was not to be. In the last 50 yards Bayardo came and took the race, with Valens collecting a worthy second.

The first weekend house party following Carnarvon's accident was just family. They went to Newbury Races to watch two of his horses and Carnarvon at least managed to come down to greet his friends. Winifred kept Elsie updated with news: 'Porchey is evidently doing well. But I wish he would be even quieter. However, he is cheerful and rather proud of the strength of his nerves which shows a great advance. Almina is very white . . .' They decided to go ahead with a larger party for the beginning of November. Most of the Carnarvon family were there. Almina's mother had been staying for much of the autumn to help with her grandchildren along with Carnarvon's brother Mervyn and sister Margaret, both of whom were happy to see their brother feeling a little stronger. Mervyn was an enthusiastic cricketer who had enjoyed a first-class season for Somerset, saving the day against Kent and enjoying a fine innings against Middlesex at Lord's.

The house party left for Newbury in a series of Panhard et Levassors. Lord Carnarvon hugely enjoyed the day and one of the four horses he entered, Aye Aye, actually won. He returned home slightly ahead of most of the party, accompanied by Beatrice Fetherstonehaugh, happily discussing breeding plans for the next season as he very much valued her opinion. She had an encyclopedic knowledge and later she and her husband would live at Royal Lodge, Windsor, as a token of gratitude from King George V who would consult Beatrice's opinions on thoroughbred horses.

As the autumn continued, Carnarvon invited various friends, including the Duleep Singhs, to shoot. He himself found the repercussion from a shotgun still too much to handle but delighted in his friends' enjoyment and ensured he had other guests such as the Hastings for debate and conversation about future plans. Christmas 1909 was a small family affair with Aubrey returning from his travels and ever more tales.

Howard Carter, meanwhile, was horrified to hear of Lord Carnarvon's accident, concerned, of course, for his health but also fearful he might have lost his patron when fortune appeared at last to be favouring him. However, Almina reassured him by telegram that Carnarvon would be back the following season, January 1910. When the Egypt Exploration Fund wrote to Carter at the end of September offering him an excavation site, he felt confident enough to decline it.

During the autumn of 1909, Carnarvon's friend Moore-Brabazon continued with his first trials of the Short biplane, none of which were very satisfactory chiefly because of the difficulty of finding a suitable engine. Ultimately, a 50–60hp Green engine was fitted to the Short biplane and on 30 October 1909 Moore-Brabazon flew it at Shell Beach, Leysdown, on the Isle of Sheppey, to win the £1,000 prize. Six months later Moore-Brabazon was awarded the first British pilot's licence. He continued flying until the end of 1910 when the news that Charles Rolls had been killed in a crash at Bournemouth caused his then pregnant wife to make him promise to stop.

Of course, all Carnarvon's hopes of being involved in these amazing flying machines had evaporated, at least for the time being, following his car crash. Recovery was a long haul. In December 1909 Carnarvon wrote to Dr Wallis Budge at the British Museum: 'So good of you to ask after my health. I do not seem to be able to shake off the results of my accident. I only weigh 8st 12 and cannot go up however I hope a change of air will do me good. It is a great nuisance as I ought to be electioneering in a discreet manner, but I feel physically incapable.' He also thanked Budge for the mounting of various antikas for him.

The end of the year was a peaceful family affair. Both Aubrey and Mervyn came to stay and left their brother resting in his study or sitting room as they enjoyed some shooting. Charlie Whincup at the stud arranged for fourteen yearlings to be sent up to Whatcombe to go into training with Dick Dawson. Mustapha and Valens were beginning to get back into work and Carnarvon very much hoped that Mustapha, who had come second in the Cambridgeshire the previous year, might go one better this year, while Valens should acquit himself well in April at the Newbury Races.

21

THE VALLEY OF THE QUEENS

STILL FRAIL, CARNARVON felt very *piano*. He had trouble speaking due to the injury to the roof of his mouth and, while he enjoyed the quiet family Christmas, he was nevertheless struggling after his accident. He was enormously grateful to Almina for her patience: she was a wonderful nurse and quietly encouraging during his terrible, intermittent migraines. However, he was entirely convinced that the sun and warmth of Egypt would do him good and determined to return to Egypt in January 1910. They sailed via Gibraltar, landing at Port Said and taking the train to Cairo before continuing on to Luxor and the Winter Palace. Carnarvon was utterly exhausted by the travel but found the warmth and his endeavours over the next few months in Egypt hugely restorative.

Carter was delighted to see them, and they had much to discuss. There were two main areas to plan and organize: the lower slope of Dra Abu el-Naga, known as the Birabi, which meant vaulted tombs, of which there were hundreds in this district; and the north side of the Deir el-Bahri valley, which contained burials predominately from the 11th Dynasty.

Carter had already prepared the work teams, some 270–300 men and boys organized into various groups, and had recruited Cyril, Harold Jones's younger brother, to help out. Within ten days working at Deir al Bahri Carnarvon noted, 'we came upon what proved to be an untouched tomb. I shall never forget the first sight of it.' He was mesmerized by the age and freshness of the find. 'There was something extraordinarily modern about it. Several coffins were in the tomb but the first that arrested our attention was a white brilliantly painted coffin with a pall loosely thrown over it and a bouquet of flowers lying at its foot. There these coffins had remained untouched and forgotten for 2,500 years.'

There were no other funerary furnishings, suggesting these were a well-off family but neither noble nor royal.

Four hundred yards away in the valley, there seemed to be the possibility of another wall. Carter began early in the morning and Carnarvon, crossing the Nile, rode out on a donkey to join them. 'Alas what had looked promising the day before turned out to be merely a walled- up sort of stable where the ancient Egyptian foreman had tethered his donkey and kept his accounts.' There was always plenty of scope for disappointment.

Despite his physical weakness, Carnarvon had come armed with his new camera and spent some time setting up various photographs, of both the landscape and the excavations. Early one morning he hired a number of donkeys and guides to transport both himself and his camera and equipment to the clifftop above the pillared colonnades of the temple of Queen Hatshepsut. Just as it is for every visitor, it is awe-inspiring in terms of architectural achievement and must have been a wonder of the ancient world in its glory 3,300 years ago. The wide causeway which led from the mortuary temple at the foot of the monumental cliff towards the Nile was lined by stone sphinxes and lions. To one side are the ruins of a temple five hundred years older whose stones were probably reused for the new temple. It was here, beneath the causeway, that Carnarvon and Carter had begun to excavate.

In fact, it was Cyril Jones who uncovered two foundation deposits which were hardly touched. Lord Carnarvon was excited as it might mean there was a valley temple associated with Queen Hatshepsut nearby, but no further leads emerged until a year later when Carter found part of a well-constructed wall alongside tomb number 9. This did indeed lead to further foundation deposits with the name Hatshepsut and the inscription of the name of the architect Puyemre on the wall. Other than that, sadly little else was found, leading Carnarvon and Carter to conclude that all the stones from the temple structure had been repurposed. Carnarvon could imagine the path a procession must have taken from the Nile, passing through this valley temple towards the great temple above with flowerbeds and papyrus pools.

Carnarvon and Carter did have one success, finding the remains of a colonnaded temple of Ramesses IV of the 20th Dynasty (1150 BC). Again, it had been demolished and its existence obscured by later Ptolemaic vaulted tombs which also extended over the Hatshepsut valley temple. The latter yielded little of interest except for two demotic texts, which were found in a sealed pottery amphora and dated to the second century BC. Carnarvon had met Wilhelm Spiegelberg, the leading demotics scholar and professor at Strasbourg University, who contributed a brief account of the two papyri for the book *Five Years at Thebes* which Lord Carnarvon later published, as well as himself publishing a longer paper in 1913 discussing the importance of the texts.

Some of the tombs in the Birabi had been reused from Middle Egyptian times and were now places of multiple burials, including coffins of nobles and officials from the 18th Dynasty. They had been considerably vandalized already and Carter noted that white ants had also done much damage. Three of the tombs, however, yielded a large quantity of funerary equipment and rishi coffins from the Second Intermediate Period (14th–16th Dynasties) when different peoples such as the Hyksos rose to prominence. The Arabic word 'rishi' meaning feather is used to describe sarcophagi adorned in a feather design and made in the area around Thebes. Lord Carnarvon was not enamoured of this period or its art but was delighted also to discover some exquisite works of art from the 12th Dynasty: a few pieces of small statuary, some detailed cosmetic equipment, such as a tiny makeup box with a mirror, and some alabaster vessels made for an official, Kemen, who lived during the time of King Amenemhat IV of the 12th Dynasty, 4,000 years ago.

In order to be resurrected after death, the bodies of the Egyptian dead underwent an embalming process, the quality and attention to detail of which would depend on the person's status and wealth. In any case, the embalming took a few weeks and began with washing the body during which the organs were removed in order for them to be processed separately.

The body was first dried out with natron, a substance found naturally in Wadi Natrun, which was a mixture of sodium carbonate, bicarbonate sulphate and chlorite. Afterwards, the body was again cleaned with herbs, ointments and resin before being filled with linen pads and sawdust-filled linen bags so that its shape was maintained. The body was then wrapped in linen sheets and long bandages and, in the case of royalty or the very wealthy, adorned with rings, gold shoes, jewelled daggers and magic amulets which were placed among the linen wrappings. Finally, the shrouded body had a face mask affixed while the organs were placed in canopic jars.

Carnarvon spent as much time as possible at his dig and was present when the men found first an ivory pin and then a piece of a box. Ordering them to stop work immediately, he called Carter over. Slowly, using a trowel and bellows to clear the sand and stone, the two men worked with growing excitement. An ivory box with ten beautiful hairpins, decorated either with jackals or hunting dogs, was eventually revealed. A little drawer safely stored the playing pieces: five pins with hounds' heads and five with jackals' heads. The upper surface had fifty-eight precise holes in it with an incised palm tree topped by a shen sign in the centre which Lord Carnarvon thought must be the goal of the game: 'Presuming the "Shen" sign . . . to be the goal, we find on either side twenty-nine holes, or including the goal, thirty aside. Among these holes, on either side, two are marked "nefer" or "good"; and four others are linked together by curved lines. Assuming that the holes marked "good" incur a gain, it would appear that the others, connected by lines, incur a loss. Now the moves themselves could easily have been denoted by the chance cast of knucklebones or dice . . . and if so, we have before us a simple, but exciting, game of chance.'

Howard Carter was tireless and patient, ably recording every detail and creating accurate plans and drawings to aid Lord Carnarvon.

Theodore Davis, of course, was still working in the Valley of the Kings, although so far his man Harold Jones had only found a used tomb (KV61) in the winter months of 1910 which was completely bare, without even any broken pottery. However, he continued to enjoy the social position acquired through his previous endeavours and in March was delighted to welcome ex-US President Theodore Roosevelt (he had left office the previous year) and to show him the tombs of Hatshepsut and Horemheb before hosting a lunch at his excavation house.

A few days later Professor Maspero showed both Davis and Roosevelt around the Cairo Museum, before, on 28 March, President Roosevelt gave a speech on law and order. Disappointing the Egyptians and their leaders such as Sheikh Al Yousef, Roosevelt spoke in favour of the British upholding the peace despite the nationalism brewing in Egypt.

Carnarvon, however, continued to lead a quiet life, asking Carter or other eminent Egyptologists to join him for dinner each evening. Apart from reading and research, he and Almina discussed how they could make the travel and work less strenuous for his still-precarious health and continual battles with exhaustion, despite his determination not to be an invalid.

One plan was easily made. Having settled down to a light supper and an excellent glass of burgundy, Carnarvon turned to Carter. 'I would like to propose that I help you build a house so that you are no longer dependent on the good offices of Professor Maspero, and you can concentrate fully on our excavations.'

'It would in fact be an enormous help to me, somewhere I can stay nearer our work, and I would like you to build a darkroom so that I can process my photographic work with somewhat more ease.' Almina added, 'I would be delighted to occasionally sit in the shade during the daytime, so it would be of much advantage to both of us.'

With the confidence afforded by title and money Lord Carnarvon continued to explain that he had a brickworks in Derbyshire near his estate at Bretby and he would make and dispatch sufficient bricks to make a solid, well-built house to Carter's design.

They both discussed the site, and the following day agreed it in person. It was on a hill, welcoming any eddying breeze to the north of Dra Abu el-Naga where they had been working, but in the direction of the Valley of the Kings.

When Lord Carnarvon arrived back at Highclere, he instructed Rutherford his agent to organize the production and dispatch of the bricks as soon as possible. For his own amusement, Lord Carnarvon ensured that each brick was stamped 'Made at Bretby England for Howard Carter AD Thebes 1910', just as all the foundation deposits from ancient tombs they had found were similarly stamped.

While Lord and Lady Carnarvon had arrived home in time to see Valens win at Newbury, there was far more serious news. Edward VII had been taken ill while staying in Biarritz in March. He had managed to travel back to London the following month but was struggling with bronchitis. His mistress, Alice Keppel, was with him until the Queen requested her absence. Despite suffering several heart attacks, he refused to go to bed. On 6 May, drifting in and out of consciousness, his son just had time to tell him that his horse Witch of the Air had won that afternoon. The King replied, 'Yes, I have heard of it. I am very glad', and died.

Rumours spread fast and the crowds outside Buckingham Palace swelled to thousands. A week later his coffin was taken in procession to St Stephen's Hall, Westminster, where soon there was a queue a mile long, stretching along the embankment by the Thames. Carnarvon's old tutor and minder Schomberg McDonnell was arranging access but allowed no special passes: everyone had to wait their turn to pay their respects.

On Friday 20 May 1910, King and Emperor Edward VII was buried in Windsor in the presence of eight kings, one emperor and Theodore Roosevelt. In the midst of the mourning was his Queen, a lone and composed figure, taking precedence in this moment of grief. More than either of the Carnarvons, the King's death sorely affected Alfred de Rothschild. Close friends for a long time, it seemed the end of an era.

It had been a momentous spring, and, in some ways, the stormy summer weather seemed to reflect the mood of the country. None of Carnarvon's horses ran especially well that year: he had a case of coming second which he found infuriating. Dick Dawson remained a constant visitor at Highclere, smoking nearly as much as Carnarvon himself, despite the fact that the latter had been really ill earlier in the year. Lord Carnarvon was, however, much cheered by his younger brother Aubrey. Somehow or other he had persuaded the beautiful and much-admired Mary Vesey to marry him. Almina had asked them to stay as well as Elsie, Mervyn and Vera and the whole weekend amused Lord Carnarvon hugely. Mary was as tall as his brother at nearly 6 foot whereas his beloved Almina, despite her love of patent-leather high heels, was not much over 5 foot.

Mary may have been a little unconventional in thought and life but was always exquisitely dressed, as was her mother, and was trying to cajole Aubrey into a new suit to meet her grandfather, the Earl of Wemyss, since he would be giving her away at the church. Her own father had died when she was 13 years old. Mary had written to Aubrey: 'I must tell you a thing or two which will make you furious with me. I am going to take you to a tailor myself and choose a stuff and make you a brand-new country suit for Gosford . . . Grandpa sets great store by dress.'

It was all quite stressful as Lord Carnarvon himself was apt to be outrageous in his dress as well and she told him that 'turned up trousers reduced [her grandfather] to a speechless rage'. Lord Carnarvon did in fact try to be helpful and to encourage his brother. He agreed with Aubrey's friend Raymond Asquith that Aubrey had done better than he deserved: 'Your luck amounts to genius . . . to be frank with you, a more glittering prize was never awarded to a more misspent life than yours.' The same could be said of either of them.

Lord Carnarvon was very fond of Elsie but, unlike her eldest son Aubrey, she was eminently sensible, and Lord Carnarvon had always hugely appreciated that she had never failed in her support of his sisters as well as her two sons. Just like Aubrey, however, she was not concerned with her sartorial appearance, focusing instead either on her charitable work or the administration of the legacies and investments left to her by her late husband. Luckily for the rest of the family she kept a tight hold on budgets whereas Aubrey, like his older brother, found that money exited from his bank account in speedy and often inexplicable ways.

Evelyn, (usually called Eve), at 9 years old, was excited at meeting her new, glamorous aunt Mary. She was allowed to join them for lunch when they came to Highclere as she was going to be a bridesmaid, one of the two holding the bride's train. Her cousins Althaea and Juliet, aunt Winifred's daughters, were also bridesmaids. It was a fun weekend and as ever Almina made her guests feel very welcome. Delicious summer repasts were set out on banqueting tables for lunch outside under a cedar tree, followed by cosy dinners in the dining room.

Much of this period was spent by Aubrey and Mary with the Souls, a liberal coterie of young people centred on the Asquith family 'bent on pleasure of a superior kind, eschewing the vulgarities of racing and card-playing indulged in by the majority of the rich and noble, and looking for their excitement in romance and sentiment'. Nevertheless, Aubrey stayed true to family tradition and was looking for a constituency as a Conservative MP, just like his father. He was offered the seat of South Somerset to contest which he did not win although he did make inroads into the Liberal majority.

At the end of the summer Lord Carnarvon invited a new friend to stay at Highclere, Francis Griffith, another respected Egyptologist. Lady Carnarvon was delighted to meet Mr Griffith's new wife, Nora, who was just as extraordinary a woman and Egyptologist as her husband's first wife, Kate Bradbury, had been. Kate founded a chair of Egyptology at University College London, of which her protégé Flinders Petrie had been the first incumbent.

From his first wife's legacy, Griffith was able to establish a post in Egyptology at Oxford and in later life became Professor of Egyptology at the university from 1924 until 1932. Nora worked alongside her husband to establish the Griffith Institute at the Ashmolean Museum. Francis tended to avoid social occasions and could be absent-minded, so entirely preoccupied was he in peering carefully at his papers through small, round glasses. An endlessly kind man, happy to help, he very much enjoyed Carnarvon's enthusiasm and desire to acquire more knowledge. Carnarvon would invite Griffith and his wife to Highclere on their own and found that he shared his love of music and was a fine pianist as well, and happy to explore the grounds in the warm late-summer weather. Carnarvon particularly wished to ask Griffith to contribute a paper on the Carnarvon Tablets 1 and 2, to be published as a record of his work at Thebes.

Both Mr and Mrs Griffith were delighted to see Lord Carnarvon's antiquities and had been most interested in the tablets in Luxor. Carnarvon had taken some photographs, but Griffith commented that they were singularly difficult to translate. However, he undertook Tablet 1 for the publication and explained that the text began with a little philosophy between a wazir (high-ranking official) and the King and could be dated to the reign of the Pharaoh Kamose, the last pharaoh of the 17th Dynasty, c. 1555 BC. It relays a speech given by the King in his palace to the court concerning the expulsion of the Hyksos from Egypt. 'I was in my ship, my heart rejoicing! When day dawned, I was on him like a hawk.' Griffith believed that 'the handwriting proved that Lord Carnarvon's tablet had been written within a few years of the events recorded in it'.

22

THE MOTH CLUB

Lord Carnarvon was really struggling with pain in his back but was determined to drive down (even if somewhat bumpily) to the foot of Beacon Hill, the Iron Age hill fort two miles or so south of the Castle. His goal was the large metal hangars built in early 1909.

A local neighbour of Carnarvon's had followed Moore-Brabazon's construction of the hangars the previous year with much interest. He lived with his two brothers and two sisters in a large rambling rectory with ten bedrooms and numerous outbuildings at Crux Easton in the hills above the Castle. They had moved there as his mother had wanted to live in the country, and her husband Charles had become Lord Carnarvon's vicar. The outbuildings were perfect for trying out engineering ideas and the neighbour Geoffrey and his brother Ivon spent hours investigating different ideas; they were especially thrilled when their father bought a second-hand Panhard et Levassor.

At 26, Geoffrey had read everything available about planes but had never seen one fly. Nevertheless, he was determined to design his own craft and to learn how to. He asked Moore-Brabazon if he could buy the hangars and if Carnarvon would be happy for him to attempt to fly from there. Brabazon readily agreed to sell one of his hangars for £150 and Carnarvon gave permission for the new aeroplane to be tried there on condition that occasional shooting parties could use the buildings.

This Highclere story marks the beginning of the career of the celebrated aviator Geoffrey de Havilland. Having studied at the Crystal Palace School of Engineering and, fascinated by cars and motorcycles, he began building his first aircraft in Fulham, southwest London. Borrowing £1,000 from his grandfather, he asked a colleague, Frank Hearle, to work with him. During this time Geoffrey de Havilland married Louise Thomas and she was co-opted into sewing all the wings for the aircraft in calico on a Singer sewing machine. From what he had read, and as he said later, from ideas in his head, De Havilland built a light wooden framework over which was stretched fabric held together with piano wire.

From his research, de Havilland was quick to see that the greatest shortcoming of most of the machines then being built was that their motors were either too large and heavy or too small and insufficiently powered. As there was no suitable engine available for the machine he was building, he set to work and built one for himself. The four-cylinder engine powered twin propellers set just behind the wings. Strong bicycle-type wheels were fixed at the bottom for taking off and landing and a basket-like seat was attached between the wings.

In November 1909, de Havilland and Hearle hired a lorry and drove the biplane down to Highclere in sections and began to assemble it for the first time in its complete form. It was a long job, trueing the piano-wire bracing and fitting the shaft-drive propeller gear and engine control. They worked in friendly silence seldom found these days, hearing only the sound of the wind and the distant bells from Carnarvon's sheep grazing on the hill above their hangar.

The resulting aircraft was a three-bay biplane with an open-truss fuselage, equal-span unstaggered wings and a four-wheeled undercarriage. Power was provided by a 45hp (30kW) de Havilland Iris flat-four engine (custom-built by the Iris Car Company for £220) driving two pusher propellers mounted behind the wings. A fin and stabilizer were carried at the rear, with a large elevator at the front of the aircraft while lateral control was provided by ailerons attached to the upper wing.

In December 1909 they took out the plane to try the engines and over the next few weeks made various sorties to taxi around the field. Many things went wrong (to, for example, gearboxes, casings and transmission) and they also had to wait for a day with a light breeze before actually trying to fly.

One day, determined to progress beyond taxiing, de Havilland proceeded along the slope and turned around with Beacon Hill on one side and the Seven Barrows down the hill on the other. Opening the throttle, he picked up speed, bumping ever faster over the grass before pulling back and becoming airborne. But it was too steep and some of the framework cracked. The aircraft fell to earth and lay in splinters. Miraculously de Havilland was not hurt, and he was able to walk away. They collected what they could of the wreckage, and de Havilland borrowed further funding from his grandfather and started again. Lord Carnarvon visited them and promised to keep the grass grazed.

It was now 10 September 1910, and a beautiful late-summer's evening. The new version of the machine was ready with a single propeller mounted directly onto the engine shaft, which simplified everything, and de Havilland managed to get the aircraft a few inches off the ground. He always said afterwards that those few inches were the most important and memorable moment of his life.

The local newspaper came along to capture the moment. 'For some time, it has been an open secret that the sheds at Beacon Hill contained an aeroplane in an almost completed state.' On this momentous day, a biplane was launched and 'behaved itself in the way that its inventors wished'. It flew for a quarter of a mile.

Delighted to hear of the success, a week later Lord Carnarvon drove down to watch. It was once more a very still evening as four men pushed the machine out of the hangar. 'Mr. de Havilland carefully climbed into the seat at the front (of the fragile machine) whilst Mr. Hearle gets the compression on the engine by twisting the propeller, and the word is given to go. He gives a quick revolution and stands well clear of the circling blades.'

Standing with Trotman, Carnarvon watched as 'slowly the flying machine bumped along the ground, but with increasing speed as propeller hums there were ever quicker bangs of the exhaust, and the elevators came into play. The tail skidded along, and the speed became great, possibly thirty miles an hour and at last like a giant bird, the machine rose until it had reached about 30 ft. from the ground. He circled overhead and then touched down and took off as he began to understand how to finesse the height and direction. Eventually it returned and stopped by the huts where they would stable it once more.'

Carnarvon was elated at the success and told de Havilland he would so enjoy being taken up but as his back was very painful at the moment he thought he would be too much of a burden. He did, however, order a specially cut track to be made extending obliquely for over half a mile from the sheds to the Winchester road in order to help them with future experiments.

Still annoyingly frail on some days, Carnarvon hated being consigned to the life of an invalid and insisted on walking over to the plane to ask for a detailed look over the mechanics if they had time.

Trials and experiments would continue through the autumn and over the next decades there would be a whole stable of planes which transformed air travel and, of course, combat.

Lord Carnarvon felt, as did everyone, that the heartiest congratulations were 'due to Mr de Havilland and to his assistant, Mr F T Hearle for their painstaking undaunted efforts . . . it can only be hoped that the trials now taking place at Beacon Hill will result in an all British made machine which will hold its own with those of other countries'.

Shortly after the first flight at Highclere, the family were in London. Aubrey and Mary's wedding took place at St James's, Piccadilly on 20 October 1910. Mary wore a beautiful white chiffon and velvet gown, and her fifteen bridesmaids wore flame-coloured chiffon over gold satin carrying bunches of myrtle. His brother Mervyn was best man. For once, Aubrey looked remarkably neat and tidy, his hair (which he seemed to be retaining rather better than his older brother) swept to one side and the same pale blue eyes. In fact, his eyes remained a problem, but they had not deteriorated further. Following the marriage, the party made its way to the reception at 29 Grosvenor Square, which had been lent to them by the Marquess and Marchioness of Bath. Aubrey gave his wife a beautiful ring and a pair of Irish wolfhounds and afterwards they left in a car arranged by Lord Carnarvon to spend the first week of their honeymoon at Highclere Castle.

Afterwards, they took the train to Pixton, which was to be their home. Given the time of year, it was quite dark by early afternoon, so a torch-lit procession took them up the drive. It was a fairytale homecoming. Almost immediately a general election was called, and they were thrown into canvassing in order that Aubrey could be elected a Member of Parliament, but he failed again – just. They then returned to London where Lady de Vesci, Mary's mother, had kindly given them her beautiful house at 28 Bruton Street, not far from the Carnavons' house around the corner in Berkeley Square.

23

CASTLE CARTER

L EAVING THEIR FAMILY behind, in January the Carnarvons returned once more to Egypt, very much looking forward to resuming the work below Queen Hatshepsut's temple and to seeing Carter's new house. Carter had worked apace to design and build an airy four-bedroomed house with a high central dome in the vernacular style and by February it was ready to move into.

Theodore Davis and Mrs Andrews came to visit, and the latter noted, 'Carter has built himself a delightful house at the north end of the necropolis and moves into it soon' . . . 'It looks like the abode of an artist and a scholar' and she commissioned a painting by Howard Carter as a memento.

Davis was again not having an especially productive season but was still nevertheless a port of call for the great and the good. This year it was J. P. Morgan who together with his sister came to lunch along with Herbert Winlock, as he was acting as Morgan's guide.

Carnarvon very much liked Herbert Winlock and as was his wont asked him and his wife Helen to stay at Highclere. Maspero had granted a concession to the Metropolitan Museum of New York to excavate in the ruins of the palace of Amenhotep III, so Winlock was working alongside the Carnarvons' site which lay next to the Met's which also had a hill a kilometre to the northeast as well as a desert valley some way distant.

Carnarvon's excavations continued at a great rate. Tomb 37 in the Valley of the Queens had yielded sixty-four coffins, domestic furniture, pottery and other works of art. In one coffin Carnarvon found the statues of two brothers: a beautiful silver-bronze statuette of a boy, Amenemhab, standing on wooden base, and a wooden statue of his brother Huwebenef alongside. From a young age, Carnarvon had been a keen collector, explaining, 'My chief aim was then and is now not merely to buy because a thing is rare, but rather consider the beauty of an object than its pure historic value. Of course, when the two beauty and historic interest are blended in a single object the interest and delight of possession are more than doubled.'

Lord Carnarvon consulted both Dr Wallis Budge of the British Museum as well as the German archaeologists Spiegelberg and Moeller concerning the results of his work. He wrote to Budge that he had found a rather amazing '5ft long bronze snake buried in a coffin' as well as many rishi-style coffins, of which he was going to sell two to the Berlin Museum. He later reported to Budge that they had discovered a temple built by Ramesses IV on an axis at Deir el-Bahri. Carnarvon found the area challenging to understand in terms of its structure as it was not easy to interpret. He had asked Spiegelberg to work on the papyri and ostraca inscriptions, requesting his notes be sent to Highclere Castle, c/o Howard Carter.

A little later Lord Carnarvon wrote to Budge telling him that he had 'just discovered a new temple of the axis of Deir al Bahri, it was built by Ramesses IV'. He then reported that he 'had come upon an enormous tomb and, as it would have taken two weeks to do it properly, in safety I have stopped'. He later added to the letter that he 'had found the most interesting discoveries a tablet with news of the defeat of the Hyksos'. It was, however, too late in the season with 'beastly south wind' to take it much further.

Sitting outside Carter's new house, in the cool of the evening, Carnarvon proposed that they produce a report of the work undertaken at Thebes. He would contribute some of the photographs and would rely on Carter to edit the paper. Carnarvon had thought he would ask Legrain, Alan Gardiner and Spiegelberg to contribute chapters as they could provide learned enlightenment for all interested in reading it. To that end, Percy Newberry was coming to stay at Highclere for Easter.

Sadly, on 9 March Carnarvon's colleague and friend Harold Jones died, losing his battle with TB. Along with Harold's brother Cyril, Carnarvon helped to arrange the burial in the Foreigners' Cemetery in Luxor before returning home to Highclere.

The usual busy social season followed with dinners, parties and racing. June the 22nd saw the coronation of King George V and Queen Mary in Westminster Abbey, an extraordinary spectacle of ancient pageantry, a gathering of royalty and emperors from around the world, with processions, rituals and music. Neither of the Carnarvons were part of the procession although many of their friends played their parts, including the Earl Kitchener who, along with the Earl Haig, bore the King's train.

They could only imagine the golden coaches as they slowly made their way through the Abbey to their seats. It was a bit of an ordeal for Carnarvon, and he could only guess how heavy the regalia and inlaid crowns were for the royal couple, especially the one worn by Queen Mary, of purple velvet trimmed with ermine in which was set the Koh-i-Noor diamond. Like other guests, they waited in the Abbey, silently bearing witness to the rich tableaus marking the continuation of history through music, through the solemnity of the church, the deep colours of the jewels and the long red velvet trains against the white dresses of the peeresses.

Afterwards, they returned to Highclere where they had arranged a party for 2,000 local children on 24 June to celebrate the coronation. Food and drink were set out on long trestle tables on the Castle lawns and every child was presented with a coronation beaker. Evelyn joined her parents in hosting the celebrations, delighted with the pretty dress and hat she was wearing, but she was missing her brother, who was away at school.

In his role as High Steward of Newbury, Carnarvon arranged various subsequent dinners at Highclere to mark the Jubilee and fortunately the good weather continued into July. This was not so good for the farms, though, and Carnarvon soon began to worry about the harvest and lack of grass for the animals. Staying at Halton House in July with Alfred de Rothschild, Carnarvon was pleased to meet up again with the barrister Edward Marshall Hall, a celebrity of the day who was renowned for his oratory and his success at saving his clients from the gallows, and who was giving Alfred advice on his estate. Marshall Hall was also the MP for Liverpool East Toxteth although he rarely spoke in the House of Commons, to everyone's disappointment. Tall and charismatic, he enjoyed his invitations to the best houses and the best parties and had stayed at Highclere for the first time the previous year. Subsequently, he became a regular guest.

Carter left the heat of Egypt for Highclere sometime after the Carnarvons, having stayed on until June in order to concentrate on the report of their works at Thebes. He wanted to be able to bring a good working draft with him to Highclere and in turn Carnarvon wished to accord him as much credit as possible.

His patron had a surprise for him. Carnarvon had dispensed with the billiard room which lay next to the magnificent green drawing room. The billiard table was now dismantled and in storage, the room refurnished and some beautiful display cabinets installed. It was now Lord Carnarvon's antiquities room.

Carnarvon very much enjoyed visiting dealers and had already acquired some antiquities before he started working in Egypt. Over the last few years, however, the opportunities to acquire pieces through excavation or local Egyptian dealers had led to a growing collection.

Carter wrote to 'Spiegie', as he referred to Wilhelm Spiegelberg, saying Lord Carnarvon wished to send all his salaams and to let him know if he had been put to any expense on his account. He later added, 'I have shown your MS to Lord Carnarvon, and he is immensely pleased, and he trusts that whenever you should come to England that you will not fail to let him know. The little collection "Specimens of Egyptian fine art" is gradually growing and beginning to become most interesting, and I am sure you will like to see it.'

Carnarvon was particularly interested in small, fine works of art, sculpture, precious metals, jewellery and glass, and the purchased items sat among those he had found and been permitted to keep. Conscious of the help given him in terms of research as well as a desire to share the beauty of ancient Egypt, Lord Carnarvon also gifted works of art to the British Museum and to the Metropolitan Museum of New York. As Keeper of Antiquities at the British Museum, Dr Wallis Budge naturally had his eye on potentially generous benefactors and was a frequent visitor whenever possible.

Lord Carnarvon also sold some of the coffins from the tombs in the Birabi to other museums to help recoup the costs of excavation and he encouraged Carter to act as agent and thereby improve his own finances. Weigall, of course, heartily disapproved of such trading. He had spent the last two years installing gates and cataloguing the tombs in order to deter thieves and wrote long, emotional letters to Gardiner imploring his help in regulating the antiquities trade according to his own thoughts and protocols. Weigall called Maspero and Kitchener philistines when they failed to offer him support but, nevertheless, despite his misgivings, he continued to accept Carnarvon's invitations to Highclere, always saying how much he liked Lord Carnarvon – mostly. Weigall expounded passionately his belief that instead of the utter selfishness of excavators making notes and copies of their finds for their own interest, 'the first instinct of the Egyptologist should lead him, to realise that he shares it with the world, present and future . . . to throw it open to all scholars'. Ironically, Carnarvon's detailed and illustrated report on his work, *Five Years at Thebes*, did in fact reflect precisely Weigall's passion and the conscientious research of the best experts.

During his time as Inspector of Antiquities, Carter had developed a good network of official and unofficial discoveries from the renowned families of dealers. Antiquities for export had to be obtained from licensed dealers and then shown to the Cairo Museum, which might grant a permit or decide to keep the item in return for some remuneration. It was not a perfect system and objects were exported on behalf of institutions as well as private individuals without any rigorous inspection. Weigall was torn between dealing himself in order to make some money and his strongly held views on the ethics of the trade, with the result that he managed almost continuously to undermine and annoy Maspero. Weigall stayed with the Carnarvons in the summer the following year for a race meeting at Newbury though nothing is known what he made of the new antiquities room, and, in any case, ill health forced him to take some time off after that.

Lord Carnarvon stayed at Highclere for much of the summer and in early August the House of Lords finally passed the Parliament Act by 131 votes to 114. The Act signalled a profound change in the constitution in that it provided that finance-related bills could become law without the assent of the Lords and that other bills could also become law if they passed in the House of Commons but failed in the Lords three times within two years. As the financial imperatives became more critical in the next ten years, it would mean that the taxes were levied without mitigation on many of the revenues which used to support families such as the Carnarvons.

Lord Carnarvon finished the preface for *Five Years at Thebes* and signed the book off at Highclere on 11 August 1911. He was always superstitious and chose the date carefully. The publication represented five years of consistent research and excavation among the dusty, rock-covered hillsides and valley floors for which Lord Carnarvon held the concessions and contained an impressive amount of detail and analysis compared to other reports. It was also the first time Howard Carter had seen his name on the cover of a book as a bona fide Egyptologist. Beautifully illustrated, it was published promptly the following year.

Feeling stronger now and in better health, Carnarvon accepted an invitation from the Mintos to stay with them near Berwick. Their house was set in a beautiful rolling parkland and close to a links golf course where Carnarvon was to be found almost every day. He very much enjoyed the bluff and honest outlook of Lord Minto, who had been appointed Governor-General of Canada in the summer before becoming Viceroy of India. He was a man who welcomed both challenges and responsibilities and much of his time in Canada had been the direct result of Carnarvon's father's work helping define and create the Dominion of Canada in 1867. The summer had turned into something of a heatwave, but they enjoyed a very pleasant couple of weeks, and it had allowed Carnarvon time to think. He had a relentlessly inquisitive mind and was balancing the options and the way ahead for his next Egyptian excavations.

Along with Carter, Percy Newberry was also always a welcome guest at Highclere. Lord Carnarvon had spent some time poring over the detailed maps of Egypt and its Delta region, which he had stored in his father's old leather-lined study. Carter had suggested that perhaps they turn their attention next to the Delta region and Carnarvon wanted Newberry's opinion on the idea. The ancient city of Xois seemed a realistic option and Carnarvon was aware that, during his career, Newberry had collected considerable information on the different phases of ancient Egyptian history. Carnarvon also valued Newberry's input into his antiquities collection.

In July 1911, Sir Eldon Gorst died of cancer and the Liberal Foreign Secretary Sir Edward Grey announced that Lord Kitchener was to be appointed to the diplomatic post of British Agent in Egypt. His own party shared the concern expressed in *The Times* about the appointment: 'The duties he has now to perform are novel to him and his countrymen will look forward with much interest but with confidence to see how he will discharge them. He has proved himself a great soldier and a great military administrator. They expect him to prove himself a great civilian.'

Gorst had been much more of a civil servant and had famously made his influential 'Egypt for Egyptians' speech at the Turf Club, always stressing that the British Government would eventually withdraw its political domination over Egypt and that Egyptians were ultimately going to fill the government positions that the British held. Kitchener was an unknown quantity in this respect.

Awarded the title Viscount Kitchener as well as the Barony, Kitchener arrived in Egypt accompanied by his military secretary Fitzgerald along with two French chefs. He was greeted with enthusiasm – he spoke Arabic and genuinely admired their culture and outlook, having lived in Egypt for fourteen years. A writer in the paper *Al-Bassir* noted, 'the dead would return to life, the poor would be rich, science and freedom would spread, and everybody would be happy', and he was greeted by crowds when his ship docked in Alexandria on 28 September. After driving in the Khedive's carriage to present his credentials to Abbas Hilmi, the following day Kitchener travelled by special train to Cairo and was driven to Kasr-al-Dubara, the British residency, with its beautifully manicured lawns and dignified setting beside the Nile.

Kitchener had a different approach to the job from Gorst. He built a ballroom and filled the residence with his collection of antiques: he loved visiting the bazaars and showing off his latest finds. He even redesigned the livery of the staff so that they were all now dressed in scarlet and gold uniforms.

For the English archaeological community, it felt like a different country. Kitchener was a dominant figure preferring generosity to English teams as opposed to those of foreigners. Davis was back, of course, but an English photographer and archaeologist, Harold (Harry) Burton, became his man on the ground organizing the excavations.

The year 1911 ended with a celebration as Aubrey had contested the South Somerset seat once more and this time was successful. He was now a Conservative MP and his brother and Almina were delighted. Meanwhile, Lord Carnarvon's son was now a teenager and had received as his birthday present that year a 16-bore, single-barrelled, non-ejector shotgun, and was allowed out with Maber, the head keeper at Highclere, and occasionally given a peg. His godfather, Prince Victor, was always very encouraging and was himself a superb shot. Unfortunately, Victor had become so large now that one of the boys had to carry a wicker seat for him as the regular shooting sticks would collapse under his weight. At one point Carnarvon also provided a pony and cart in which to convey the Prince from stand to stand. On one occasion, as he climbed in over the shaft of the cart, it broke and both Prince Victor and the footman driving the cart ended up in a tangle on the ground. Luckily neither was hurt and it was the source of much laughter.

24

FIVE YEARS AT THEBES

In January 1912, the Carnarvons arrived back at Luxor. Carnarvon went to review the work at Deir el Bahri to find Herbert Winlock in quite a state. Normally a relaxed, happy man, he was on edge due to the imminent arrival of J. P. Morgan. These excavations were larger than so far undertaken by the Metropolitan Museum and had been funded through the support of both Morgan and Mr Edward Harkness, who wanted to see how their money was being spent.

With the help of Maspero and his French deputy Georges Daressy in the Antiquities Department, Davis was preparing a report on the tombs of Horemheb and the alleged Tutankhamun tomb. Davis wrote a preface summarizing the work since 1903 and reflected that he had found seven important decorated and inscribed tombs as well as nine undecorated or unassigned ones. He famously concluded: 'I fear that the Valley of the Tombs is now exhausted.'

Horemheb's tomb KV57 was indeed Davis's last great discovery, and it really should have been attributed to Harold Jones. Davis did remember to thank Harry Burton who took over one hundred photographic records but never mentioned Jones, preferring to keep the glory to himself.

Davis's final two short chapters concerned a note on the life and reign of Tutankhamun. Maspero begins: 'Very little is known about the origin of this King.' Many eminent Egyptologists, including Wilkinson, Leeman, Rougé and Mariette, had concluded, from vague inscriptions left on disparate monuments, that his father was a pharaoh and he had married the lady Ankhesenamun a daughter of the Pharaoh Akhenaten. Davis concluded from the linens he had found that Tutankhamun's reign had lasted at least six years. Flinders Petrie thought that he had lived at Tel el-Amarna but had not been buried there and that, following his residency at Thebes, Tutankhamun had been very active in restoring the supremacy of the old religion based around Amun although part of his work may have been usurped by his successor Horemheb. Maspero concluded he may or may not have had children: 'Aiya replaced him on the throne and buried him. I suppose that his tomb was in the Western Valley, somewhere between or near Amnenothes III and Aiya . . . his mummy and its furniture were [later] taken to a hiding place . . . Davis found what remained of it after so many transfers and plunders. But this is also mere hypothesis and, the truth of which we have no means of proving or disproving.' All in all, a triumphantly academic way of saying that really not much was known and certainly nothing had really been proved.

Carnarvon had returned to his endeavours with much enthusiasm though his knee was bothering him – a legacy of his accident – and riding a donkey each day was not a good way to improve it. However, life soon took on a more morose tone. First, Almina received the sad news that her brother, Captain Alfred Wombwell, had died. He was only 42, but his health had been compromised after an injury in the Boer War. He left a wife and young son and was buried in the church near Carlton Hall, his widow's family home. Their mother Marie was devastated as her brother and sisters had also all passed away and, while she saw as much as she could of Alfred, her daughter and her beloved grandchildren, she was lonely.

Shortly afterwards, Almina herself became ill and the Carnarvons had to return to Cairo where she had an operation, needing some time to recover. Carnarvon spent his time lunching and gossiping with the various Egyptologists in town. One particular lunch during that time with Dr Wallis Budge went along typical lines: that Brugsch was going to stay on in his job to please Kitchener, that he thought Maspero would sell the Tuthmosis III sarcophagus, and he had doubts about the provenance of a flint knife he was thinking of buying – did it look right?

While his wife's health was improving Lord Carnarvon visited his friends the antiquity dealers in Cairo. He had become a familiar client and was even name-dropped by dealers such as Yusef Hasan to lend credibility to their credentials. Some Cairo families had export licences at time of purchase which made things very straightforward. Lord Carnarvon became ever more experienced and thoroughly enjoyed the ritual of being shown into a room – eventually – because there was something exciting to see. Collecting had become a real passion and occupation.

Luxor dealers such as Mohammed Mohassib and Abd el-Megd would also say they had kept back something special for Lordy. In fact, it was estimated that anything between 10 and 20 per cent of discoveries from any excavations were stolen or just found their way to traders, and certainly some objects from Davis's excavations ended up in their shops.

Carnarvon did not want to exhaust his wife with the long journey home until she was strong enough, but they eventually sailed back in the company of J. P. Morgan and his family, Lady Wingate and Sir Frederick Milner among others. From London, they left for

Highclere and every day Almina felt a little better. They, like millions of others all over the world, then heard the shocking news of the sinking of the *Titanic* in April 1912, but hadn't directly known anyone on board. Almina asked her sister-in-law to come to stay with her son but otherwise spent the next four weeks quietly at home.

By June, and Ascot, Carnarvon was pleased to see his wife looking stronger and was delighted to welcome the Duleep Singhs who had come over from Paris for the racing. He had a busy racing season with a number of horses in training. Nevertheless, every house party comprised one or more of his archaeologist friends: Leonard Woolley, Sir Arthur Evans, Howard Carter, Percy Newberry, Dr Wallis Budge, Sir William Garstin and even General Sir John Maxwell as Carnarvon tried to work out where he should next venture.

Lord Carnarvon had never forgotten the memory of watching the archaeological work at the tumuli by Beacon Hill, Highclere, thirty years earlier. His life had taken a very different route from that of his father, but he had taken up his father's archaeological and anti-quarian mantle.

One of the frequent guests was Leonard Woolley. Carnarvon found him excellent company, a good raconteur and acutely intelligent despite Woolley being some fifteen years younger than him, and he had asked Woolley to join him in Egypt. Sadly, Woolley had to decline as he had already accepted the offer from the British Museum to lead an expedition to Carchemish, in Turkey. However, Carnarvon then decided to ask Woolley to help him excavate a section of the Iron Age fort on Beacon Hill. 'My friend Mr Woolley having a few days spare and the weather for this year being quite pleasant we decided to try the camp on the top of Beacon Hill.'

Carnarvon had also asked Arthur Evans to stay for a few days. Evans was the famous archaeologist of the day and Woolley had worked for him in the past as his assistant at Oxford. In 1900, Evans had uncovered evidence of a most sophisticated Bronze Age civilization in Crete: Knossos. His work was one of archaeology's major achievements, which he painstakingly recorded. As a result, he had just been knighted by King George V.

With such experts on hand Lord Carnarvon was also keen to open one of the smaller barrows at the foot of Beacon Hill, which looked as if it was still intact. Unfortunately, they found nothing of distinction except that the form of the barrow with an open stone ring recalled the structure of a long barrow.

Their main effort was within the fort itself, looking at each of the two types of circles which suggested dwelling places within the nine-acre site. Woolley summarized their endeavours for later publication. 'On the top of Beacon Hill is a fine contour fort; the vallum ditch and counterpart are well preserved along their length.' They 'distinguished circles of two distinct types small round sinkings having a diameter of 9 foot and much larger ones with a shallow depression forming the circumference'. Despite cutting down into the chalk and trying different areas it was, as Carnarvon put it, all 'most disappointing'. Other than large numbers of flintstones the only object found 'was a fragment of black Bronze Age pottery'.

Woolley stayed on several other occasions and records have him writing to a young man, T. E. Lawrence, on Highclere note paper. Lawrence was going on ahead to begin work at the excavation site before Woolley joined him. Given Lord Carnarvon's passion for collecting, Woolley stayed in touch, telling Lord Carnarvon if he found any interesting pieces.

Carnarvon's wide reading was now married to a great deal of experience and a number of years rubbing shoulders with the best experts, while he himself was ever more widely respected. It was a time of increasing discovery. Some baked-clay tablets with cuneiform writing, ploughed up by chance at Tel el-Amarna and initially dismissed as nothing of much import, had been found by Budge to be diplomatic documents, adding hugely to the knowledge of life and politics of the times.

In November 1912, Winlock and his new wife Helen came to stay at Highclere. As neighbours in Egypt, Carnarvon spent the time exploring and discussing where to apply for a concession to excavate. When Lord Amherst, another notable Egyptian collector, had needed to realize some money, Carnarvon had put him touch with Winlock, suggesting that he purchase the so-called Amherst Papyri (279 documents) for the Metropolitan Museum. The transaction duly raised £8,000 for Lord Amherst, who wrote to thank Lord Carnarvon.

Winlock could not help but be envious of Carnarvon's ability to source and fund his collection without reference to endless committees. Because he was able to act quickly as a private collector, Carnarvon had just managed to acquire three bracelet plaques from the reign of Amenophis III (1360 BC). Their acquisition had been an object lesson in diplomacy and negotiation. Acting on a tipoff, Carter had bought them from Yusef Hasan in Luxor. Yusef wanted £600, 'swearing by all the Gods he had accepted £400'. Actually, Carter bought them, as well as kohl pot, for £350 and had outmanoeuvred the The Neues Museum in Berlin with his prompt action.

Two of the plaques were made of carnelian, with finely carved miniatures representing royal ceremonies, while the third showed an openwork sphinx in a 'purplish tawny coloured sard', which Newberry thought was probably the depiction of Amenophis III's principal wife Queen Tye holding a cartouche bearing her husband's name. Carter wrote, 'the latter one is really superb' and would have been part of the most magnificent piece of jewellery, adding, 'I know of nothing like them'. Carter believed they were from his tomb in the 'second Valley of the tombs of the kings'.

A month later, when Carter was looking round the antika shops again in Luxor, he reported that Yusef had two very fine coffins which the locals had found that summer in a tomb that had been hidden behind one of the large ones in Dra Abu el-Naga. Yusef also had an interesting shabti box of Amenophis I, but Carter did not think it was from his actual tomb: an interesting mystery and perhaps from a reburial. In addition, Mohammed Mohassib still had a lion, but Carter thought Carnarvon should see it and make up his own mind. In the meantime, he had also bought for Carnarvon a gold ring from one of Theodore Davis's finds.

Lastly, General Sir John Maxwell had written to say he had heard that a Frenchman, Comte de St Ferrières, had a very interesting collection which was really worth looking at and that he might be willing to part with.

Given he thought there was no hope of Tel el-Amarna, Carnarvon spent some time trying to persuade Maspero to give him the concession at Dahshur where there were two great pyramids of the fourth century. They had a heated argument about it, but Maspero was treading a difficult course between both the British and French factions in Egypt, a number of powerful men, the usual wheelers and dealers plus the integrity of the monuments themselves.

Lord Carnarvon had even prevailed upon Frank Rattigan, who was attached to the British Embassy in Cairo, to lobby on his behalf. Rattigan was immensely charming and determined but he wrote to Carnarvon saying: 'I have done all I can to get you the concession at Dashur', adding he had 'attacked Lord K' who referred him to Maspero, whom he then lobbied suggesting the 'warmth of Lord K's support' but that 'Lord K seemed to be staying out of it'. Later on, Carter also tried to argue the matter with Kitchener in person but to no avail.

In the meantime, Carter had discovered a charming little head in dark green basalt, which may have been Amenhotep II or Tuthmosis IV, and was thrilled to receive 'Lady Carnarvon's wine'. On a more positive note, Carnarvon had organized a new camera for Carter who was trying out a plate and was pleased to report it was not fogged and, on that basis, would order more of them.

As Carnarvon later wrote, 'the Dahshur business is in a very unpleasant state . . . I had a great passage of arms with the professor . . . I was pretending to be very angry and Brugsch came to the door, lifted his hand to heaven and bolted.' 'There is a lot of archaeological scandal I should love to tell you . . . I am better – the fact is there had been an epidemic of influenza this year and I got it.' He was, however, not enormously surprised when he received a less pleasing letter from Maspero. He agreed Lord Carnarvon could continue the concession and confirmed he would receive a positive letter about beginning work at Tell el-Balamun. Maspero acknowledged he had received 'un mot de Lord Kitchener recommandant votre demande'; he had, however, explained in essence that he was following Lord Cromer's protocols. He hoped he would see both Lord and Lady Carnarvon soon and sent his and his wife's best wishes to both of them.

Newberry was back in London as well and, while he had been exceptionally busy with ministerial work, would really like to see Carnarvon before he went out to Egypt. Meanwhile, Leonard Woolley wrote from Carchemish saying he thought Turkey would fall but that he might return with a few nice antiquities if he (Carnarvon) was interested.

The Carnarvons' house party that Christmas was overflowing with a disparate collection of friends from the worlds of archaeology – Leonard Woolley – as well as the world of racing represented by Carnarvon's trainer Dick Dawson, old friends such as the Marshall Halls and Frederick Duleep Singh and family: Almina's mother, Marie, as well as Lord Carnarvon's sister Winifred and her family. Carnarvon was very proud of his sister's historical endeavours – she had just published the first part of her book on James, 1st Duke of Ormonde, an extraordinary, complex historical figure who, rather like their father, 'weighed himself not by opinion, But conscience of a noble action'.

For both Porchey and Evelyn it was fun to have their cousins staying. Winifred's youngest daughter was also called Evelyn, so they loved muddling themselves up, pretending to be each other for the hapless adults who didn't know better. The new year began with a party for the children. All the families around were asked, making some five hundred guests who, in line with Carnarvon's fascination with all new technology, were entertained by a cinematograph show.

25

CAMPING

At last Carnarvon had opened a letter from Maspero confirming he was authorized to excavate at a Delta site; there were no hotels, so everyone would need to camp.

On 1 January 1913, Howard Carter began work once more in the area in front of Queen Hatshepsut's temple, uncovering more of the Ramesses IV temple and finding a fine sandstone stela. He had 180 men and boys working for him but hoped to recruit many more in the next couple of weeks when Carnarvon came out to join him.

Carnarvon and Carter spent some time working out what they would need. The main party would consist of Carnarvon, Carter, Newberry and Dr Johnnie, each of whom needed their own tent. Then there were two living tents, WC tents, bathroom tents and a kitchen tent. Each tent had to be appropriately provisioned, and men and boys were hired both to set it all up and to work in the allotted area. Carnarvon organized a list of goods to be sent out to Egypt, from biscuits to four jars of marmalade, tins of apricots and pears, soups, consommé, chutney, bacon, smoked salmon and caviar.

The weather was humid and the site full of snakes so the excavation only lasted two weeks.

Undaunted, the next site was Tell el-Balamun, a large earth mound further north and nearer the Mediterranean Sea. Carnarvon worked on in Luxor and then fell ill: 'I finished up at Luxor yesterday in a blaze of disaster, found really nothing and was in bed for the last week a sort of influenza bronchitis – altogether a dreadful fiasco. I think I go to Diospolis next week or so, but the weather is icy so far.'

Diospolis Inferior was the more recent name for the city of Smabehdet or Behdet, an ancient port from 2400 BC or earlier. About 1200 BC, during the New Kingdom, it was named Paiuenamun, meaning 'the Island of the god Amun' which was the ancient form of the name of Balamun. Tell el-Balamun was located in an agricultural area in a port city of an estuary of the Nile. Today there is no water near it, it has all receded.

Carter wrote that camping there was much more pleasant and cooler than Cairo. The land was low-lying with beautiful birds, but that also meant the excavation work was challenging. It seemed to be an ancient town with temple buildings and it looked as if where they were working was part of the old palace. On 17 May 1913, Carter commented they had found some silver bracelets with an intricate design and a large pottery jar. They also discovered a fragment of a statue confirming the name Smabehdet.

Carnarvon took the statue and some other objects to show Dr Budge at the British Museum, but then decided he would like to keep the statue as 'it is my chief record of Balaman'.

Meanwhile, Theodore Davis had returned once more to Luxor and this time employed Harry Burton to carry on in the Valley of the Kings. However, it seemed that Davis's energy and direction had lapsed since his glory days. He seemed tired and preferred to spend the day quietly on his boat. On 2 January 1913, Harry Burton broke through to Siptah's burial chamber, but he wrote that 'it looked as if the ceiling might collapse at any moment'. (The Pharaoh Siptah was the penultimate ruler of the 19th Dynasty.) A supporting column was hastily built, and Davis later learned that they had found a splendid granite sarcophagus.

J. P. Morgan had also arrived and engaged a suite of rooms for his party at the Winter Palace with Herbert Winlock standing by for instructions from one of the Metropolitan Museum's most important donors. But Morgan changed his mind and left suddenly for Cairo where he suffered a complete breakdown of his health. Such was his political and financial influence in the United States that on 17 February 1913 the stock market plummeted. He left for Rome where he died two weeks later.

Despite the papers reporting another successful season for Carnarvon, he returned home rather disconsolate, believing that he had not really achieved what he had hoped for in his excavations that year. Despite this, he enjoyed his summer in England. He had rather a good horse called Rivoli who won at both Newbury and Ascot, and the Duleep Singhs had returned to share in his racing success.

He also spent a great deal of time that summer putting together albums of all his photographs, both those he had taken at home and in Europe as well as his Egyptian ones. He had what we would today consider quite a romantic style of photography: beautiful women with hat ribbons floating in the breeze, but also some very atmospheric ones of Egypt, taken at his digs and showing as many Egyptians as Europeans. Carnarvon was very loyal to his workforce and kept the same three reises for much for his time there. There is also a particularly nice photograph of his son holding his new fox terrier puppy, Susie.

Almina, however, was worried about her mother, who spent much of the summer staying at Highclere tended by Dr Johnnie. In July, she unveiled a beautiful stained-glass window in the church at Highclere which was dedicated to the memory of her brother, Captain Alfred Wombwell, and then, as a change of scenery, the two ladies went, together with Dr Johnnie, to a spa town in the Pyrenees where Lord Carnarvon later joined them. Sadly, Almina's mother died on 30 September and the Carnarvons accompanied her body back to Paris where she was buried in the family vault. The Duleep Singhs joined them at the service and then returned to England with the Carnarvons. Alfred de Rothschild rented a house in Northamptonshire, not far from Highclere, where he and Almina could grieve quietly away from the eyes of the world.

Marie's executors were Alfred de Rothschild, Lord Carnarvon and her nephew. Bar a few legacies, her estate was valued net at £72,000, which was to be invested in trust for her grandchildren Lady Evelyn and Lord Porchester.

In December, Carnarvon wrote to Carter: 'I have had an operation and cannot go out. If you could come here and see me any time between 4 and 6, I should be pleased to see you.' Lord and Lady Carnarvon would set off for Cannes as soon as they could and from there travel on to Egypt.

After the previous rather unsatisfactory season, Carnarvon and Carter decided that they would again apply for a new concession. This time they were thinking of Hawara, where Flinders Petrie had excavated in 1888–9. Carter had heard that Georg Steindorff, Professor of Egyptology at Leipzig, was giving it up and that it therefore might be available. However, Carnarvon had heard that Theodore Davis was not at all well and was going to relinquish the Valley of the Kings concession, which would be even better. Carnarvon and Carter therefore needed to carefully consider their best approach to the Department of Antiquities.

26

THE VALLEY OF THE KINGS

DAVIS DID RETURN to Egypt and Burton moved the excavation on to the temple of Medinet Habu, but he was a far better photographer than excavator, having neither the experience nor the interest. Not much later, in 1914, Davis went up to Cairo and sat down in Maspero's office to tell him he would be finally retiring from Egypt.

Carnarvon and Carter were on hand and Maspero granted the rights to work in the Valley of the Kings to Lord Carnarvon. Unusually, Carnarvon also managed to persuade Maspero that he would need a share of any finds to 'sufficiently recompense him for the pains and labour of the undertaking except in the extremely unlike event of finding an intact tomb'. It was the moment Carnarvon had been waiting for.

The Valley of the Kings was first inaugurated by Pharaoh Thutmose I at the beginning of the 18th Dynasty, a desolate and isolated site designed to protect the royal tombs from grave robbers.

The move may well have represented a new set of religious beliefs in which the coffin was the most important item in the tomb, protecting the mummy inside and thus ensuring safe passage through the underworld, and marked a move away from the grand funerary temples along the banks of the Nile at Thebes. The valley also represented the place of death and the start of the journey through the underworld.

Like any good adventure story, Thutmose I and his successors laid false trails, built secret passages and cleverly disguised entrances in the cliffs to try to preserve their tombs intact. The Egyptian afterlife consisted of all that was best from earthly life and so the body was accompanied by everything the individual might need for a successful afterlife, from food to jewellery, chariots, spears, games, statues, shabtis. The royal tombs would naturally be full of the greatest treasures.

Over the following thousands of years most of the tombs were repeatedly plundered, sometimes the kings and queens were reburied, some simply buried together in the remains of their coffins, which may also have been robbed of any gold. The trappings of the afterlife were stolen and reused by the living.

As mentioned, an essential source of information for all archaeologists, including Howard Carter, was the list of kings compiled by Manetho of Sebennytos. In around 300 BC he wrote a collection of three books about the history of ancient Egypt, dividing the 150 pharaonic kings into thirty dynasties. Each pharaoh had five Egyptian names and Manetho was not always consistent in his lists, but his research was derived from records, most of which no longer existed.

The 18th and 19th Dynasty pharaohs who chose to be buried under the pyramid-shaped cliff in the Valley of the Kings were some of the greatest and most successful kings of Egypt and included Tuthmosis I, Tuthmosis III to Amenhotep III, Seti I, the first Merenptah and the Ramesses succession.

Maspero also had some news for Lord Carnarvon. After holding the office of Director for nearly nineteen years, Maspero was also retiring. He wished to return to Paris to concentrate on his writing. It was the end of an era and would take two years for the post to be filled, in time by another Frenchman Pierre Lacau.

Maspero was an extraordinary man of diplomacy and learning who had instigated and overseen a period of extraordinary change in Egyptian architecture. He had worked with English, French and German archaeologists, sometimes backed by their governments, sometimes working through their own passion and intellectual curiosity, but all competing for the privilege of exhuming the past. Enormously intellectual, Maspero had the often unenviable task of acting as mediator between the rival claims of, among others, the French Archaeological Institute, the Egyptian Exploration Fund, the German Oriental Society, the Americans and myriad museums, along with the hugely challenging task of ensuring methodical explorations. He was so highly regarded that in 1909 he received a knighthood, being made a Knight Commander of the Order of St Michael and St George, a British order of chivalry and an exceptional distinction for a foreigner.

The First World War brought deep sorrow to him as a French patriot, as a European and as a father. His talented son Jean, who was following in the footsteps of his father and had already achieved an outstanding reputation as one of the most brilliant of the younger scholars, fell in battle on 17 February 1915. Professor Maspero wrote: 'Until now I was considerably younger than my age. I cannot tell you how I aged in a few months.' It undoubtedly hastened his own death.

Carnarvon and Carter were immensely cheered by the prospect ahead of them. In early 1914 they decided to look for the tomb of the Pharaoh Amenophis I of the 18th Dynasty and his mother Queen Ahmose Nefertari. According to the official tomb records found in the Abbott Papyrus in the British Museum, this most likely lay outside the Valley of the Kings.

The tomb records suggested it may have been partly violated in the 20th Dynasty, but Carter had chanced upon a lead to it during negotiations over some broken alabaster fragments with a local dealer called Gad Hassan. Eventually Carter persuaded him to lead him to a tomb entrance on the hill above Dra Abu el-Naga, on the edge of the area of Lord Carnarvon's concession. Carter returned with a small team the same day to find a tomb choked with debris and thoroughly plundered in antiquity. Fires had even been lit inside it and all that remained were some charred remains of funerary equipment.

Nevertheless, this was a cursory inspection and, in the spring of 1914 both men thought it would be worth sifting through the debris to see if any further clues could be found. They were not sure whether it was just the Queen or the tomb of the King and Queen. Carnarvon wrote to Dr Budge in the British Museum where the Abbott Papyrus is preserved: 'I believe I really have found the tomb of Amenhotep I at all events a great deal of inscribed stone and its being a royal tomb there is no possible doubt. Could you get one of your underlings to copy the passage of the Abbott papyrus (About A1st) in the hiero-glyph and if you could just add the translation, it would be very kind. I imagine it is only a few lines, but I want very particularly the various signs such as the determinative of a tomb . . . All this will help a good deal. It will take a month or so to work out so I shall not finish it off just at once.'

They carefully cleared the tomb, each basket sifted as it was hauled up but, despite the immense amount of work, the result was disap-pointing with little more than dust and a few fragmentary antiquities to show for their efforts.

In the meantime, the outline agreement for the concession to exca-vate in the Valley of the Kings was agreed in June 1914, although the final authority in detail was not signed until 1915. It was undoubtedly amazingly lucky timing. Maspero favoured Carnarvon over others, his successor Pierre Lacau was not yet formally appointed and, while Lord Kitchener did not wish to be involved directly, it was well known that he was a personal friend of Lord and Lady Carnarvon.

Lord Carnarvon was as well versed as Maspero in the Egyptian antiquities laws that had been set out in 1912. The premise was that 'except as provided below [in the code] every antiquity found or in the ground belongs to the state'.

The permit (or concession) defined the locality and length of life of the excavations and were given by the Minister of Public Works on recommendation of the Director General of the Antiquities Service. Permits were only granted to experts sent or recommended officially by governments, universities, academics or learned societies and to individuals who gave proper guarantees. The latter, if not known through previous work in Egypt, must guarantee the direction of their excavations by a well-known expert. Holders of permits must work for at least sixty days in a season. Moveable antiquities found on site were to be divided between the permit holder and the government according to the Antiquities Laws division taking place on site or at the museum and 'The Excavator to pay the cost of transport to the Museum'.

'The holder of a regular permit to excavate could receive half the objects found or their value. In case of disagreement as to what the excavator's share shall consist of the Antiquities Service shall set aside the objects it wishes to retain. The remainder the Service divides into two parts of equal value between which the excavator may choose.'

The concession to excavate in the Valley of the Kings was drawn up by Gaston Maspero, with a certain amount of input from Lord Carnarvon. It was defined by the efforts and knowledge of two decades of the site on the part of Gaston Maspero and of the last eight years of Lord Carnarvon and was for a term of ten years. Maspero assessed there was little still to find in the valley but that it would keep the Englishman away from other sites. Carnarvon's record of work in *Five Years at Thebes* and his ability to call upon the best experts in the world of Egyptology gave Maspero sufficient comfort that the excavation work would be both well recorded and shared. Carnarvon agreed with Maspero about his ability to run a dig properly but not with his view that there was nothing left to find.

Carnarvon therefore had the right to a share of what he found even from a royal tomb as long as it had been previously partly opened or robbed and was not intact. Maspero's analysis was that this was all perfectly safe, and Carnarvon thought he was in with a chance. Given what else was available, he could see the opportunity rather than the obstacle. There would always be something better ahead, something even more beautiful to collect or find.

Eager to begin, Carnarvon and Carter thought that, following Maspero's supposition that Tutankhamun might have been buried in the Western Valley somewhere between Amenophis III and Ayia, they would start to clear down to bedrock in front of the tomb of Amenophis III, although the real excavation work would have to wait for confirmation of the contract.

27

JUNE 1914

Standing in one corner of the dining room as the house guests drifted in for breakfast, Streatfield, the house steward, seemed hardly to have changed at all over the last twenty years. Still very upright, he seemed if possible to have become of even greater stature, a consequence no doubt of his experience of managing the Castle staff and from welcoming so many prestigious guests over the last decades.

Two footmen were on duty as breakfast was set out in chafing dishes for the guests to help themselves. Lord Carnarvon had remained in his rooms partaking of his usual light breakfast of toast and marmalade, catching up on the newspapers and some essential reading from the Egypt Exploration Society.

There was the usual unconventional mixture of family, friends, racehorse trainers and Egyptologists. Carter and Woolley were both there, as was the famous barrister Mr Marshall Hall. Sir William Garstin was spending a little time here away from his work in Egypt,

James and Dorothy de Rothschild were visiting and, of course, there was the ever-present Dr Johnnie. Breakfast trays had been delivered to the ladies in their bedrooms and there was a relaxed, desultory pace before the departure for church.

The summer of 1914 was almost golden in its beauty, the air smelled of roses, the French windows of the library were already open, the grass tennis courts waiting and the combination of friends and sunshine led all to feel summer would never end. Yet the newspapers that morning reported the most appalling news: Archduke Ferdinand and Duchess Sophie of Hohenberg had been assassinated in Sarajevo on 28 June. Ironically, they had survived one attempt in the morning and with great courage had continued their programme for the day. They had been killed returning home. It left their three very young children, Maximilian, Sophie and Ernst, orphans and was to precipitate a cataclysmic war.

The archduke and his wife had been in England just six months earlier. The visit had been 'to promote a closer approximation to a common understanding' and the papers commented how 'no man worked harder, both by study and travel to prepare himself for his future inheritance on the throne of the dual Empire'. He also brought an invitation from the Emperor Franz Joseph for King George V and Queen Mary to visit Vienna the following autumn to express the shared desire for friendly relations and continued peace.

Later that morning, their Serene Highnesses and family were mentioned in the prayers at Highclere church and in a single day the tone seemed to have turned to one of disquiet, even in England. Nevertheless, it was a beautiful warm summer's day and Lord Carnarvon had many other projects to occupy his mind. There had been a race meeting the previous day and he was considering the next plan of campaign for his horses. Even more importantly, given he had finally been awarded the concession to excavate in the Valley of the Kings, he wished to spend time discussing his plans for the forthcoming season. There was no man Carnarvon valued more highly in his excavations than Howard Carter and both men were interested in Garstin's views of the changing topography in the valley, caused by either water or rock, and how it might relate to or help with archaeological discoveries.

Everyone returned to London the following week. Mr Alfred de Rothschild was using all his influence and contacts to orchestrate meetings in various embassies in London and writing to his cousins in Vienna and Paris to try to urge calm. Kaiser Wilhelm, who immediately proclaimed support for his devastated allies in Vienna, was impetuous and bristling in his competitiveness and neither Carnarvon nor Rothschild were under any illusions about the precariousness of European politics.

The unwieldy Austro-Hungarian Empire was unravelling, with real or manufactured hostilities spilling over. Ironically and tragically, Archduke Ferdinand had been the one liberal leader for a new era who might have been able to renew a federation, unlike his tradition-embedded father. Carnarvon was aware of the reports that the Germans had been building a global navy which could be used to threaten Britain and that, logically, food shortages might be likely. He therefore refused a very good offer for his harvest at Highclere and stored it instead. He bought more chickens and cattle, one and a half tonnes of cheese and a huge quantity of tea. Following Mr Alfred's suggestion Carnarvon also went to the Bank of England to withdraw £3,000 in gold but, by a lucky fluke, the clerk suggested his lordship increase it to £5,000, which he did and then deposited it in his bank in Newbury.

Almina, meanwhile, had embarked on planning a different contribution to the war effort. She had become a proficient and experienced nurse given her husbands' on-going medical challenges and she had become interested in learning and implementing the best medical and hospital practice. Almina had, for example, visited the new King

Edward VII's Hospital for Officers, established by Agnes Keyser, the king's friend, lover and advocate of her nursing efforts. 'Sister Agnes' funded the hospital herself. She had a genius both for organization and for grasping the connections that helped secure the cooperation of the most distinguished doctors and surgeons. A well-respected humanitarian, the hospital provided an excellent learning experience for Almina.

With the prospect of war, Almina realized her experience and skills could be applied to a whole new medical facility at Highclere. With the help of Alfred, Almina persuaded Earl Kitchener, Sirdar of Egypt, to come to lunch as she wanted to establish preliminary authorization to transform Highclere into a hospital, given the war looked ever more unavoidable. Kitchener was a busy man on a short visit home from Egypt and he wished to return to his command as soon as possible to prepare in case of war. Arriving in an immaculate tweed suit, accompanied by his military secretary Colonel Evelyn Fitzgerald, he politely agreed with his enthusiastic hostess that, were there to be such a need, he would help to ensure patients would be referred to Highclere.

The last weekend house party at Highclere for nearly five years was thrown on the 18 July. Almina had asked her brothers-in-law Aubrey and Mervyn, close friends such as General Sir John Cowans, General Sir John Maxwell, Viscount Lascelles and, of course, Howard Carter, to attend. Winifred and her husband had set off for to Vichy for a month-long visit but they turned round, arriving back at their house in Charles Street, Mayfair, on 25 July to find that, in Winifred's opinion, she had perhaps enough servants to contrive 'a picnic existence'. With serendipity, Winifred wrote to her brother that it was 'the last Sunday morning of the old world'.

On 27 July Lord Kitchener wrote to Adjutant General Birdwood in India, 'Every chance of war all round on the continent and civil war in Ireland', but he doubted the Prime Minister would offer him a meaningful role and, rather than hang around, he prepared to return to Egypt.

Alfred de Rothschild never stopped trying to use his influence positively, but the news was depressing: Germany, Russia and Austria were all introducing conscription and hurriedly constructing more railways to transport the soldiers. Alfred and the Carnarvons went to Covent Garden on 1 August for the closing night, Mr Alfred as ever with a red carnation in his buttonhole and a large box of chocolates on the ledge of his box to offer any evening guests. He showed them a copy of the telegram he had sent earlier that afternoon to the German Emperor:

'Sirs – I am fully aware that your Majesty is straining every nerve in favour of peace, and it is because I am aware of this and because I have always been such a warm and devoted admirer of your Majesty's policy that I venture to address your Majesty at such a very critical moment when the blessings of peace or the horrors of war are evenly balanced. Will your Majesty therefore send me a proposal which I could at once lay before my friends and which would be of such a nature to find favour both at St Petersburg and at Vienna and which could be warmly supported by my friends? I venture most earnestly to hope that your Majesty will most graciously reply to one who begs to describe himself your Majesty's most faithful and obedient servant, Alfred de Rothschild, 1 Seamore Place.'

Kaiser Wilhelm read it but commented from 'an old very respected acquaintance' perhaps it was now a young man's time . . .

Almina had already discussed her desire to contribute to the war effort with both her husband and her father. It was, nevertheless, a leap in the dark for all of them, and above all a radical change to family life and home. They would share their home, Highclere, with a continual stream of badly wounded soldiers and airmen who had survived the journey back from the front.

As a practical organizer, Almina was very much aware that the first thing she needed was significant financial support given the standard of medical care she wished to provide. Thus she arranged for a car to drive her to the Rothschild offices in New Court, St Swithin's Lane. For all his anxiety about the state of the world, Alfred thought that this was something positive and he agreed to write a cheque for £25,000, for his daughter's humanitarian project. It was an astonishing amount of money.

Almina and Dr Johnnie spent several days in London advertising for, interviewing and recruiting trained nurses for whom Almina commissioned some cheerful raspberry and white uniforms. She gained introductions to the best surgeons, such as Mr Robert Jones, to enquire what surgical equipment would be needed and a whole operating table with instruments soon arrived at Highclere and was installed in the Arundel bedroom. In addition, Almina bought all the comforts she could think of in terms of extra sheets, pillows, blankets, towels, as well as the everyday medical supplies from bandages to wooden crutches and wheelchairs, all of which she was sure would be vital given the patients who would soon be arriving at Highclere.

Meanwhile, Mr Alfred was in continual talks at Downing Street to help prepare the country's finances for war. Carnarvon's decision to buy gold had been very well judged. As the nation realized with horror that war was now very possible, from 31 July there was a run on the banks. On 28 July, Austria declared war, Russia mobilized on the 31st against Austria, Germany declared war against Russia on 1 August and against France on the 3rd. Given that Britain had signed an entente with both France and Russia, technically she was also at war with Germany and, given the latter had invaded neutral Belgium, the whole house of cards toppled over and Britain declared war on 4 August. The Foreign Secretary Sir Edward Grey stated in the House of Commons, 'We worked for peace until the last moment and beyond the last moment'.

Lord Carnarvon opened the Highclere guest book for his visitors to sign and scrawled 'August 1–4 WAR!' in a shaky hand across the top of the left-hand page. Only a few friends were staying but it was as if all the clocks in the world had slowed down, waiting.

While Alfred had done all he could to avert conflict, as practical as his Almina, he offered his beloved Halton House to the war effort with the proviso it would be returned six months after peace was signed.

Aubrey declared he was going to enlist.

'Your country needs you!'

As soon as war was declared there was an explosion of activity.

Earl Kitchener was already at Dover about to board a steamer bound for France en route back to Egypt when he received a telegram from the Prime Minister requesting his immediate return to London. On 5 August, he formally accepted the post of Secretary of State for War. He was now honoured with further titles: an Earldom as Earl Kitchener of Khartoum and of Broome. In short order, the British Expeditionary Force (BEF) was preparing for its departure for France, commanded by Sir John French and under the direction of Lord Kitchener, who was not convinced that the French would hold any line against the Germans.

The British had never had a large army and the entire strength was 250,000 men, of whom nearly half were stationed overseas. The Territorial Army, founded in 1908, could contribute a further 250,000 volunteers, some of whom had even attended short training camps. Some 14,000 extra horses had been secured by General Sir John Cowans, the General Quartermaster, and his logistical ability to feed and supply the Army was unfailing. In contrast, though, the German professional army was 700,000-strong and by 10 August an additional three million men had been called up.

The British, however, had their hero: Earl Kitchener commanded their hearts even while he struggled with the politics of the Prime Minister and his Cabinet. To the Cabinet's surprise and scepticism, Kitchener said that he thought the war would last at least three years.

The British Expeditionary Force began to cross the Channel on 9 August to strict press silence so as to avoid attack from German warships. They disembarked in France with their beautifully groomed horses, smart uniforms and laughter and enthusiasm to set out on an expedition to a war, the scale of which none of them could foresee.

Wasting no time, medical director Dr Johnnie and Almina made all ready at Highclere. They placed adverts and called on all the nursing agencies in London, between them recruiting thirty nurses. Almina had a decided preference for Irish nursing staff and seems to have decided that pretty nurses would be good for morale. She relied heavily upon Mary Weekes to help her. Mary had already proved herself as a very useful secretary but she now took on the role of deputy hospital administrator and found herself liaising with visiting doctors, Army medical boards and patients' relatives.

Streatfield instructed the maintenance department to construct blinds that could be attached to all the Castle's south-facing windows. Arundel was scrubbed down and a lino laid instead of carpet for the operating theatre. Opposite the stone staff stairs, it was well situated to bring in supplies as required. Mrs Macnair the housekeeper was tasked with organizing beds for all the nurses on the servants' floors.

All the guest bedrooms on the first floor were readied for use, as well as some of those on the floor above. The patients were treated as house guests, sleeping in proper comfortable beds with soft down pillows, cotton sheets and soft blankets.

Almina had decided that the library would be the best option as a day room and dining room for the patients. Lord Carnarvon was very happy in his antiquities room and study and it left the dining room and drawing room for the family. Some of the furniture was moved out of the central saloon, leaving just the sofas and chairs so that it could also act as a reception area.

The first patients arrived in mid-September, members of the Seaforth Highlanders wounded at the First Battle of the Marne and the Royal Artillery who had fractures, gunshot wounds and no doubt a large dose of what would soon be called shell shock, what we now describe as post-traumatic stress disorder (PTSD).

Almina was dressed in her nurse's uniform and was head matron, greeting each new arrival, taking their names and those of their family and settling them into their bedroom. No wonder so many patients from the very beginning felt as if they had arrived in paradise. The food was excellent, good beer and whisky and, most importantly, the treatment was designed for each patient, from diagnosis to surgery and recovery.

Across the country, dozens of society ladies in similar circumstances to Almina were establishing hospitals either in Boulogne or at home. Queen Alexandra's Imperial Military Nursing Service only had 463 trained nurses when war was declared. Every duchess and countess was writing in to ask Kitchener's personal advice and aid for a hospital and sometimes to obtain favour, and fairly swiftly Kitchener tasked Sir Alfred Keogh, who had been Director General of the Army Medical Services, to take the muddle in hand and create a proper process, from increasing the Territorial Nursing Services to organizing convalescent homes.

Lord Carnarvon, to his chagrin, knew that his weak and battered constitution would not allow him to enlist. He had hoped that his languages might enable him to be useful as a liaison officer, but he was not accepted by reason of his poor health. He found himself in the position of so many others, working behind the scenes to keep everyday life continuing in order to supply and support those at the front. He kept abreast of what was happening where he could through his great friend General Sir John Maxwell and, of course, his brother Aubrey.

Disqualified from active service because of poor eyesight, Aubrey enlisted the help of his friends in the Irish Guards. He went to his tailor to get a uniform made and, as they left Wellington Barracks in London, he fell into step with the Guards and was smuggled along by his friends, to be discovered only once the troop ship was en route to France. Given the situation the commanding officer, Colonel George Morris, reluctantly signed Aubrey on as a lieutenant and interpreter.

Aubrey's wife Mary had helped him prepare for France but was terrified of losing him and, with her mother-in-law Elsie, tried to see him off on the train though they couldn't find him among the sea of khaki. Both Mary and Elsie wrote to him daily. If their marriage had begun with romance, it deepened into an essential, unwavering love over their life. Mary began, 'My darling it's not to be believed that our perfect life has broken up this way. It still feels as if it is one of our small partings and I shall find you in London tomorrow – oh my dear it's too awful the time before us.'

Aubrey wrote as cheerfully as he could and his eldest sister Winifred received a letter he had written as he prepared to leave:

'My dear one, it was so dear of you to have sent me the lovely flask. I was on the point of going out to buy one. I had given up the foolish habit of believing one could do without a drink. I suppose it will be very uncomfortable without a servant etc., but one really has the time of one's life before one goes. This war is a most extraordinary thing. It has made the government popular, the House of Lords popular, the House of Commons popular, the Church popular now that the Bishop of London is going, the King popular, the Army popular etc. Thank you again so much my dear, and all love to all of you.'

Mary decided to lend her house in Bruton Street to Belgian refugees and moved with Elsie into Vera's (the younger sister's) house in 5 Stratford Place so that they could all be together. On 20 August,

Mary wrote that she lunched at Downing Street: 'the Prime [Minister] was so depressed . . .' Violet Asquith was one of Mary's best friends and related how much of the Cabinet disliked Kitchener who puffed his cigars in their meetings and was not interested in any of their other business.

Accounts from the front were muddled but it was not long before Aubrey was posted as wounded and missing. Elsie sent telegrams to the few Germans she knew, to the embassies and the War Office. Carnarvon was miserable: he adored his brilliant, madcap younger brother and would not believe he was dead. Deciding he couldn't wait any longer for news, he loaded up his largest motor car for all eventualities, from blankets and food to provisions and not forgetting his revolver, cigarettes and a decent medicine chest. With Trotman beside him, he set off for France to rescue Aubrey.

Carnarvon had tried to cable his friends in France and, of course, Colonel Fitzgerald at the War Office but in the end it was Sir Mark Sykes, a great friend of Aubrey's who was working with Lord Kitchener, who received the news. He immediately cabled the Carnarvons.

Almina cabled Winifred: 'Aubrey last seen in vicinity of Compiègne lying wounded in abdomen. English surgeons advised leaving him to care of Germans as to move under existing circumstances too risky. Two things in Aubrey's favour were having had no food for considerable time and assurance that when wounded are tended by Germans they are well looked after. That is all I know of Aubrey so far. I have personally requested American Ambassador, French Councillor and Swiss Minister to make every possible enquiry. Am in London for two or three days, wire if you want me to do anything. Elsie and Mary lunching. Am doing all I can. Almina.'

Telegrams were charged by the word, thus messages were usually abbreviated so as to pack the necessary information into the smallest (and cheapest) possible number of words. The average was around twelve, the exception being Almina's, to the amusement of her relations.

Aubrey had been part of the British force sent to protect the Fifth French Army's flank and thus prevent the Germans from a rehearsed pincer movement to cut off the Allies. Once the French Army lost Namur (a supposedly impregnable Belgian fort) and took the unexpected decision to retreat, there was nothing for it but to fall back, fighting rearguard actions and blowing up bridges all the way to the outskirts of Paris.

His story was fantastical, as always. Marching north had been a journey through villages owned by kind farmers, through orchards, harvests and a side diversion to buy an ex-racehorse. Having engaged in a number of skirmishes, the battalion was outflanked and ordered to retreat. Despite the professionalism of the soldiers, the regiment seemed ill-equipped and messages were carried on horseback by men such as Aubrey.

Aubrey's luck had held until 1 September when a bullet punched a hole in his side. Unable to carry him, a Royal Army Medical Corp orderly levered him onto a stretcher, tried to dress the wound and dosed him with morphine as he slipped in and out of consciousness.

When he came to, Aubrey said he found himself being prodded by a gun belonging to a German soldier. As Aubrey replied in fluent German, he became, luckily, an object of interest and was taken to a German-run field hospital before eventually being moved on to the town of Viviers and deposited with other wounded officers in a makeshift triage station. Lying on bloody straw and locked up, he was lucky to survive.

But with even greater luck, the British advanced under Sir John French and took over the German medical station. Through his elder brother's influence, Aubrey was allowed to be transported to Le Havre by road under the care of a nurse rather than in the somewhat rough troop hospital trains. He was operated on to remove the bullet from his stomach and sent back home. In fact, ironically the bullet he had received saved his life: his commanding officer Colonel George Morris and the entire battalion had continued the campaign but were mown down and all were killed on 1 September.

Lord Carnarvon and his car had been about to board a boat from Southampton when he heard the news. Lord Carnarvon wired back to Winifred, 'Aubrey wounded in the stomach; left behind when army retired; will wire'.

Almina's next telegram to Winifred read: 'Aubrey found; disembarks at Southampton today.' He was met by Elsie, Mary, Lord Carnarvon and Dr Johnnie. Carnarvon wanted to take him straight to Highclere but Mary and Elsie preferred to have him in town with them so the family, overjoyed, set off slowly in convoy for London

Mary had written, 'Oh my dear, war is abominable. One can hardly imagine the horror of men killing each other.'

28

KITCHENER'S ARMIES

IT WAS A jobbing artist for the newspaper *London Opinion* who drew one of the most iconic images of the First World War: that of the clear-eyed Lord Kitchener staring from the front page, a large, gloved hand with the index finger pointing out and beneath it the caption 'Your country needs you!'. Thousands flocked to the call. At Highclere, Carnarvon promised his staff and workers to continue to pay their wives half their wages and that every volunteer would be guaranteed his job back when he returned. Gardeners, foresters, gamekeepers and grooms signed up. Lord Carnarvon made the same offer to all those working on his other estates but wished to keep the colliery going near Bretby to supply power for essential industries.

On 22 October, as High Steward of Newbury, Carnarvon, along with special guest Lord Charles Beresford, MP, admiral and a naval hero with his famous bulldog, opened a mass public meeting in which he expressed the belief that, although the war had been forced upon Great Britain, it would all be over soon provided the nation stood firm. Even if well over 100,000 men had already volunteered, Kitchener knew he needed many more.

By December 1914 over one million men had enlisted in Kitchener's New Army, and recruitment was maintained at 100,000 a month for the following year. Equally, however, every week 24,000 men were returning wounded.

Now, to the great debates of military strategy and manpower were added the essential ones of logistics, munitions and medical support. Initially, the Royal Army Medical Corps had only 1,509 officers and 16,331 other ranks and all its procedures were based on experience gained in the Boer War, where conditions were very different from the muddy, gangrenous trenches in France and Belgium. The Army had decided that the hospitals should be well back from the front line so that the logistics to the front was entirely focused on the soldiers, although to start with, as with Aubrey's experience, whole companies were annihilated and the number of wounded survivors small. Six clearing stations were quickly established but equipped only with stretchers and minimal supplies.

This would be gradually rectified during 1915 but still the journey from the field to a dressing station and thence to the clearing station was precarious. From there it was back to the general hospitals where operations could be carried out. Head and abdominal wounds were considered too complex to treat and patients like Aubrey were simply dosed up with morphine and left to die. Fracture injuries were considered treatable and then the wounded would travel back to England, which might well take some two to three bumpy weeks.

In England, there was no public health care and the gap was filled by a melange of charitable organizations, well-meaning society ladies and a small number of some large, swiftly arranged military hospitals. Southampton was one of the principal points of return for the injured soldiers, and from there they were dispatched all over the country, some of them to Highclere.

The first few patients arrived in August and more in September 1914. Almina assessed each patient on arrival and assigned them a nurse to bathe their feet and clean and dress their wounds. A telegram was then sent to their families to let them know that their son, husband or brother was safe. Inevitably she didn't skimp on her words, wanting to tell the family every possible detail so as to reassure them.

Meanwhile, Carnarvon found he had ever more work to do to keep the farm and estate going as more of the men volunteered for Kitchener's Army. His main concern was that if there were no men left, there would be no one in the kitchen garden supplying the hospital and no harvest planted. On the other hand, he very much enjoyed the other side of this life, going round the bedrooms to see the patients, taking the time to recommend a book to read or a painting to look at. Patients whose 'nerves . . . were utterly wrong', even this early in the war, wrote later to express their enjoyment of the Earl's company. Saturday was visiting day, which was all part and parcel of Almina's deliberate attempt to resist the anonymity of big hospitals and to look after the men in every way possible. She understoood that treating the patients as individuals in need of space, time and comfort as well as medical attention was the key to success.

Almina's approach may have been admirable but it was also extremely expensive. The papers reported that Lady Carnarvon, 'one of the most beautiful women was establishing her hospital' and had been entirely reorganizing it to welcome more patients. Lord Carnarvon was full of admiration for his wife's endeavours but also entirely thankful he was not funding it. So it was with some foresight that Almina set off once more to the Rothschild offices to ask Mr Alfred for further funds. Alfred's remonstrance was gentle: 'Darling, it was only last month I gave you £25,000, what on earth have you done with it? I know it's all in a good cause, but please do be careful.' Nevertheless he wrote a cheque for a further £10,000. Alfred was also on the board of Princess Charlotte's Hospital, and such support was a family tradition. Almina's next move was to equip her operating theatre better and install an X-ray machine.

By mid-October, Robert Jones was operating in the Arundel bedroom on a succession of men with broken bones. Already an experienced orthopaedic surgeon, he had learned how to treat fractures from years working as the Surgeon-Superintendent on the construction of the Manchester Ship Canal. He devised the first comprehensive accident response service in the world and implemented it along the length of the canal, so he was accustomed to treating many people in stressful conditions.

Two-thirds of all casualties during the First World War (those who survived long enough to reach a hospital) had injuries to bones from shrapnel and gunshot wounds so there was plenty of work for orthopaedic surgeons. Jones was adamant that by using a particular technique called the Thomas splint, which had been developed by his uncle Hugh Thomas, in the treatment of compound fractures, the mortality rate could be reduced from 80 per cent to 20 per cent. It seems odd to us that a broken leg could kill you but on the battlefields of the Great War it frequently did. The femur is the longest bone in the body and the muscles surrounding it are correspondingly strong. When the femur breaks, the muscles contract, pulling the bone ends past each other, causing additional injury, dangerous loss of blood, nerve damage and a great deal of pain. Jones's idea was to use traction to ensure that the two broken pieces of bone were held end to end so that healing could take place. It was a brilliantly successful treatment and it saved countless lives at Highclere and throughout the war. The patients who benefited were so grateful and so conscious of others' needs that they frequently returned their splints to Almina's hospital once they were done with them.

Another eminent medical man to come down to the hospital was Hector Mackenzie, a renowned chest surgeon. Despite all his best efforts, one of the patients he operated on, a man called Thompson, died. When it became clear that her patient was not going to recover, Almina wired Thompson's daughter and invited her to stay at Highclere. Agnes Thompson wrote to Almina later: 'I will never forget my few days visit to Highclere and that I saw the death of Daddy and the very kind treatment that he received from your hands. I do hope you are feeling better . . . you looked very ill.'

The pressure on the Western Front had increased since the Russians had suffered a heavy defeat on the Eastern Front. The Allies were holding the line, but it was already abundantly clear that, with more than a million men on both sides dug in across Belgium and northern France, this war was definitely not going to be over by Christmas.

Then came the news no one wanted to receive: two of the young lads who had volunteered from the estate, Harry Garrett and Harry Illot, had been killed in action in France. They had both been gardeners under Mr Blake and Harry's family had been part of the estate for the past twenty years. Blake, horrified, wanted to enlist but Carnarvon was adamant he should stay.

Winifred's nephew Bar (William Fuller Maitland) had also been killed by a shell. His brother Dick, a delicate boy who suffered from pneumonia most winters and was an artist, volunteered to take his brother's place. He obtained a commission in the Scots Guards and, luckily, he survived.

Amid the relentless news there was one happy event to mark the end of 1914: on 12 December, Lord and Lady Carnarvon walked into Westminster Abbey and along to the Henry VII Chapel at the far end. They were not the first guests. Princess Mary was already sitting in the front pew with her lady-in-waiting. She was wearing the prettiest crushed strawberry coat trimmed with a rich brown and was very happy to be supporting her great friend the Hon. Mary Sidney Katharine Almina Gardner, Winifred's daughter, at her wedding to the Hon. Geoffrey Hope Morley. The register was signed by Princess Mary, the Earl of Carnarvon and HE the French Ambassador Paul Cambon. Given the war, however, there was no reception afterwards. The King and Queen were unable to attend but sent the bride a beautiful pendant.

The family and patients spent Christmas 1914 together. With the help of all the nurses and servants, Almina did her best to decorate the house and to keep everyone's spirits up. The kitchens produced turkeys and a goose, a Christmas tree was put up in the library and the vicar was asked to lead them in carols and prayers one evening. Lord and Lady Carnarvon went to matins on Christmas Day with those who were able to. Carnarvon was low and depressed; his headaches would not ease and he always got coughs and bronchitis at this time of year. They had invited a few friends to stay as well but nevertheless Carnarvon annotated the visitors' book: 'Seeing the New Year in . . . the saddest and most trying owing to the awful war.'

Christmas Day on the Western Front had been stranger still. It began when German and British soldiers called out Christmas greetings to each other across the barbed wire before, extraordinarily, they negotiated their own unofficial truce for the day. Unarmed soldiers from each side clambered over the top to collect their dead. Meeting in the shattered land that lay between them and shaking hands, they buried their fallen comrades together. Somebody suggested a game of football and food was exchanged: sauerkraut, sausages, chocolate and cigarettes. German and English voices rose up from the trenches to sing 'Silent Night' in both languages and for twenty-four hours there was peace.

Despite pressure from the French generals, Lord Kitchener had delayed taking part in any fresh battle until the new troops were armed and trained in 1915. As a result, the First Battle of Ypres began much later in the year.

In November, to Aubrey's great sadness, Turkey entered the war on the side of the Germans. The coming year would see the war expand to Italy, the Balkans, the Middle East and wider conflict.

Aubrey's wounds had healed remarkably well but his appalling eyesight was now an open secret. Hatching schemes to return to the battle, and given his friendship with General Sir John Maxwell through his brother, Egypt was Aubrey's new goal. He was accepted, told to report to the Arab Bureau in Cairo and sailed in December.

29

EGYPT

JANUARY 1915 HAD begun with a disaster at sea for Britain. On New
Year's Day, HMS *Formidable* was torpedoed in the English
Channel by a German U-boat and tragically only 199 men of the
750 on board were saved. One sailor had a miraculous escape, which
Lord Carnarvon related in a letter to Winifred. As the ship went
down, a man named Saxton managed to cling to the propeller despite
his injuries and the immense waves which threatened to wash him
away. He then tried to swim for the pinnace which was not too far,
but when he eventually made it, he was too exhausted to haul himself
up the side of the boat. He was about to give up and resign himself
to drowning when a huge wave caught him up and swept him over
the side. Saxton arrived at Almina's hospital with broken bones,
shock and hypothermia. He was one of the lucky ones.

Undeterred by the increasing threat of the German torpedo boats
and increasingly anxious to at least be doing something, in mid-
January Lord and Lady Carnarvon too decided to set sail for Egypt.

In the meantime, Aubrey had arrived in Cairo with his usual haphazard wardrobe and his typewriter to find life carrying on much as before. He reported to the Arab Bureau and was none too complimentary about the chief, Colonel Newcombe, but knew Leonard Woolley, 'a good sort', from Highclere, and had met T. E. Lawrence, 'an odd gnome, half cad and a touch of genius'. Lawrence for his part wrote: 'Then there is Aubrey Herbert, who is a joke but a very nice one: he is too short-sighted to read or recognise anyone but speaks Turkish well, Albanian, French, Italian, Arabic, German.' Understanding of each bred affection.

Staying at Shepheard's Hotel, Aubrey was joined by his brother and Almina and later by his wife and mother-in-law as well. Despite the war, the social life in Cairo was intense even if the parties seemed rather surreal. There were troops from New Zealand and Australia riding their incredibly well-trained horses perfectly in line through the streets, sunburned youths from England trying to recreate home in the officers' clubs and a number of shadowy new government intelligence bureaux all rather inexpertly competing with each other. At the same time, a pageant of ceremony greeted the accession of the new Sultan of Egypt, a colourful spectacle for all to watch.

The Carnarvons had brought gifts of port and pâté de foie gras for General Sir John Maxwell, who found time to dine with them despite being busy preparing to defend the Suez Canal against a German-led Ottoman force. The battle took place at the end of January 1915 and the Suez Canal was successfully defended but the relatively swift success probably compounded the British Government's continual misjudgements about the Turkish fighting capacity later in the year.

Carnarvon and Almina left the politics of Cairo behind and set out for Luxor where they settled into the Winter Palace Hotel and met up with Howard Carter. The Egyptology scene was now very different from that of pre-war and the loss of the competent Germans from the the Neues Museum in Berlin who had been forced to return home had left a gap. Although to an extent the teams all competed with each other as to who could unearth the greatest finds, it was a small world in Luxor and Cairo and the Europeans and Americans mixed and socialized together.

The Valley of the Kings was actually made up of two separate valleys and both Carnarvon and Carter were interested in the more remote, less-excavated Western Valley, at the far end of which lay the tomb of the great 18th-Dynasty pharaoh Amenhotep III, which had been discovered in Napoleonic times.

Carter had already reconnoitred it and, although strictly speaking the formal document allowing them to excavate within the Valley of the Kings had not yet been signed, nevertheless in February they decided to begin work in the Western Valley.

Clearing the watercourse below the entrance to the tomb of Amenhotep III, they fairly quickly found five foundation deposits. Some bore the cartouche of Tuthmosis IV (the father of Amenhotep III) who had clearly abandoned this site in favour of one in the Eastern Valley (his tomb had been discovered eleven years earlier by Theodore Davis), while other fragments bore the cartouche of the great Queen Tiye.

They then turned their attention to the well and the area around it, finding some small objects such as a wooden rope knot, model chisels, adzes, knives and blades as well as cartouches of faience plaques. The wooden fragments bearing the name Queen Tiye (Great Royal Wife of the Egyptian pharaoh Amenhotep III) were covered in bitumen and there were some other fragments of shabtis of Amenhotep III.

The next two weeks were spent carefully cataloguing what they had found but they ceased their excavations on 8 March when they reached the bedrock without finding any further evidence of a burial. Returning to Cairo, the Carnarvons set sail for Highclere while Carter stayed on to see if he could do anything to aid the war effort in Cairo, promising to stay in touch should there be any developments. It had been a brief and rather unsatisfactory sojourn and both men were feeling equally frustrated.

Back in England, Carnarvon promptly fell ill and sought the sea air in Penzance, Cornwall. Rutherford was also not well. 'Very sorry to hear that you are ill but hope you are better. I came down here for 2 or 3 days and I fear I have got flu.' He then signed it off, 'Yours truly, Carnarvon PS I have been so ill. I could not send [this] off or do anything!'

The spring of 1915 marked the opening salvo of an ill-judged and poorly executed engagement. The British and her allies launched an attack on the Dardanelles, the idea of which had begun as a purely naval strategy in order to secure Constantinople and thus the route to Russia via the Black Sea. The goal was to ensure the Russians fighting on the Eastern Front could be properly supplied and that some pressure would be taken off the Western Front, which had reached a hopeless stalemate. However, as a land attack, history would judge it a catastrophe, with the deaths of hundreds of thousands of courageous men on both sides.

As spring became summer in Egypt, Elsie and Mary began the task of planning the logistics for the hospital ships that began to ferry the first of the 100,000 wounded men back to Alexandria's port. The Army had commandeered large halls, clubs, hotels and any spacious building that could stand in as a temporary hospital. It quickly became obvious that the casualties were shattering and Elsie telegrammed Almina asking for her help in recruiting nurses to come out and help. The bureaucracy proved ridiculously difficult since the nurses had no permits to work or visas to stay and the military authorities were initially more concerned with the rule book and the budget than anything else.

Carnarvon stepped in to try to help through General Sir John Maxwell and, in May 1915, twenty-seven nurses left Tilbury Docks in London for Alexandria on board the P&O steamer *Mongolia*. Mary and Elsie argued that they were prepared to pay the wage bill of £2 2*s*. per week per nurse, which removed one obstacle and, given that the nurses were already in Alexandria and certainly desperately needed, perhaps it was time to change the rules on visas and permits.

Elsie Carnarvon had become a formidable woman who never allowed the intense heat of a Cairo day to bother her. When there was a shortage of stretchers, she went out and scoured the city for sewing machines and fabrics, organizing work teams to make up the equipment that was so desperately needed. She started a canteen for the Anzac forces and provided all the cutlery and crockery herself. One day the men became so rowdy that plates and cups were smashed and Elsie took it upon herself to march into the canteen and ask what they thought they were doing. Something in her manner brought the fracas to a halt and when the men realized who she was and what she had done for them, they lined up to apologize to her. Later in the summer Sir John Maxwell commented to his staff on the good work she was doing and she was given a motor launch to meet the incoming ships, which made her job easier.

Carnarvon left the operating theatre and the nursing to his wife but spent the afternoons listening to the patients' stories, thus gaining a harrowing insight into the course of the war. David Campbell was one such patient. He had arrived at Highclere in the middle of September 1915 having endured a painful journey by ship and ambulance. During a mission to take a summit at Suvla Bay, he had been shot in the calf. As a comrade was helping him dress the wound, that man was shot in the foot. In turn, David now helped to dress the man's wound but fire was still raining down all around and David was hit again, this time by a bullet through his foot. Unable to move and losing blood, he passed out while the man who had been helping him died. Regaining consciousness, David crawled back towards his lines, falling in with a stream of other wounded before collapsing again. A Gurkha picked him up and continued to carry him down but David was shot a third time, again in the leg. Two hours later the Gurkha deposited him at a First Aid Post where his wounds were dressed but there were no stretchers available. Finding a stick, he then hopped and crawled down the hill, eventually reaching a Field Ambulance station. Here there were stretchers but almost no stretcher-bearers as they had all been targeted and killed by enemy snipers. Eventually David realized he would only survive by dragging himself in the dark across to the evacuation point.

At this point his wounds were dressed immediately, there being little pressure on the medical staff because so few soldiers made it to them alive. While the hospital ships were full, an officer managed to commandeer a fishing trawler and David was one of the men loaded onto it. From there he was transferred onto a British Army hospital ship. He was assigned a cabin with three other officers but all of them died during the night. Repatriated home from Alexandria, he was left in his cabin with minimal attention. Like everyone else he got dysentery. As his foot was in a terrible way, it was marked for amputation but the surgeon fell sick and was too ill to carry out the operation, so he arrived at Highclere with both legs attached, even if one was swollen, black and almost too painful to touch.

Shrunken, gaunt and in constant pain, an operation removed the last splinters and foreign objects and he began to get better. He wrote to his family, 'there can be no better solace than to wander over the cool green grass and sit under the cedars'. Luckily for him, Alexander Fleming had visited Almina's hospital a little earlier and had expounded his theory that the use of strong antiseptics on wounds did more harm than good, recommending instead that they simply be kept clean with a mild saline solution. Later, Fleming would be commissioned into the Royal Army Medical Corps where he worked as a bacteriologist studying wound infections in a laboratory, which led, in due course, to the discovery of penicillin.

Listening to such tales, Carnarvon grew ever more worried about his brother, who was in the thick of it. In March 1915 Aubrey Herbert spent a few days in Cairo with his Mary, who was working as a nurse, before he was due to sail to the Dardanelles. Although half blind, Aubrey was in the thick of the battle for the next nine months.

Aubrey's letters home expressed increasing fury about the incompetence of the military and his futile attempts to influence the course of the war through various friends. While he had liked Prime Minister Asquith, Aubrey now wrote that he was a 'dilettante', with 'a mind of granite and the soul of a rather bad bridge party'.

Eventually Aubrey managed to instigate an armistice to bury the dead. Approaching the Turks with a white flag, he was taken hostage and blindfolded while Kemal Bey Ohri was taken to negotiate the date and length of the truce with General Hamilton. On 24 May Aubrey walked up through gullies filled with thyme and the awful sight and smell of 4,000 Turkish dead. Equally, English, Australian and New Zealand companies had also been annihilated. The Turkish captain walking with Aubrey said: 'At this spectacle even the most gentle must feel savage and the most savage must weep.' The ceasefire ended just before 4 p.m. and for once Aubrey kept his thoughts to his diaries rather than share them in any of his letters. He remained at Gallipoli at Anzac Cove until the end of August, haunted by the voices of men crying out that they were being murdered and writing, 'One feels ashamed of being alive.'

Increasingly feverish and ill, Aubrey was sent back to Alexandria and to Lady Howard de Walden's nursing home where his mother Mary and Mervyn all danced attendance, but then he returned to Gallipoli, finally leaving it for ever in the dismal evacuation just before Christmas 1915. Glad to hear better news from Elsie, Carnarvon was cast down by the death of his aunt Gwendolen. 'What a blank' would the absence be 'of that little figure in grey'. She had been the last of the siblings left connecting him to the memories of his parents and childhood.

David Campbell left Highclere having been ordered to appear before the Army medical board on 4 November where he was given one month's leave before he had to report again. The journey to Ireland to see his family proved too much too soon for his foot and he ended up back in hospital in Dublin, but the Carnarvons later found out that he not only survived the war but fathered a son, also called David.

Gallipoli was just one field of battle. On the Western Front, 1915 was dominated by the Battle of Ypres and a new weapon of war: gas. Artillery shelling was followed up with the release of 168 tonnes of chlorine gas into the Allied positions. It was totally unexpected and terrifying: 5,000 French soldiers died within ten minutes of the gas dropping into the trenches. A further 10,000 were blinded and maimed as they tried to flee. All was chaos as the Germans advanced, fitted with their rudimentary gas masks, picking off the desperate French soldiers as they went. The Allies were completely wrong-footed and over the next month the Germans gained three miles, repeating the gas attack with the same devastating results on the British Expeditionary Force. A hundred thousand men died, more than two-thirds of them Allied soldiers, and thousands more were sent back to Britain with a whole new raft of symptoms for the medical staff to treat. The gas attacks, however, were sometimes inaccurate and gas drifted back into German positions. It was not the solution the Germans sought.

In Egypt, in December Elsie and Maud left Alexandria to stay in Luxor at 'Mr Carter's house in the desert at the entrance to the Valley of the Kings'. Elsie wrote: 'He [Carter] has been kindness itself and sent his servant and we have his donkey and [Carnarvon's] to ride and his old guide near to show us what we came to see and the desert with all its peace and far awayness and sense of the smallness of human things, to rest in. It is a little mud house like a glorified native one – all brown – a studio, 3 bedrooms and a dining room and it seems to have grown out of the sand . . .'

30

BRYANSTON SQUARE

INCREASING NUMBERS OF surgeons had come out of retirement and were working achingly long days, based mostly around the hospitals in Central London and in Harley Street. Almina, recognizing that a London base was a more practical situation, secured the lease on 48 Bryanston Square, a delightful town house in Mayfair overlooking a peaceful garden behind railings, and moved her hospital out of Highclere and into the new building. As ever, Alfred helped her equip it with first of all a lift, a purpose-built operating theatre and a room for an X-ray machine. The bedrooms became wards so as to accommodate more patients and, to her husband's amusement, each ward was named after the Highclere bedrooms: Stanhope, Sussex, Arundel, etc. Then she transferred all her staff from the country up to town and put them under the charge of Sister Macken, the head matron.

The New Year began with a sense of unalloyed gloom: on the Western Front the Allies had lost nearly 90,000 men compared to the Germans' 25,000 and Sir John French, the commander of the British Expeditionary Force, continued to dither and to fall out with both his own colleagues and the French command. In December Lord Kitchener recalled him and replaced him with Sir Douglas Haig. Winston Churchill, who had been one of the Gallipoli campaign's principal proponents, resigned his position at the Admiralty. As Secretary of State for War, Kitchener was hit hard by these two failures and the great hero never recovered his reputation for invincibility. The country was at a desperately low ebb.

At Highclere it had become obvious that steps would have to be taken to ensure that the tree planting was kept up even though so many of the estate staff were serving: wood was used for all aspects of the war, but above all as pit props. Carnarvon wrote to Rutherford, the Estate Agent, 'with regard to the planting I would try & get some German prisoners. There must be a good many foresters about I have no doubt you could put them up somewhere, but I should give no guarantee as to their not escaping, probably it would not be asked for. Most of the agricultural schemes I see mooted are too foolish for words. As if you could sow wheat on commons in that casual way.' Another possibility could have been an increased use of machinery on the estate but, despite his passion for motor cars, in March Carnarvon wrote again to Rutherford: 'I heard a poor account of the motor plough . . . zigzagged all over the place.'

With most of the gardeners having joined up already, in April Carnarvon was further dismayed to discover that Blake, the head gardener, had also volunteered. He promptly instructed Rutherford to 'point out to him that it is far more important that the Hospital should be supplied with vegetables & fruit than to be put to some possibly unsuitable form of labour', adding, 'will you please see Streatfield & impress on him the need for rigid food economy'.

The following year, still worrying about food supplies, Carnarvon saw the advantages of having poultry on the estate, writing on

21 February, 'According to the *Daily Express* poultry can be put on the land & can then be eaten. If that is so we must have chickens & will you please see to it at once . . . why should we not have some ducks & geese.' Rutherford evidently took prompt action, because the estate accounts record that some poultry houses were bought at a sale at Fyfield Farm, and Wyandotte and Light Sussex eggs were also bought; soon eggs were being supplied to the Castle and to the house in Seamore Place, while some were sold to Venner & Son. Lord Carnarvon also encouraged others to keep poultry, contributing to a Christmas poultry show prize fund. Meanwhile, the dairy farm in the Park was also updated. A new dairy had been built in 1904, and further work was undertaken on the buildings in 1914–15 in order to be able to supply the hospital.

March 1916 found the Carnarvons at Le Grand Hôtel Cannes. Carnarvon was most worried about his wife, who, 'I am sorry to say, has been laid up with a chill on the liver. I thought she was getting well, but she does not mend as quickly as I should like.'

Aubrey had sailed for Mesopotamia in the company of the Commander-in-Chief of Egypt, the Commander-in-Chief of the Mediterranean and the Prince of Wales. It was the first time Aubrey had met George V and Queen Mary's eldest son, Edward (later briefly Edward VIII before the abdication crisis some twenty years later) and, clearly somewhat underwhelmed, his only comment was that at least 'he was more imaginative than I expected'.

British military involvement in Mesopotamia had started out as an operation to safeguard the oil fields in what is now Iraq, crucial given that the naval campaign in particular was heavily oil-dependent. The 6th Indian division had been dispatched to the region under the command of General Townshend but they were woefully supplied both in terms of food and transport. As the military problems escalated such cost-cutting proved catastrophic. Aubrey had a very bad feeling about the whole thing but was hoping to be proved wrong. When he arrived, he wrote back to his great friend Sir Mark Sykes at the War Office: 'Well, the position here is absolutely bloody.'

General Townshend had retreated to Kut al Amara, which he was trying to defend against the vastly superior Turkish forces. Attempts to relieve him and break the siege had failed. His troops were starving; some aerial drops of rations were made but even so, by April, the men were down to 4oz of food a day and riddled with disease. There was no choice but to surrender.

Aubrey wrote to Colonel Beach, the Head of Military Intelligence in the region, offering to accompany General Townshend to the negotiations as he knew some of the leading Turks very well. Colonel T. E. Lawrence had arrived and was sent with Aubrey to talk terms with the Turkish high command. The two men's hopes were limited to being able to secure a truce to allow the wounded soldiers to be shipped out but the British Government seemed to have a more long-term goal in mind. The men were authorized to offer £2 million and the promise not to launch further attacks on the Ottoman Empire. This offer was rejected and although there was a truce to allow for an exchange of prisoners, on 29 April 1916 General Townshend surrendered. Thirteen thousand British and Indian soldiers were taken prisoner and, despite agreeing to all terms, the prisoners were treated appallingly, with more than half dying of starvation or at the hands of their captors.

Carnarvon wrote of his fear that 'my boys from the Stud Farm and Estate have been taken prisoners in Kut Al Amara. If this is the case, I should propose trying to send them out either money or some small comforts. There are organizations for this object and I can get in touch with them easily.' As ever, anxious to do all he could, there was also a possibility, he continued, that 'I may go to Ireland, how long I shall stay there if I go is, I imagine, in the lap of the Gods. It may be very interesting and possibly I may do some good.'

The whole incident was a tremendous humiliation for the British Army. Aubrey continued to visit Turkish prisoners of war in the British Army camps where morale was high. They believed that after Gallipoli, Salonika and now Kut, they were going to win. Aubrey's response was typical of the bullish determination that persisted in the British forces and public despite the shocking failures. He informed the confident Turks that it was his country's 'national habit to be defeated at the beginning of every war and to win in the end'.

Almina continued to make liaison with the patients' families a priority and sent telegrams and letters with regular updates when patients were themselves unable to do so. True to her vision for the new hospital, the men could spend time in the residents' garden in the square and they still dined on the vegetables and cheeses sent up every day from Highclere.

The Carnarvons' life in London now settled into a vague routine. Lord Carnarvon would spend most afternoons at his wife's hospital talking to the patients or sitting quietly with the more traumatised among them. Each evening he would return to Berkeley Square while his wife lived between the two houses, depending on her operating programme. He was immensely proud of her and all her nursing work, but her unflagging devotion and its consequent impact on her health worried him.

At this point, Kitchener promoted the introduction of two new additions to the war effort, first the tank and second the Royal Flying Corps. With the Flying Corps and its obvious role in reconnaissance, Carnarvon finally got the brief role in the war effort which meant so much to him.

He had been elected President of the Camera Club in early 1916 in recognition of his skill and expertise as a photographer. Photography was an interest he could pursue during his many frequent bouts of illness and then practise as soon as he was up and about because it was not too arduous. It combined both his artistic flair and practicality and was the perfect hobby for a man who was fascinated by new technology, an adventurer at heart locked in a rather frail and uncooperative body.

He was thus the perfect choice to advise the Royal Flying Corps (RFC) on the subject of aerial photography. Despite initial scepticism, vertical aerial photographs became invaluable both for accurate mapping as well as intelligence gathering. A School of Photography had been established at Farnborough in September 1915 to provide men with the necessary skills in processing and camera maintenance and a new science of interpreting features, light and shadow. The Model 'B' camera was developed and introduced in mid-1916 and made it possible for aerial prints of ground features to be made for military commanders. The first Photographic Section was formed attached to 1st Wing, and Lieutenant-Colonel Moore-Brabazon led the way, leaning out of the plane, a wooden camera with a strong leather strap around him angling the camera downwards and changing plates in the freezing air. By now the better lenses allowed the photographs to be taken at a higher and thus safer altitude, which was very relevant given the slow flying speed of biplanes. Carnarvon spent three days with the RFC at Gouy-Saint-André near Calais offering his advice and demonstrating his experience. He wrote to his sister Winifred saying how much he enjoyed it and that it offered him some consolation for not being in combat.

Carnarvon continued on, accepting from time to time that he would be confined to reading in bed before resuming life at a rapid pace. At no point did he ever seem to contemplate taking the advice of his friends, his family or his doctor to give up smoking, or at least to stop when he was feeling ill. Today it would be clear that as a born asthmatic with a weak chest, a very heavy smoking habit was about the worst possible thing for him.

As President of the Camera Club, Carnarvon was asked to contribute some of his work to the Adelphi Camera Club exhibition of photographs and he spent some time sifting through his collection deciding which ones to present. Inevitably, most of the pictures were of beautiful women but he did include a striking portrait of Lord Ripon holding an ancient vase in his hands, entitled 'The Connoisseur'. This exhibition was followed by another, shared between the Royal Institute of Painters in Water Colours and the International Exhibition of the London Salon of Photography, at Pall Mall East, in September. Of the portraits 'nothing better could be desired than those shown by Lord Carnarvon'.

On 14 May 1916 King George V received a cable from his cousin the Emperor of Russia asking if Lord Kitchener could visit. He agreed to this in the spirit of continuing to fight the Germans on both fronts. Despite sailing in the armoured cruiser HMS *Hampshire* and taking an unorthodox route rarely used by warships via the Orkney Islands, the ship hit a mine in a storm and sank on 5 June. Only twelve out of the 600 men aboard reached shore. Kitchener was not among them.

The King and Queen were grief-stricken – Kitchener had been a personal friend – and the country was stunned. With his fluent French much appreciated by all 'allies' and enormous personal standing, it is possible that, had he lived, he may well have been able to change the course of the twentieth century – to be the 'architect of peace', to quote the Prince of Wales. Kitchener had always spoken bitterly of the German atrocities yet he also told his friends that the Allies must not make a vindictive peace but a peace of reconciliation.

Lord and Lady Carnarvon were among friends and guests at the funeral service at St Paul's Cathedral which took place on a freezing day in June. The King and Queen arrived in an open-top carriage followed by many other royals, soldiers lined the way and everyone was visibly upset.

Still worse was to come with the Battle of the Somme, which began in July. While General Haig planned it as a decisive breakthrough in the stalemate of trench warfare in France, it has instead passed into history as the epitome of the futility of war. On its opening day, 1 July, 60,000 men were killed, the highest losses ever sustained in a single day of combat. The Canadian 1st Newfoundland Regiment was annihilated, with 500 out of 801 men killed. Four hundred doctors were killed and injured in July, increasing the pressure on the already horrifically overstretched medical corps The same story was repeated over and over again for a further two months. Kitchener's Army, taken from bands of men from tight-knit communities, was wiped out, a lost generation back home, the impact of which was felt for decades to come.

The Somme was characterized by the use of very heavy artillery but also saw the debut of a new weapon – the tank. As well as their physical injuries, the troops mentally feared the mechanical monsters and the human frame couldn't withstand the impact of this new, fully mechanized slaughter on a grand scale. The number of cases of mental breakdown began to increase exponentially. Like everyone, Carnarvon and Almina could see the disintegration in body and spirit as men returned from the front, some of whom wished to talk while others were too haunted physically and mentally to speak.

Every family and community was affected and suffering. Equally, the war effort had to be paid for. Governments in every country were raising money and increasing taxes. In common with other landowners, the workforce on the Carnarvon estates was hugely impacted. Very few of the workers and tenants hadn't lost at least one family member to the point where every single aspect of running the land and the great houses had been affected from farming to the gardens and the maintenance of buildings. Adored all her life by Mr Alfred and cosseted by his wealth, Almina did not know the meaning of the word economy and if she did not realize which way the wind was blowing, it was becoming increasing obvious to Lord Carnarvon.

To Rutherford at Highclere, he wrote the following:

'My dear Rutherford, I feel we must have a long talk on the subject of retrenchments. The super tax is over £7,500 so that will have to be found. The economies must I think be made over following:

- Estate
- Household
- Stables
- Subscriptions
- Golf
- Garden
- Management
- Stud Farm
- Racing

and anything you can think of. The last item has generally paid. Think the whole thing over. As you will see, further calls are expected to be made on us. The Government seems unable to do more than increase the income tax.

Yours truly, C'

Racing was minimal during the war years but it did continue on the basis that otherwise it would not survive, despite the fact that it was loved by millions in Britain. Inevitably, this decision attracted some negative press and lobbying.

Without trivializing the horrors of the First World War and its effect on millions across the world, it did present the Jockey Club with challenges, and serious decisions had to be made to ensure that, when hostilities were over, there would still be a racing industry to return to.

A rumour circulated that wounded servicemen being treated in a makeshift hospital occupying Epsom Grandstand would have to be evacuated so that the Derby could go ahead. This was untrue, but it did help to sway public opinion against the racing industry.

Lord Carnarvon had obviously significantly reduced the number of horses he had in training during the war years but despite that he did have some good winners, notably Julian during the 1916 season, although the *Sportsman* summarized it as follows: 'Lord Carnarvon has long been the principal patron of the Whatcombe stable and continues so but had a comparatively lean year with only seven wins to his credit – worth a combined total of £2,368 – and three of those were due to the prowess of Julian, who ran eight times, and was only once unplaced.' Julian was sold at the end of the year for 2,000 guineas, which helped improve Lord Carnarvon's books.

As the war ground on, more and more horses were requisitioned. Kitchener had ordered that every horse must be a minimum of 15 hands as many children were so distraught at losing their ponies. Carnarvon had both to comply and yet try to keep some of the horses he loved and knew so well. Six million horses joined the war and very few of them survived much beyond it, either through injury, death or trauma.

31

SERVE TO LEAD

CARNARVON ADORED HIS children. As they grew up, he enjoyed their company and was proud that his son was becoming a very good shot and a first-class jockey: visits to racecourses at top speed were a shared passion. Likewise, he doted on his daughter. If she was ever ill, he would admit, 'I really can't sleep or eat'. Pretty and as well dressed as her mama, she also very much enjoyed racing and took as much interest as her brother in the breeding and care of the horses at the stud.

In spring 1916 Henry (Porchey) had tackled his father and said he would like to enlist. The columns of *The Times* were reporting more and more deaths of friends and their sons and Porchey, like so many other young men of his generation, could not bear to be left behind at home. Porchey had met Kitchener at a lunch with his parents while still at Eton and had told the great man then that he would very much like to join the Army. He sat the Sandhurst entrance exam and failed the maths abysmally. However, with the mention of Lord Kitchener's name that was duly overlooked. He was then deemed medically unfit: he had flat feet, fallen arches and twisted toes. In the end he persuaded them to accept him because, as he said, he was joining the Cavalry and therefore didn't need to march and, while he was not very tall, he was an excellent rider.

Porchey had a lot of charm and he enjoyed Sandhurst even if he felt consistently underfunded by his father. Ironically, given his own history, Carnarvon's view was that his son invariably overspent his allowance.

During his six-month training period, he also took the time to fall a little in love with a very pretty auburn-haired nurse at Highclere. She in turn was having a dalliance with one of the patients and Carnarvon relates that his wife had had to let the nurse go with the words: 'Look here my dear, I'm afraid you'll have to go. I cannot have my nurses behaving in this fashion. It must have put a great strain on the patient's heart. He might have died as a result!' The flame-haired beauty left, much to both the patient's and young Porchey's sorrow.

So, against all Army regulations (17 was too young to volunteer and he should certainly not have been sent abroad), on Boxing Day 1916 Lord Porchester sailed with the 7th Queen's Hussars for India. Carnarvon wrote: 'Porchester left on Christmas Day for India. I cannot help being very very anxious not only for the journey out, but for anything that may happen in India he is so very young to go there or anywhere as far as that goes.'

Just 18 when he landed at Bombay, Porchey was a boisterous, self-important teenager with a young man's inability to grasp the fact that he might die. To give him his due, he always recalled the awful sinking sensation of scanning the casualty lists for the names of his school friends but, being a young man, he was quite capable of resisting the melancholy and sense of hopelessness that his uncle Aubrey could not.

In addition, nothing Porchey found in India robbed him of his good-natured expectation that his life would continue to work out very well indeed. As he wrote in his memoirs, the changing pattern of warfare on the Western Front hadn't filtered through to India. The Indian Army still trained and drilled to a pattern that hadn't altered in 200 years: sword-play exercise, mounted combat with lances, revolver practice, and polo to practise horsemanship. The niceties were meticulously observed out in Meerut and the Anglo-Indian military's way of life was entirely immune to the austerity that was biting back home. There were four changes of kit a day and dress uniforms were worn for dinner, which was always served on the best silver plate by a retinue of staff that put Highclere to shame.

Despite enjoying himself immensely, gradually a degree of frustration began to creep in, as it did for the whole regiment, that, despite the awful news from France and the Eastern Front, there was no sign of them being called up and given any work to do. The fact that he was stationed in the backwaters of India did, however, give his parents some relief. They had been devastated by the death of Carnarvon's cousin Bron Herbert, just the worst news among an appalling death toll of friends over the past year. Despite having a prosthetic leg from the Boer War, he had joined the Royal Flying Corps in 1915 and had had some very lucky escapes. Carnarvon was also desperately worried about Aubrey, who had adored Bron and who was always throwing himself into danger. Aubrey's wife wrote, 'I am so unhappy for you and for all the others who loved him'.

Against this background Lord Carnarvon would treasure the pencil notes that arrived back at Highclere from his son, usually ringing up his sister Winifred to share the news they contained. The little fox terrier his son left behind never left Carnarvon's side.

Porchey remained in India until October 1917 when the regiment was sent to Mesopotamia, to Basra in modern Iraq. He wrote to his father of the soaring heat, the desperate search for shade during the route marches, carrying all the supplies on their horses and pausing to eat the cold bully beef, weevilly biscuit and using brackish water to make tea. They crossed arid deserts, the stifling heat of the daytime giving way to extreme cold at night until they reached Kut, with its debris of broken buildings and carts, barbed wire rocking in the breeze above old trenches marking where General Townshend had surrendered in April 1916.

32

IN FLANDERS FIELDS

In August 1916, a rather serious 21-year-old Cambridge-educated linguist was sitting reading a map on the edge of a trench trying to locate the final resting place of the battalion they had been sent to search for, when a sniper shot him in the face. The bullet entered directly between his eyes, passed through his palate and shattered the right-hand side of his jaw. Part of the bone severed an artery in his throat. Instinctively he clutched his neck and, finding the place where blood was gushing, he tried to stem the flow as he staggered back in the direction of the head-quarters dugout.

Almost unconscious when found, he was evacuated back to the base hospital at Le Touquet, a once elegant French town on the coast. The hospital was funded by the Duchess of Westminster and, in another of the surreal contrasts of the Great War, had been set up in the casino. Since Charles Clout had been unlucky to be hit on his first day in the new post and lucky enough to survive, the patients had not yet flooded in. He was given a lot of morphine to slow his heart rate and stem the blood loss.

He survived an operation to remove part of the bullet lodged in his jaw and two weeks later, once he was stable, he was transferred to a hospital ship and taken back to Britain. From Dover he went by train to Victoria station and there, as he lay on the platform with hundreds of other wounded men, he was labelled for the Countess of Carnarvon's hospital at 48 Bryanston Square. Clout tried very hard to insist that he would rather go to the general hospital in south London, which was nearer his family, but that was ignored.

Clout always recalled it was very different from the field hospital. The beds were comfortable, breakfast excellent and above all he remembered the kindness. Two weeks after his arrival, he was able to sit up in bed and the swelling and pain in his face had improved enough for him to take an interest in the world again.

At Le Touquet, Matron made her ward rounds at the crack of dawn but, in the slightly more tranquil surroundings of Bryanston Square, the men slept until breakfast and then saw the medical staff. Clout was there until November and made a reasonable recovery although he had to return in January for a series of operations to continue removing fragments of bone and shrapnel. He later had reconstructive surgery to enable him to eat solids, but his speech was impaired for years, so much so that in his embarrassment he took to wearing a bandage on his throat so that people would appreciate it was the result of a war wound.

Charles Clout noticed that Almina had a very charming assistant who accompanied her on her rounds, taking immaculate notes as Almina directed. Mary Weekes, rather tall, neatly dressed, kind and efficient, had been with Almina first as a secretary and then, from 1914 onwards, as the hospital administrator.

Mary and Charles were married in July 1918, when Charles 'believed that the war might drag on for years yet'. They had decided to wait until Charles's recovery was complete and all the work on his jaw was finished, and both Lord and Lady Carnarvon attended their wedding.

Lord Carnarvon lent the Clouts Milford Lake House on the estate at Highclere for their honeymoon and, as a souvenir, Almina gave Mary a specially made fan, painted with a view of the building. It is a beautiful house, an elegant, low villa right on the water's edge, and a peaceful idyll for two people who worked surrounded by death and destruction. Almina, who was good on detail, made sure that food and staff were laid on so that the couple would not have to lift a finger. Furthermore, she set them up in a house in Paddington, buying the furniture for the main rooms. Charles never returned to the front line. His injury was too severe and he spent the rest of the war helping to train battalions of new recruits. They went on to have three children, but to begin with Mary continued to work for Lady Carnarvon.

In the global arena, 1917 was a momentous year. In Russia, the abdication of the Czar and the Bolshevik Revolution led eventually to a Russian armistice. Outside Russia, the Americans were drawn into the conflict, the Greek king, Constantine, was forced to abdicate and the horrors of Passchendaele shattered even war-hardened soldiers.

For those in Britain, the increasing menace of U-boat attacks had eventually made travel effectively impossible for anyone for whom it was not absolutely essential. Germany had resumed unrestricted submarine warfare and more than 500 merchant ships were sunk in little more than two months. There would be no trip to Egypt this year for Carnarvon.

Lord C kept in touch by letter, though. Carter wrote that he was carrying out 'sundry war jobs' in Cairo which was enlivened by various trades in antiquities. He acted as the agent in the acquisition of some precious treasure found in the tomb of the wives of Tuthmosis III from the Luxor dealer Mohammed Mohassib. The Cairo Museum was not interested in the objects and Carnarvon helped Carter by putting up the money needed to secure them. Between December 1917 and February 1918, Carter continued excavating in the Eastern Valley between the tombs of Ramesses II and Ramesses VI, finding only shards and fragments and effectively spending his time clearing up after Theodore Davis.

Those on the Home Front were also playing crucial roles. Britain's war effort depended on industry and agriculture. For example, before the war Britain imported over 60 per cent of its total food supply, including 80 per cent of its wheat. Now it had to feed itself.

Many of the men from Highclere were at the front, which left fewer and obviously older men at Highclere to help on the farm. Crucially, women from the Women's Land Army joined to fill the void on the farms and tractors began to do the work of many hands. Carnarvon ploughed up the pasture in the park to allow space to grow more arable crops and abandoned work in the formal gardens in favour of keeping the vegetable gardens going. It marked a seismic shift in how houses such as Highclere were maintained and run. Things would never be the same again.

Winifred Burghclere's nephew Richard Maitland, whose brother had already been killed, was also serving at the Somme. He was badly wounded in the leg and sent back to Southampton and from there to Bryanston Square. He spent five months in hospital and survived the war, though even after his final operation in 1917 he walked with a limp because of a stiff knee.

William Garstin and Alan Gardiner joined Lord Carnarvon at Highclere for several weekends, allowing Carnarvon to catch up on all the news from Egypt where General Allenby was now in command of the Egyptian Expeditionary Force. The British and Australian forces had been augmented by the Egyptian Camel Transport Corps. Between 1916 and 1918, more than 170,000 Egyptian volunteers and 72,000 camels brought food, water and medical supplies to the troops on the front lines.

Having replaced Murray after his two disastrous attacks on Gaza, Allenby was a major success, improving organization and morale. Just as importantly, he brought reinforcements at a time when Turkish superiority was gradually being eroded by the Arab Revolt, aided and abetted by the efforts of Aubrey's friend Colonel Lawrence, now better known as Lawrence of Arabia. By October, the British outnumbered the Turks by two to one in terms of infantry and eight to one in Calvary regiments such as Porchey's. This was vital as Syria was one of the few arenas in the First World War where mounted troops could still be used effectively. Successfully reaching Jerusalem by December of that year, Allenby's was perhaps one of the few really successful campaigns of the First World War.

It wasn't all work, of course. In May, Carnarvon drove up to Newmarket and much enjoyed his visit bar the, by now somewhat predictable, fine for speeding that he accrued.

33

GO GENTLY INTO THE NIGHT

Lord Carnarvon walked out to shoot in the early grey light of a January morning, brittle, frosted leaves blown across the drive underfoot, a white frost touching the edges of the deep green cedars. The game was always challenging at this time of year but the rabbits and pheasant would be most useful for the Castle and hospital kitchens. Rutherford was already there waiting by the shooting brake, a true country gentleman grown older and greyer with worry over his sons in France, one of whom, currently on leave, would join them. Carnarvon had been complaining of pains around his lower stomach but hoped that a good walk and the distraction of a shoot would cure it.

After lunch, however, Carnarvon collapsed with excruciating stomach pains. Rutherford telephoned Almina who rushed down from London with Dr Johnnie and a nurse. Collecting her husband and instructing Rutherford to call Major General Sir Berkeley Moynihan, who, despite his honourary military titles, was in fact the leading abdominal surgeon, to meet her at 48 Bryanston Square, she drove at some speed back to London.

Carnarvon was rushed into the operating theatre and his appendix was removed. By now, this was becoming a standard operation and the main risk was infection if it burst or as result of the operation. Moynihan's opinion was that another half an hour and his patient might have died and Carnarvon certainly believed his recovery was entirely due to his wife.

Lord Carnarvon remained seriously ill for some time and spent three weeks at his wife's hospital, Almina by his side and willing him to pull through when her father sadly had not. Mr Alfred had died in January 1918 with Almina at his side and she was still mourning him.

Mr Alfred had not been well for the last two years. His elder brother Lord Nathaniel Rothschild had died in 1915 and his younger brother Lionel in May 1917. His cousin James de Rothschild, a close friend of Carnarvon, lived in France and had managed to enlist in three successive armies, the French, then the Canadian and finally the British, while another cousin was building ambulances in France and taking them to the front.

At the outbreak of hostilities, Mr Alfred had offered the glorious parkland around Halton House to the Army and, due to the acres of flat land and ideal location, large numbers of men were billeted and trained there. Then, in January 1917, Mr Alfred learned that the Allies were short of pit props for the trenches and wrote to Prime Minister David Lloyd George: 'I am not an expert as regards what sort of timber would be suitable for pit props, but I cannot help thinking that, as there are so many pine trees in my woods at Halton, some of them at least would be suitable for the purpose. May I ask you very kindly to send down your expert who would very easily be able to report fully on the subject, and I should indeed be proud if my offer should lead to any practical result.'

In London, Mr Alfred had packed parts of the offices in New Court with sandbags to protect the bullion room below while an air raid shelter had been built in the corner of the Drawn Bond Department. The Rothschilds had held the lease and run the Royal Mint Refinery since 1852, but Alfred now converted it to munitions production along with a special system designed to relay air raid warnings to New Court and the surrounding offices.

Like many others, the Rothschilds subscribed to charities, sending parcels of food and luxuries to troops at the front and every Christmas he sent turkeys and champagne to the Red Cross Hospital and British Expeditionary Forces in France. Anything that might help.

Mr Alfred had always been something of a hypochondriac but, as the war wore on, he was increasingly ground down by it, becoming gradually frailer. He began the New Year in 1918 low in both health and spirits, his health having been strained by his relentless war work for the government. Almina was in London in any case at her hospital and so was able to visit him every evening. He died on 31 January with her by his side.

He may not have died in the conflict but, like many others, perhaps died too young as a result of the war. He had been offered a baronetcy, refusing it, but was honoured to have been made Commander of the Royal Victorian Order and to have been awarded the Legion d'Honneur and the 1st Class Order of the Crown by Kaiser Wilhelm and the Grand Cross of the Order of Emperor Franz Joseph of Austria-Hungary. He had had so many interests outside the word of banking and in all aspects was a life enhancer: an exceptional, unconventional man in many ways, of whom his equally unconventional son-in-law was immensely fond.

Just as Alfred de Rothschild's family had found itself on two different sides of the conflict, so the British royal family had to contend with the perception that some members might have split loyalties. The issue came to a head in the summer of 1917 when anti-German sentiment was so insistent that King George issued a proclamation changing the name of the royal family from Saxe-Coburg-Gotha to Windsor. Similarly, Admiral Battenberg was a German prince and a cousin of George V who had served in the Royal Navy for forty years by the time war broke out and had been First Sea Lord since 1912. He began to draw up the Navy's plans for war but a huge wave of anti-German feeling forced his retirement.

Evelyn had spent all the time she could helping her mother in London, returning to stay at Berkeley Square each evening. It was the first time she realized that Mr Alfred was more than just a beloved family friend. Porchey was still away on active service and the same realization only dawned on him on his return a year later.

By 1918 the spirit of endeavour and confidence was not entirely dead, but there was a mental exhaustion, a moral tiredness about the country. There were no more men at Highclere who could be called up: they were either already fighting or dead. Virtually every family in England had suffered bereavement and every battalion on the front in France was nervously aware that Germany was gathering itself for a final breakthrough.

The Germans were probably correct in considering themselves in a reasonable position with over three and a half million men deployed in 191 divisions and certainly with more successful generals. On 26 March, General Foch was appointed as supreme commander of the Allied forces to coordinate their efforts while General Haig (Britain), Marshal Pétain (France) and General Pershing (USA) retained tactical control of their respective armies. On 11 April Haig issued an order telling his soldiers, 'With our backs to the wall and believing in the justice of our cause each one of us must fight to the end'. The Germans thought they had victory in their sights.

Almost miraculously, with the help of the Americans, the French managed to hold the Marne line against the Germans, and German morale began to fail – they had expected an Allied collapse now. They also knew that 200,000 more American troops were arriving every month and they could no longer match that. Equally, the British blockade had finally ensured their food supplies were failing.

By the end of March, Carnarvon was well enough to return to Highclere and Dr Johnnie spent much of the spring there as well. However, in June, Carnarvon suffered another setback with the premature death of his best and oldest friend, Prince Victor. The last twenty years of the Prince's life had been a succession of poorly suppressed scandals but Carnarvon never wavered in his friendship. After several brushes with bankruptcy, to the despair of both the Crown and the Army, both of whom were left to pick up his debts, in 1898 Prince Victor married Lady Anne Coventry, the daughter of the Earl of Coventry and sister of another of his friends from Eton. It was the first mixed-race marriage between an Indian prince and an English noblewoman and it caused a sensation. The Queen had to personally intervene with the bride's family to allow it to take place and although she gave the couple her blessing, she also allegedly told Lady Anne never to have children with the Prince. Whatever the truth, the marriage remained childless.

In 1902, Prince Victor was declared bankrupt with debts of £117,900 (nearly £13 million in today's value), largely attributed to bad investments, and gambling, something that he indulged in all his life. He died aged only 51 and was buried, appropriately, in the Anglican Cemetery above Monte Carlo. In his will, the sapphire ring given to him by Lord Carnarvon was given back to Lord Porchester as an heirloom.

In September, the Allies had a significant victory at Verdun. The Austro-Hungarian Empire was collapsing, the different constituents announcing their independence, and the Germans had to decide how they would surrender and sue for peace.

Porchey was still out in Mesopotamia. Recovering from a bout of sandfly fever, he was summoned to Baghdad for a most unusual enterprise. He was to take £1 million in gold to the White Russians some 400 hundred miles across northern Persia to Enzeli and the shores of the Caspian Sea where it was handed over to an ill-kempt bunch of Cossacks. His Majesty's Government had decided to fund their struggle against the Bolsheviks who had surrendered and negotiated peace with Germany and Austria.

Lord Porchester returned to his battalion having escaped what he described as an epidemic of influenza. In fact, it was the beginning of the Spanish flu epidemic which would go on to kill perhaps as many as fifty million people worldwide over the next three years.

Almina was exhausted and also went down with the flu herself; her husband wryly commented that he was 'an inept nurse'. It was time, though, to close the London hospital. From rumours and indecision came the gradual realization on Lord Carnarvon's part that he needed to balance the books. It was a new era and with the war gradually winding down, like most governments Britain's was all but bankrupt. During the First World War the British Government had been forced to borrow heavily to finance the war effort. The national debt, £640 million at the start of the war in 1914, had ballooned to £7.4 billion by 1919. The standard rate of income tax, which was 6 per cent in 1914, stood at 30 per cent in 1918, with super tax on the highest incomes adding another 47 per cent, though this did fall after the end of the war in the early 1920s.

Carnarvon decided he would sell the contents of Bretby and the house. He felt it was far from ideal in terms of realizing good prices but, talking to Rutherford, felt that on balance it was better to go ahead with it now than wait. Rumours about Bretby had circulated for some years but now Elsie wrote to her brother that, sadly, 'Porchey and Almina are selling or have sold Bretby . . . it has caused a certain agitation in the family, tho' to my mind only men matter now not things'.

Carnarvon was very happy for his sisters to choose what they liked but otherwise hoped to raise some money. The sale took place over three days and Sir William Beechey's *Portrait of a Girl with a Dog*, dressed in white muslin with a pink sash and red shoes, sold very well for £5,985, a record for the artist. Some items from Bretby were retained and taken to Highclere, including Sir Joshua Reynolds's immense portrait *Mrs Musters as Hebe*, which was given a commanding position on the Oak Staircase and remains there to this day. It is probable that the longcase clock by John Shelton, one of the most renowned precision clockmakers of eighteenth-century London, now in the dining room at Highclere, also came from Bretby.

Happily, though, on a positive note, in 1918 Lord Carnarvon was finally appointed a member of the Jockey Club.

34

'DULCE ET DECORUM EST PRO PATRIA MORI'

KAISER WILHELM ABDICATED on 9 November 1918 and on 11.11.1918 the guns finally stopped as the Armistice was observed. The most devastating war the world had known was finally over. The international map had been partially redrawn and, for most of the upper classes of Europe, life would never be the same again.

In October 1919, the Highclere War Memorial Fund was launched, which paid for a stone cross in the churchyard and a tablet within the church. Carnarvon was almost the first donor, with an initial gift of £25 on 27 October 1919; he made a further gift of £29 1s. 2d. on 29 December 1920 and was one of the final two donors on 30 March 1921, giving £10 in order to help complete the fundraising. This made a total of £64 1s. 2d. out of the total sum raised of £346 14s. 10d. Carnarvon also contributed to the peace celebrations at Highclere while Lady Carnarvon gave £1 towards the Burghclere peace celebrations in 1919.

Carnarvon was particularly insistent that a Roll of Honour be produced to commemorate those from Highclere who forfeited their lives and instructed Rutherford that it was to be given priority. The frame was made from walnut grown on the lawn at Highclere Castle and it was written by C. H. Smith from the estate office. More than eighty men from the estate fought in the Great War, of whom at least thirty died. Many of those who returned were either physically or mentally broken by their experiences. Elsie took great interest in helping those who had been left unable to speak through shell shock, becoming Vice-Chairman of the Vocal Therapy Society, which aimed to give them back their voices through singing.

Absolon, Pte L, 74th Bn, MGC

Annetts, Pte A, 3rd Devon Regt

Attwood, Driver G J, RASC

Adnams, Pte C, 1/4th Hants Regt, killed

Barton, Pte E, 2nd Dorset Regt

Bartholomew, Pte W, 2/4th Hants Regt

Bartholomew, Pte H, 2/4th Hants Regt

Blanchard, Pte G, RASC

Bendle, Pte W, Labour Corps

W Bendle in woodmen wages list by Aug 1915,
entry in Jul 1916 marked 'enlisted'

Broomfield, Pte F, 2/4th Hants Regt

Bowsher, Pte F, 2/4th Hants Regt, killed

Bowsher, Pte E, RAF

Butler, Pte F, Wilts Regt

Butler, Pte A, R West Kent Regt

A Butler in gamekeepers' wages list by Aug 1915, leaves Feb 1916

Ballard, Pte W, RE

Brindley, A/m C, RAF

Berry, Pte H G, RE, died

Bridle, Pte E, Hampshire Regt

Choules, Pte C, Labour Corps

Cox, Steward C, HMS Chatham

Cox, 3/Writer A E, HMS Egmont

Cox, Pte G, 6th R Berks Regt, killed

Cram, Pte L, 1/4th Hants Regt, killed

Cram, Pte A, Hants Regt

Cummins, Pte G, 1st Dorset Regt

Cummins, Pte A, R W Kent Regt, killed

Digweed, Pte G, 1/4th Hants Regt, killed

G Digweed in garden wages book, Mar 1910–Sep 1914

Etwell, Pte E, RASC

Etwell, Pte H, RASC

Fisher, Sub-Conductor C W, RAOC

Fifield, Pte F, 2/4th Hants Regt, killed

Fifield, L/Sgt A, 2/4th Hants Regt, killed

Garrett, Pte H, 1/4th Hants Regt, died

Greenaway, Trooper Hants Ha

F, 2nd R Gloster Hussars

Girdler, A/m A, Royal Air Force

Herrington, Pte S, 1/4th Hants Regt, killed

Hilderley, Pte F, 1/4th Hants Regt

Hodgson, Pte P, 1/4th Hants Regt

Hunter, Pte A, 12th RB

Huntley, L/Cpl E, RGA

Hall, Pte A, Royal Defence Corps

Ilott, Pte W, 15th Hants Regt

Ilott, Pte H, 1st Wilts Regt, killed

Kewell, Pte W, 7th Worcester Regt

Knight, AB, G, HMS Renown

Lewis, Pte A T, Labour Corps

Maber, L/Cpl C H , 2nd Bn MGC

Maber, A/m N, RAF

Painting, Sergeant C, 2/4th Hants Regt

Painting, Driver S, RFA

Rutherford, Major J A, 4th Hants Regt, mentioned for valuable services

Rutherford, Lt J S, 1/4th Hants Regt

Rivers, Bombardier W H, RGA

Smith, Corporal C H, 7th Somerset L I

Smith, L/Corporal W G, 1/4th Hants Regt

Smith, Gunner H, R Marine Artillery

Stratford, Pte A W, Grenadier Guards

Sheerman, Pte H, R Wilts Yeomanry, drowned on HMS *Leinster*

Sheerman, Pte F, RE

Sims, Pte A, 3rd Hants Regt, killed
Steer, Pte C, 1/4th Hants Regt
Sheppard, Pte H, RMLI
Stevenson, Pte A G, Hants Regt
Sadler, Pte F, Coldstream Guards
Taylor, Pte W, Royal Berks Regt
Thirkill, Tr M G, 15th Hussars
Thirkill, Sapper J W, RE
Tanner, L/Cpl G, MGC
Whippey, L/Cpl A, 4th R Berks Regt
Woodley, Trooper R W, 15th Hussars
Woodley, Trooper J A, 4th Hussars, killed
Williams, Driver J, RASC
Whincup, Pte T C, 1/4th Hants Regt
Waugh, Trooper J, 15th Hussars
Young, Pte T, 1/4th Hants Regt, killed

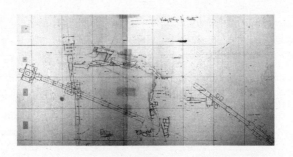

35

LAND OF LIGHT – 1919

Lord and Lady Carnarvon and their daughter Evelyn were up on deck of the ship as it slowly docked at Alexandria. Eve was leaning over the side of the deck rail, enthralled by the colour and noise of the mass of small boats bobbing round the ship. The smells of the salty sea air and the heated land were so entirely different from anything she had ever experienced. The donkeys and turbaned men and boys were waving to attract attention to the colourful shawls or jewellery they were selling.

They were very glad to have moored up. The journey had been no easy matter and their ship had been escorted across the Mediterranean because there was still a risk of floating mines: only recently a French ship had been sunk. Even more dangerous, however, were the unsanitary conditions on board as the ship had served as a troop ship during the war but had not been disinfected. Despite it being only a short journey, there had been much sickness and some deaths.

Alexandria was soon left behind as they boarded the train for Cairo. Carnarvon had been happy to leave the grey, depressing English winter behind and his daughter was so excited to be travelling with her parents. Porchey, her brother, meanwhile, had also sailed from England but in his case for Constantinople where he was posted as an aide-de-camp within the embassy. This year, though, there was a different, restless atmosphere in Egypt which was perhaps not surprising. Despite their invaluable help with the Camel Corps during the Syrian campaign, no delegation from Egypt had been permitted to join the peace conference which had just commenced at Versailles following the end of the war.

The leaders of the Wafd ('The Delegation' in English), the best-organized mass political party in Egypt, found this unconscionable and, as a result, were gathering and stirring up public support through rousing lectures, noisy meetings and unruly marches. They had taken their inspiration from the speech by the American President Woodrow Wilson to Congress the previous January. As the war was moving towards its end, he had introduced Fourteen Points, one of which was self-determination. Not all the Allies agreed with his principles and Georges Clemenceau, the French Prime Minister, commented 'Fourteen Points? The good Lord himself had only ten.'

Having briefly introduced himself to M. Lacau, the new head of the Department of Antiquities, Carnarvon promptly departed with his wife and daughter by train to Luxor so as to be able to spend as much time as possible supervising his excavation work away from the political challenges of Cairo.

For the most part, Carnarvon stayed with Carter in his house by the Valley of the Kings, while his wife and daughter stayed in the Winter Palace Hotel. Evelyn was enthralled by Luxor, exploring the temples and walking along the Nile watching the bright canoe-like boats steering along it. Some mornings she would get up early to ride through the desert as the extraordinary pink light warmed the sands, usually accompanied by some of the Army officers still stationed around Luxor.

During the summer of 1918, Carnarvon and Carter had spent a great deal of time working out the details of their campaign. Carter had drawn up a grid map of the Valley of the Kings and their plan was to clear back to the original bedrock in a number of areas in the two valleys.

In addition, however, Carter had already been excavating this season at another site, at Meir in Middle Egypt, halfway between Luxor and Cairo on the west bank of the Nile, having set up camp there at the beginning of December. Aylward Blackman had worked there under the auspices of the Egypt Exploration Fund and before that a local landowner had also excavated there. Carter had persuaded Carnarvon that the previous works had been carried out in too relaxed a fashion and that, with a well-organized and documented approach, it could be most interesting. Carnarvon had acquired Blackman's published records of his years at Meir and Carter had written to the archaeologist asking him for any advice; this was not in the least well received and no help was given.

Nevertheless, Carter asked Arthur Callender, a friend of his and an engineer in the Egyptian State Railway, to join the expedition. It turned out to be very welcome as Carter found the local people at Meir hostile and he thought the wages and cost of provisions high. He had set out a budget to which Carnarvon had agreed and, in addition to the quarterly payments already made to Carter, Carnarvon had wired him a further £250. By the time the excavations closed on 15 January, Carter had made meticulous notes but found nothing of interest at all.

It was therefore with some relief that Carter returned to Luxor to begin work in the main Valley of the Kings, clearing in front of the area of the tomb of Tuthmosis I where they found some foundation deposits. The boys and men from previous seasons were once more as happy to see 'Lordy' as he was to see them. Most of Lord Carnarvon's photographs follow their work rather than those of the artefacts found. Some of their names are recorded by the notes of payments – Hussein Abu Awad, Ahmed Gerigar, Gad Hassan or Hussein Ahmed Said – but the photographs were not annotated as to who was in them.

However, the political situation was worsening. The Egyptian Prime Minister had resigned amid general unrest and demonstrations, and violence was increasing. Carter was commandeered by the military authorities to work for them in the Nag Hamadi which lay to the north of Luxor, and Carnarvon sent his wife and daughter home although he remained in Cairo. He had gathered Rutherford was not well and wrote to wish him better, relating 'that there was rioting and shooting and things are rather demoralised at the present moment'.

Carnarvon knew the leader of the Wafd, the highly respected figure of Saad Zaghloul, reasonably well, but on 8 March the British took the rather incendiary decision to exile him along with other supporters to Malta. This had the effect of exacerbating the rioting and attacks on the British in Egypt for the remainder of March and made Zaghloul a national hero. On 9 March 1919, a more serious demonstration took place by the students at the Egyptian University and students at Al-Azhar. Carnarvon wrote, 'we are in the throes of a sort of civil war here with strikes and other outrages etc chiefly caused by the Home Govt. I am very glad my belongings are on their way home.' Carnarvon stayed in Cairo, attending many meetings with different government factions, in some instances able to promote discussion simply because he had no official role.

Carnarvon was much interested in Egyptian politics and he had a great liking for the Egyptians and a sympathetic interest in those who were trying to restore her as a nation. They responded in kind, which allowed him to act as an unofficial bridge to the British officials. He appreciated both what the Egyptians had contributed during the war and what they had suffered, and was very conscious of how difficult it would have been for the Allies without their help. On 15 March, more than 10,000 students, workers and professionals marched on Cairo's Abdin Palace where they were met by thousands more protesters discontented with British rule. The next day, the wives of the exiled leaders Safia Zaghloul, Huda Sharawi and Mana Fahmi Wissa organized a march of thousands of women wearing traditional garb.

The British High Commissioner in Egypt (the new title for the post occupied before the war by Lord Kitchener), Sir Reginald Wingate, had been recalled to London. Arthur Balfour, Foreign Secretary and a good friend of Lord Carnarvon, appointed General Lord Allenby as the new High Commissioner on 25 March. Allenby was renowned for his notorious temper and impatience, yet he arrived and declared his aims were threefold: to bring the present disturbances to an end; to inquire carefully into all matters which had caused discontent in the country; and to redress such grievances as appeared justifiable.

Determined to put a stop to all rioting Allenby proposed that Zaghloul was recalled from exile on 7 April. The Egyptian delegation immediately left for Paris and the Versailles Peace Conference, but, to their enormous disappointment, arrived in Paris the day the USA recognized the British protectorate over Egypt. Nobody in Paris seemed to care. Demonstrations broke out again in Egypt and Allenby struggled to find an Egyptian willing to take a government posting for fear of being assassinated.

In the end, Allenby recommended a mission to be headed by Lord Milner, the British Colonial Secretary, General Sir John Maxwell and Sir William Garstin. Acknowledging that Carnarvon was a well-respected expert, and had a deep interest in Egyptian politics and a liking for many Egyptians, they persuaded him to attend a number of dinners and meetings.

In 1919, Carnarvon helped fund some photographic studios at 43 Dover Street, London, with Bertram Parke, his wife Yvonne Gregory and the children's society photographer Marcus Adams. They shared darkroom staff and facilities and were known as 'the Three Photographers'. It suited Lord Carnarvon very well to have a London studio and darkroom and he hoped it might be a sensible investment. Highclere was already well set up with a north-facing studio at the back of the Castle and an adjacent darkroom which he had had fitted with teak a few years before the war. Bertram Parke later took a photograph of Lord Carnarvon in a heavy fur-collared driving coat to reflect his love of motoring. By this time Carnarvon thought he may have purchased as many as sixty cars although the majority had now been either sold or given to museums.

In September 1919, Carnarvon invited Howard Carter, the American archaeologist James Henry Breasted and Percy Newberry to Highclere and, while he enjoyed showing off his collection of antiquities, he equally enjoyed carrying his guests off to see his horses. Porchey was there as well and exceedingly friendly although Breasted commented he was not a man of letters. The weekend offered a packed agenda with a dinner at 8.30 and continuing into the small hours. Breasted was delighted to be asked to take Lady Carnarvon in to supper and appreciated how kind and thoughtful she was to each and every guest.

Two weeks later, Carnarvon asked Breasted to visit again, this time with Alan Gardiner; as there was a train strike, Lady Carnarvon sent her car for them all. It was a typical Highclere weekend with old friends as well as new from the worlds of racing and Egyptology. Rather than go racing, however, Breasted and Gardiner set off into the park to visit Beacon Hill and survey the remains of the Iron Age fort.

They both much enjoyed the walk and Breasted remarked that he thought the park one of the loveliest in England. He wrote to friends of how included he felt in the house party with such unaffected friendship and that he found Lady Carnarvon's devoted attachment to her husband both refreshing and unpretentious. Conversation after dinner revolved around Egyptology. Carnarvon did not believe that everything that could be found in the Valleys of the Kings and Queens had yet been found, and had long been trying to piece together the information in both the Abbott Papyrus in the British Museum and the Amherst Papyrus. Together they formed a record of the tomb robberies relating to the earlier 18th-Dynasty pharaohs which had occurred during the 20th Dynasty under Ramesses IX. Alan Gardiner thought they were one and the same script. Lord Carnarvon already had a translation but wanted to discuss his thoughts with Breasted in case he was missing some subtleties. To his mind it suggested that Amenhotep's tomb was along a passage into the mountains 120 cubits deep from its superstructure north of the 'House of Amenhotep of the Garden', i.e. at Deir el-Bahri.

Breasted was fascinated listening to William Garstin and his stories about Lord Kitchener. Kitchener had been a good listener himself; the word 'impossible' had to be eliminated from anyone's vocabulary, and his energy and force of character acted like a 'magic wand'. In addition, he'd had a huge interest in antika and any spare time would be spent among the native antique dealers who were filled with such awe at 'El Lord' that allegedly their prices would collapse. Carnarvon wished he had the same effect but in the meantime was delighted to show Breasted some of the exquisite works of ancient art and Breasted was thrilled just to be able to look at each antika and take his time. Carnarvon had a tremendously inquisitive mind as well as always looking for the next quest, the next beautiful object to find, the next fragment of information casting a new light on an extraordinary civilization.

General Sir John Maxwell also stayed several times over the autumn before he left for Egypt in order to work with Lord

Milner to investigate and draw up proposals for the future relationship between the two countries. Zaghloul, determined that
nobody but himself should deal with the British commission,
initially boycotted negotiations.

Meanwhile, Carter and Carnarvon spent long hours in the study
discussing what to do next. Carnarvon wanted to focus on the Valley
of the Kings and not seek other concessions, and both men were
looking to concentrate on areas covered by workmen's huts or by
stones and a depth of chippings and stone which had accumulated
from flash floods. In either case, any older tomb entrances might
have been forgotten or covered over.

On a windy, wet day at the end of January 1920, the Carnarvons
once more sailed for Egypt. After meeting Sir John Maxwell, they
went on to Luxor and the Winter Palace Hotel where, among other
engagements, they had a long dinner with James Henry Breasted,
discussing the political challenges in Egypt.

There was good news from England. Carnarvon was thrilled to
hear his son had ridden in and won the Paddock Chase at Kempton
Races with his horse, Gracious Gift. The papers happily noted that,
although during the war Lord Carnarvon had relinquished his
interest in racing, his colours would surely once more be to the fore.

This season, Carnarvon and Carter had decided to work at the
entrance to the tomb of King Merenptah, the son of Ramesses II,
exploring under a watercourse. The tomb itself was large and had
been damaged by flash floods long ago but Almina was very happy
exploring and observing the tomb with its long descending corridor,
painted walls and stars decorating the ceiling. It had been open
since antiquity but Merenptah was a 19th-Dynasty pharaoh and so
Carnarvon and Carter were looking to see whether there might be
earlier works that had been covered up by this later tomb. With
some excitement, on 26 February they discovered a cache of thirteen
alabaster vessels which Lady Carnarvon enthusiastically helped

dig out with her own hands. Her daughter Eve was fascinated. The vessels had been placed side by side in a group and would have held the sacred oils used in the funeral. Now, centuries later, they were all somewhat crushed by the weight of accumulated stones and debris above.

In Cairo, a political fight had developed between the Egyptian Government and King on one side and the Wafd led by Saad Zaghloul with Adly Yeken on the other. By the time Lord Milner left for London, the commission and Wafd were still at loggerheads. Carnarvon had known Zaghloul for a few years now and, despite wholly different backgrounds, each appreciated the other's company, not least perhaps because both had serious smoking habits. Carnarvon was not a politician but he listened and he knew many influential British ministers and it was a way to share ideas.

In contrast to the antique grandeur of Highclere, Zaghloul had been born in a village called Ibiana in the Delta before studying law at university in Cairo. By the age of 42, he had been appointed a judge in the Court of Appeal and had married the daughter of the Prime Minister, Mustapha Fahmi Pasha, bringing him into the centre of government circles and to the attention of Lord Cromer, the British Consul-General. Appointed Minister of Education in 1906, he aimed to extend literacy by increasing the number of schools as well as pushing for the Arabic language to be the language of instruction.

Before Carnarvon left Egypt in the spring of 1920, he invited Saad Zaghloul to stay at Highclere later in the year. Arriving in London in June, Milner was able to negotiate informally with Zaghloul and draft a memorandum of essential points for a treaty between an independent Egypt and the British Government. Zaghloul then said he would not support the memorandum as it would compromise his nationalist credentials but claimed that it had established his right and place to negotiate for Egypt. This was not what Milner thought he had achieved but, invited to lunch in the House of Commons, Zaghloul then spoke cordially and frankly, saying he truly hoped for a successful outcome from the talks. He then left London to stay at Highclere.

The Egyptian delegation duly arrived by train on Saturday 3 July accompanied by Sir William Garstin and included, as well as Zaghloul, Mohammed Mahmoud, Adly Yeken and Ahmed Lutfi el-Sayed. Carnarvon arranged for several cars to collect them and met them at the station himself, Zaghloul as usual wearing his red fez. Carnarvon had created a very careful house party which included General Sir John Maxwell, Alfred Duff Cooper and his wife, the very beautiful Lady Diana Cooper, the Carisbrookes (Lord Carisbrooke had been known as Prince Alexander of Battenberg before the royal family relinquished their German titles, and was a grandson of Queen Victoria), Howard Carter and two members of the Conservative party, Lord Massereene and Ferrard and the Hon. Harry Lygon. Eve was a huge help to her mother in orchestrating the weekend but she had also managed to ensure that a young man, Brograve Beauchamp, was also invited. Like her mother, Eve was rather petite but vivacious and a good conversationist. Beauchamp was well over six foot, a very good golfer and bridge player and Eve was mad about him.

Almina asked Ahmed Lutfi el-Sayed to take her into supper. Fluent in French and an outstanding scholar, he was also director of the National Library in Cairo and very much enjoyed browsing through Carnarvon's library. Perhaps to his surprise they got on very well: Almina was well read and had always delighted in visiting Egypt.

One of the highlights of the weekend for the Egyptian delegation was a visit to see Carnarvon's racehorses at the stud and to show off his mares and youngstock. Carnarvon had bred most of the horses he raced himself and his two stallions, Valens and Volta, had enjoyed remarkable success. He explained the great personal interest he took in the management of his stud, introduced his excellent and painstaking stud groom, Charlie Whincup, and related how, in order to keep the grass in the paddocks in the best condition, each of them was ploughed in rotation and duly cropped. Zaghloul had a farm of his own, albeit with somewhat more sun, and the guests seemed to enjoy themselves, caught by Carnarvon's enthusiasm. Carnarvon always found the stud something of a haven. Zaghloul liked to gamble (largely unsuccessfully) on both the horses and cards, but at Highclere he could relax and was not able to lose at either.

At the end of the weekend, everyone signed the visitors' book before departing for the station. As a good and patient listener, Carnarvon had kept the confidence of the Egyptians who appreciated his hospitality and consideration. The Egyptian delegation left for Paris and Carnarvon retired again to his reading and racing, enjoying the company of a few friends who came down over the summer. Howard Carter was naturally a frequent visitor, as were Leonard Woolley and Sir Rennell Rodd, who was part of Lord Milner's delegation in Egypt and was the British delegate to the League of Nations at this time. A strikingly good-looking man and a brilliant scholar, he came to stay with his wife and daughter Gloria, a friend of Eve's. Coincidentally Gloria later married the painter Simon Elwes who, in the future, was to paint Porchey's young American wife. Carnarvon had also asked the Allenbys and William Garstin as every insight into the options for future relations between Britain and Egypt was invaluable.

Carter spent much of this summer at Highclere, helping Carnarvon prepare a catalogue of his Egyptian collection, very much at ease and enjoying being at the centre of things. In September he wrote: 'Have been here practically the whole time, shooting and arranging antiques. Today we shot again and Friday and Saturday racing at Newbury.' Carter's mother had died and in many ways his home was now Castle Carter in Egypt, with Highclere acting as a base in the UK. Lord and Lady Carnarvon had moved into Alfred de

Rothschild's magnificent house in Seamore Place and Carnarvon decided to commission new vitrines in which to present his collection. One of his most exquisite and favourite pieces was a yellow jasper fragment of Nefertiti's face, the lower portion which he considered exemplified the fundamental beauty of Egyptian art, how it eliminated the inessential and shared the essence.

Mr Alfred had always employed a policeman to guard the house and Carnarvon maintained this, but only during the night. Almina had inherited not only the house itself but many of its treasures. Naturally she had decided to redecorate. Carnarvon much enjoyed the view from the back of the house, overlooking Park Lane and Hyde Park, giving a green and leafy view while the front entrance was in a very peaceful cul-de-sac.

Lady Evelyn was also staying in London and Seamore Place was not far from Beauchamp's mother who lived nearby in Grosvenor Square. Just like his father, Beauchamp hoped to enter politics and become the prospective Liberal candidate for his father's seat, although it took a little time as he was not, at first, the invited candidate.

In October 1920 Aleksandar Stamboliyski, who had been elected Prime Minister of Bulgaria the year before, visited England in order to foster good relations between the two countries and to look for factors behind Britain's economic and industrial strength that could be applied to his country. Bulgaria needed to modernize its agriculture and industries, while being faced with the loss of territory and an obligation to pay war reparations under the Treaty of Neuilly-sur-Seine. Stamboliyski wanted to visit modern farms, and Lord and Lady Carnarvon invited him to Highclere, suggesting to Rutherford that he should visit 'Mr Boniface as my most modern and energetic tenant'; John Boniface had taken over Burghclere Farm two years earlier. Lord Carnarvon commented to Rutherford 'by trade [Stamboliyski] is a brigand but at the same time he is an agricultural' and he wanted to show him the best farming methods and livestock, adding that he was 'pro-British and should therefore be encouraged'.

Stamboliyski arrived at the Castle on 16 October, accompanied by the Bulgarian Chargé d'Affaires, Minister Plenipotentiary and Secretaries of the Legation. Also in the group was the journalist James D. Bourchier, who reported for *The Times* on events in Bulgaria and the eastern Balkans for many years, before unofficially representing Bulgaria at the Paris Peace Conference in 1919. T. E. Lawrence and Leland Buxton, both of whom were well known to Aubrey Herbert, were also included. Buxton's book sympathizing with Bulgaria's treatment under the treaty had appeared earlier in the year with an introduction by Aubrey.

Aubrey never stopped championing various causes, one of which was the independence of Albania following his travels through the country in 1912 and 1913. He had struck up many friendships and had even been offered the crown of Albania at that point in time; now in the autumn of 1920 he was again offered the crown. He had discussed it with his brother and when the offer became more serious, sent a telegram asking whether he should accept. 'No – stop – Carnarvon.'

The New Year celebration began with a shoot, which all much enjoyed (except for 'poor old Porch' who couldn't join in as he had an ulcerated tooth) before the Carnarvons and Evelyn set off as usual for Egypt. Both Carter and Carnarvon had been anxious about the change in policy regarding the share allocated to excavators of their finds, which had been highlighted by the case of the alabaster vessels found the previous year. In the end an equitable division was agreed with the Department of Antiquities and Pierre Lacau, who kept six of the thirteen vessels for the Cairo Museum. Carnarvon's concession was extended according to its original terms of 1915, which was very important to him in order to ensure he had a share of the finds so

as to recompense him for the costs of excavation. Other new concessions were not necessarily being agreed on this basis.

Excavation resumed in the Valley of the Kings. It was too crowded
around the tomb of Ramesses VI, which was a real attraction for
tourists, so Carter concentrated instead on the extreme end of the
valley and began sorting through the rubbish mounds left by
Theodore Davis's rough and ready excavation of Siptah's tomb in
1905. Just to remove the detritus took forty men and twenty boys
some ten days. Very little was found except scraps and potsherds.
They stayed longer than usual, and in April they were still in Cairo
to attend a dinner party given by Lord Allenby for Mr Winston
Churchill, who had succeeded Lord Milner as Colonial Secretary
in February.

The most exciting family news that spring was that Eve's uncle
the Hon. Mervyn Herbert, the First Secretary of the British Embassy
in Paris, was to marry Miss Elizabeth Willard, daughter of the
American Ambassador in Madrid. Her elder sister had married
Kermit Roosevelt, and the wedding took place in June that year in
Madrid. They then moved into Tetton House in Somerset near
Mervyn's brother Aubrey.

May saw the death of Lord Burghclere, a much-loved man who
always saw the upside in life, which was a good counter to his more
serious-minded wife, Winifred. The entire family gathered at St
Margaret's Westminster for his memorial service.

Howard Carter spent much of the summer of 1921 in England.
He was preoccupied with trying to place the sale of the Rev. William
MacGregor's Egyptian collection and nearly fell out altogether with
Percy Newberry who was also hoping to do the same thing. In
addition, Carter was not at all well. He turned to Lady Carnarvon
for help, and it was established that he needed an operation to
remove his gall bladder. On 16 October he travelled from Highclere
to Leeds Hospital accompanied by Almina, who had arranged once

more for the eminent surgeon Sir Berkeley Moynihan to undertake the operation. Almina had got to know Moynihan quite well through her work with her own hospitals, and he had of course removed Lord Carnarvon's appendix.

Carter could not have been in better hands for this was a serious operation. He spent six weeks in hospital after which he convalesced at Seamore Place for a further six weeks with the help of Dr Johnnie and various nurses recruited by Almina. As a result, his departure for Egypt was much delayed and he only finally booked his passage in January (1922). He immediately launched himself into a flurry of visits to the antique dealers in Cairo, recording a number of purchases both for Lord Carnarvon and one or two other collectors.

Carnarvon spent the autumn of 1921 preparing the proofs for the catalogue of an exhibition which was being organized by the Burlington Fine Arts Club. He had also been asked to exhibit and was engrossed not only in deciding which photographs to display but also how he should photograph some of the other pieces of art for the catalogue. Percy Newberry, visiting Seamore Place, kindly wrote the introduction. Newberry dwelt on the practicality of Egyptian art and its relationship to the world in which they lived. Each piece communicated and informed through pictorial description, and the words for painter and scribe were essentially linked in the language of ancient Egypt. Much of their art dealt with the spiritual world, with life after death and the works of art required for death.

In September 1921 Carnarvon entered some photographs in the London Salon of Photography exhibition which was held at the Royal Institute of Painters in Water Colours in Pall Mall East. As the *Pall Mall Gazette* reported: 'There were some really lovely photographs in the collection, and never before have there been so many entries. The Earl of Carnarvon had two rather nice studies. Spring and Autumn.' Gratifyingly, that same month Carnarvon was asked to be

The Colossi of Memnon
(photographed by Lord Carnarvon).

A portrait of Howard Carter.

The pyramids in flood
(photographed by Lord Carnarvon).

Excavation, c.1910 (photographed by Lord Carnarvon).

Coffins from Deir el Birabi, photographed by Lord Carnarvon on self-timer.

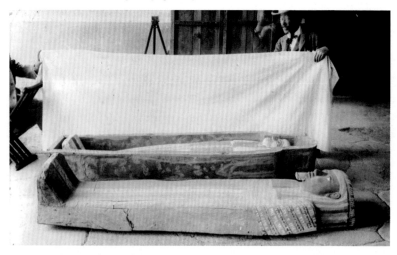

The immense depth and work of the excavations c.1910, captured by Lord Carnarvon.

Excavation photos with the crossed 'c's' at the entrance to the Tomb of Tutankhamun 1922 (photographed by Lord Carnarvon).

Extraordinary painted scenes of Tutankhamun in the afterworld on the walls of his tomb, which are important works of art in their own right.

The canopic chest, each compartment a miniature coffin for the pharaoh's organs.

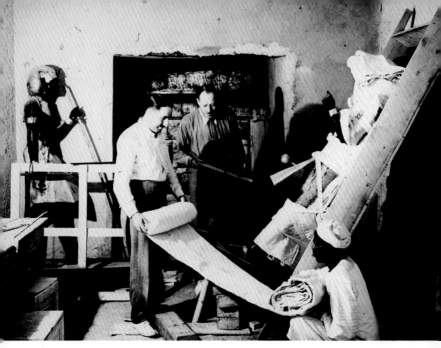

Unrolling wadding.

Howard Carter examining the mummy of Tutankhamun.

The treasures of the tomb are loaded, to be carried along the Nile to Cairo.

The death certificate of the 5th Earl, issued in Egypt.

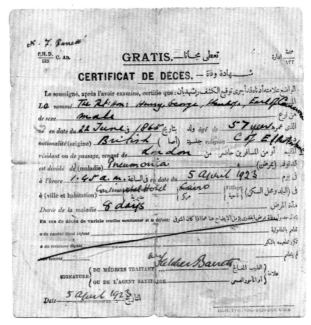

Howard Carter opening the
inner golden shrines after
Lord Carnarvon's death.

one of the judges in a new photographic competition. The *Daily Record* observed: 'That the art of professional photography has made great advance since the "keep perfectly still and smile please" days is undoubted. The £1,000 competition which the Wellington Ward Company is inaugurating should yield satisfying confirmation of the growth of artistry in photographic portraiture. It is particularly interesting to find that the Earl of Carnarvon is one of the three judges [alongside Lady Diana Duff Cooper and Mr. Alfred Ellis] who, while being an "amateur" can certainly give points to most professionals, as his exhibits in the salons strikingly demonstrate.'

In November 1921, the *Sporting Times* carried an amusing piece on Lord Carnarvon's hats: 'It is extraordinary how the average insular Briton – even such as have travelled and lived abroad – stare and comment on anything in the way of hats or wearing apparel, to which they are not accustomed. Among my own collection of Continental head-gear, I possess several Spanish sombreros and Italian Borsalino felts which I dare not wear here. Lord Carnarvon's much criticised grey felt is one of those wide-brimmed, sensible hats worn at Biarritz and San Sebastian, made to shade the eyes and neck from the sun, and the very thing to wear on the Nile where the noble Earl spends so much of his time. I shall see him, this week-end, in that Stewards' crow's-nest at Newbury, and think of that great temple built by Amenophis III dedicated to the Theban triad: Ammon, Chons and Mut at Luxor. Not to be confused with our modern Mutt and Jeff.'

In some ways the article on practical hats demonstrated how little was known about Lord Carnarvon's work in Egypt every winter. He never sought to promote himself but simply to consider and explore (and perhaps wearing quite a rakish hat) the history and understanding of an ancient world.

Howard Carter belatedly left for Egypt on 18 January 1922 while Carnarvon left soon after, arriving in Luxor on 7 February. Carter had rested part of the time in Cairo, and had spent further time making purchases with Carnarvon. Lord Carnarvon had also met numerous ministers, writing to Rutherford that he had twelve courses at some lunches and no time to eat them. He did not think it very good for his digestion. On 22 February 1922 the British Government had formally ended its Protectorate and declared Egypt an independent sovereign state. There were reservations but, overall, it was the beginning of a new era.

With limited excavation work or time, Carnarvon returned to England in April.

On 8 June the marriage was announced of Lord Porchester 'of Seamore Place and Highclere Castle, of the Queen's own Hussars' and Catherine Wendell. His godfather had been Alfred de Rothschild, whose generous bequests to him were listed with much detail and it seemed the groom was a keen amateur rider. There was also much excitement in the New York newspapers because the young Lord Porchester appeared to be unbelievably wealthy, aristocratic and with thousands of acres of land including real estate in Melbourne. He was marrying an equally wealthy American, who would inherit a large property fortune apparently. It seemed as if everything was smiling sweetly on the engaged couple. Catherine in any case looked radiant and dressed beautifully.

The details of the fortune, however, were not strictly true. In fact, Lord Carnarvon had expressed his reservations to his son. Wasn't he quite young to marry? Did he really want to marry an American and especially one with no money? He himself had done neither and had enjoyed a very happy and successful marriage.

Lord Porchester and Catherine were married on 17 July at St Margaret's Westminster, the same church as Almina and Carnarvon, and naturally it was once more a 'society squeeze'. The list of guests included Prince George (later Duke of Kent), Lord Mountbatten, the Marlboroughs, Cholmondeleys, the American Ambassador and many other friends. The bride's father had died when she was 10 years old so her brother Jack gave her away. They left the church to Mendelssohn's 'Wedding March'. The reception was at 31 Grosvenor Square and following family tradition spent their honeymoon at Highclere. Porchester was in the Army and they knew they would soon be posted abroad.

Later that month, Howard Carter returned to Highclere and also met the young bride. Carter relished his visits to Highclere. As he arrived in the park, he wound down the window of the motor vehicle which Lady Carnarvon had kindly arranged to bring him down for the weekend. The very air smelled of summer, the delicate English warmth of the eddying scents from the trees, and the drive wound for well over a mile through the park, past a lake and temple until the familiar redwoods and cedars marking the beginning of the drive up to the Castle emerged into view. Almina never failed to make each guest feel welcome at another weekend house party and, as ever, had done 'all that anyone could possibly do to make everyone have a very happy time'. There were always plenty of servants to help, lawn tennis to the east of the Castle and reading, with lovely walks.

Carter enjoyed these racing weekends; sometimes he joined the party at Newbury or wherever; at other times he would find another guest and go off on a good walk. Like so many people he was very fond of Lord Carnarvon and very much appreciated being asked to stay at Highclere; nothing was too much trouble for Lady Carnarvon and he wondered idly who else would be there. It was a good distraction as he was worrying that Lord Carnarvon was going to give up the excavation concession in the Valley of the Kings. It was becoming a more complicated world in which to work and, equally, he understood that Lord Carnarvon, like everyone else, was facing ever-increasing taxes and financial challenges. He hoped Lord Carnarvon's handsome homebred colt Franklin would continue his winning streak as that might help his case to continue. As a 3-year-old Franklin had won both the Royal Stakes at Newbury and the Hardwicke Stakes at Ascot. Two weeks earlier, he had won the Coronation Cup in excellent style, easily beating the field, and hopes were high that he would win the prestigious Gold Cup at Royal Ascot.

They all went to church on Sunday morning and, following lunch, Lord Carnarvon suggested to Carter that they go to his study to discuss how, and indeed whether, they were going to go on in the forthcoming season in the Valley of the Kings. Carter did not feel very confident since the horse had not run very well the previous day but he really wanted to have one more attempt to find the tomb of Tutankhamen, and so anticipated a long discussion. In desperation Carter said he would offer to pay Lord Carnarvon the ongoing costs for this one last season, still leaving Carnarvon as the excavator. A generous man who did not want to ask so much from Carter, Lord C agreed to continue but stipulated that this would have to be the final season. Carter was immensely relieved and yet again they discussed the map of the Valley of the Kings which lay across the desk.

They made the fateful decision to return to the area in front of the entrance to the tomb of Ramesses VI as they knew no one had ever worked there under the workmen's huts. In order to make the best of the final season Lord Carnarvon agreed to send Carter the funds to begin early, before the main tourist season, which would allow the best opportunity for uninterrupted work.

On 4 July Lord Carnarvon opened an exhibition of Egyptian antiquities at the Society of Antiquaries at Burlington House. The works of art had recently been excavated by Mr C. L. Wooley who had led an expedition at Tel el-Amarna to the palace of Akhenaten. There was a plan of the site, the house and home life with a large number of richly decorated objects illuminating the home life in the fourteenth century BC. Lord Carnarvon explained that the buildings had beautiful coloured pavements and there was an enormous amount of further archaeological work to do on this site.

The summer of 1922 revolved around racing and travel and Lord Carnarvon was very much enjoying the company of his daughter, Evelyn, and she was happy to travel with somewhat less luggage than her mother. Accordingly, in August, off they set for Deauville in possibly his favourite car, a 1912 16-valve Bugatti (registration: XD 9971) which he had bought from Jarrott & Letts. He was so impressed because he had driven it in two tours of France, cruising at 60 to 70mph, three up, and in 14,000 miles suffered only a broken petrol pipe, a slight radiator leak and the inevitable punctures. He very much enjoyed its 'road holding and springing' He had written to this effect to Ettore Bugatti who used the 5th Earl's letter as publicity. Carnarvon therefore hoped to negotiate an advantageous price for his next car and thought he would order a Type 30, given that two of these exciting Bugattis had come second and third in the July 1922 French Grand Prix. Bugatti promised delivery the following spring.

While Evelyn was no photographer, she very much appreciated her father's artistic endeavours and in September 1922 she was thrilled when he was asked to open the International Exhibition of Photographs at the Prince's Gallery, Piccadilly.

'PHOTOGRAPHIC ART. EARL OF CARNARVON ON MODERN IDEALS. The Earl of Carnarvon, is opening the International Exhibition of Photographs Prince's Gallery, Piccadilly, the London papers explained and said he hailed three epochs of photographs. The first was when dry plates came in, making the processes easier, simpler, and cleaner; the second was the epoch of the film and the Kodak, when everybody became a photographer. In the third and modern period photographers had left behind the original ideals, which consisted chiefly in a most accurate reproduction of landscape or portrait, and they are now aimed at a more artistic conception of photography. He congratulated the Professional Photographers' Association on that, the first international exhibition of its kind.'

As Carnarvon had explained to Carter, money worries were now an ever-present part of his life. In September, it was reported that 'the Earl of Carnarvon has decided to offer for sale by auction the remaining portions of Bretby estate, Burton-on-Trent, comprising 1,309 acres. The property includes ten freehold farms, fully licensed inn, building and accommodation land, and a number of residences and cottages.' Despite his interest in all the advances, the way of life at Highclere and the other estates was rooted in the past. Cocktails and shorter skirts had arrived but the question was how to finance this new way of life. Lord Carnarvon was acutely aware that Mr Alfred had gone and was sorely missed not just for his resources but for his business sense.

He was, however, pleased with his racing endeavours because, following the loss at Ascot, Carnarvon and Dick Dawson sent Franklin racing in France and Spain, turning him into a bit of a globetrotter. Among other successes, he won the prestigious Grand Prix de la Reine Victoria at San Sebastian for a lucrative prize of £2,400. Returning to England, he landed the Champion Stakes (10 October) at Newmarket. The *Daily News* reported: 'Steve Donoghue later gave his followers a good turn when he won the Champion Stakes, on Lord Carnarvon's Franklin by half a length from Torelore . . . Franklin, who has been racing in Spain during the autumn, has grown into a fine-looking horse, and Lord Carnarvon is very proud of him.' In total, Franklin was to win Lord Carnarvon over £11,000 in prize money, some £666,000 in today's money.

36

CARTER LEFT CAIRO straightaway for Luxor, catching the night train. It was still early when he reached the dock to cross the Nile in one of the brightly painted boats. For every visitor this was not only a physical crossing but a metaphorical one as well, transitioning from the bustle and amenities of modern-day Luxor to the sand and ruins of ancient Thebes. From this point on travel was by donkey, neither comfortable nor very dignified for Europeans whose longer legs dangled rather comically close to the ground. Carter usually ended up walking part of the way simply to stretch his legs.

The paths taken by the reises, donkeys and Carter cut across the fields, every square foot of fertile soil contributing to local life. In the distance the mountain's shoulder descended into the plains at the place known in Arabic as Bab-El-Moluk (the Gate of the Kings) just near his house. Carter never tired of the extraordinary colours, the groups of palms clumped together, wattle fences around family's homes with cows tethered on long ropes.

He had the map that he and Lord Carnarvon had studied so closely together in his bag. Their plan was simple – to work where no one else had worked. While happy to be back, Carter was also anxious as he knew that his extraordinary partnership and work with Carnarvon was likely to finish at the end of this season. Carnarvon was more than just his employer: he had become a friend and a mainstay of his life, enabling him to hold a better position in life than ever before, with more financial security and a reputation allied to that of Carnarvon. In turn, perhaps subconsciously, Carter had acquired in his sense of dress the accoutrements of a fastidious gentleman: a fondness for bow ties, along with a cigarette holder and a walking stick, just like Carnarvon.

Without further ado, Carter gathered the reises and their excavation teams to begin as planned by the corner of the tomb of Ramesses VI, trenching southwards. He removed the three metres of detritus above the remains of the ancient workmen's huts and then begun to excavate underneath them. Three days later, on 4 November, Carter could begin to see what lay below these old walls. In fact, one of the workmen rushed towards him: he had found the step of a sunken staircase under the very first hut and it soon became apparent to Carter that it was the start of a 'steep excavation cut into the bed rock'. By the end of next day Carter and his teams had cleared down to a plastered and sealed door which was clearly the entrance to a tomb. Carefully examining it, Carter could not find any seals revealing the owner. It was both frustrating and exciting.

Carnarvon, needless to say, was racing at Newbury, irritated as his star colt Franklin had got himself boxed in and, as a result, it had all been rather unexciting. Returning home for dinner on the 5th, however, he found a momentous telegram awaiting him: 'at last have made wonderful discovery in valley. A magnificent tomb with seals intact. Recover same for your arrival. Congratulations.' This might have erred on the side of enthusiasm and over-optimism at this stage but his patron would have been delighted to receive such promising news after working for so long in Luxor.

Carnarvon hurried to find his wife to share the news. Almina was resting in her room with terrible toothache and a painful jaw which she suspected was caused by her wisdom teeth. She thought she might need an operation. After some debate, they decided that Evelyn should accompany her father to Egypt and Almina remain at home. Carnarvon sent a telegram back to Carter firstly saying he would 'possibly come soon', and then confirming he would arrive in Alexandria on 20 November. Carnarvon knew, of course, that it could easily be no more than a false tomb but it was the nearest he had come to a major discovery and, for now, immensely cheering news, whether or not eventually a dead end.

Carnarvon was composed but quietly excited. He wired Gardiner to ask if he thought it could be a tomb and Gardiner promptly offered to travel out too. Carnarvon related that Carter had said it was an undistinguished, insignificant entrance, not what might otherwise be associated with a king, but promised to wire should it prove otherwise. Arriving in Egypt, Eve decided to stay in Cairo as she had a secret scheme she wanted to organize. Carnarvon went straight on to Luxor without further ado and crossed over to Gurneh to stay at Castle Carter with both Carter and Callender, who by now had also arrived. Shortly afterwards, Evelyn also made her way across the Nile from the Winter Palace Hotel bearing a gift for Howard Carter: the sweetest little canary in a cage which she hoped would be a welcome addition to his house.

On 24 November the entire party rode on donkeys down to the tomb. Carter had informed Reginald (Rex) Engelbach, the local chief inspector of the Antiquities Department, of the initial discovery of the steps and he had been present with some friends to witness the clearing of the debris. Carnarvon was ready with his camera and tripod to record the various stages of the excavation, at one point asking one of the boys working at the site to stand on the rock-cut shelf with the top of a plastered door defined behind him.

Once more, Carter cleared the debris off the steps up to the first doorway and then around the bottom of it. Brushing away the plaster dust in silence, they could all see the seal impressions bearing the cartouche of Tutankhamun. What was of concern, however, was that it was also apparent there had been two sections of the doorway that had been opened and re-closed.

Carter decided it would be prudent to sleep in the valley by the tomb that night and took shifts with Callender. Hopefully the carpenters would not take too long to make a robust grill which could be fitted as soon as possible; or, even better, they would be able to get hold of one of the heavy metal ones which were now being deployed in front of some of the tombs in the valley.

Carnarvon returned early the next morning and they began to clear the sloping passageway of rubble. Among the debris were shards of broken jars, seals, fragments of small, coloured vases and alabaster vessels, a few of them still in one piece, as well as water skins. The passageway descended for about 30 feet but, on 26 November, the small team found a second sealed doorway similar in every way to the first one. Once more the seals of Tutankhamun were visible and once again the door bore the suggestion of several re-openings and re-closings as the doorway had certainly been replastered.

It was early evening and the light was fading. Carter and Callender made a tiny breach in the top left-hand corner of the door into a dark void. The iron testing rod told the excavators that ahead there was an empty space. Perhaps another descending passageway and the all-important 'tell-tale' was held up to check for foul gases as was the practice when first opening an ancient tomb. Carnarvon, Carter, Eve, Callender and the reises all waited together in anxious expectation.

Carnarvon's notes recalled: 'We were very doubtful and it was a very exciting moment.' Standing close together, Carnarvon turned to Carter: 'Well it is no good speculating. We must look in', continuing, 'I fully expected we should find another staircase' Carter made a small hole through which he could insert a candle into the space beyond.

Carter put his hand holding the candle through the hole to offer some sort of light and then leaned forward, pressing his head in. He remained silent for what seemed an eternity but really was only perhaps one or two minutes. The suspense was painful. Eve was holding her breath. Carnarvon asked, 'Can you see anything?' 'Yes,' came the thrilling reply. 'Wonderful things.'

Later, Carter tried to put down words to describe the moment, explaining that presently his 'eyes grew accustomed to the light, details of the room within emerged slowly from the mist, strange animals, statues, gold, everywhere the glint of gold. For the moment an eternity . . . [he] was struck dumb with amazement.'

Carnarvon said, 'I could with difficulty restrain my excitement', looking through with the aid of the dim candle '[it] was a most extraordinary sight: colossal gilt couches with extraordinary head . . . beds, chariots, boxes of all sizes'. At the north end of the chamber were two large statues of the 'King'. They were so overwhelmed they could hardly express their exhilaration and excitement More prosaically, Carnarvon later wrote: 'It would be impossible to exaggerate the beauty and workmanship of some of these treasures . . . I never dreamt of finding such a prize as Mr Carter and I have found.'

Carter then widened the hole so that they could each see in using an electric torch. 'We enlarged the hole, and Mr. Carter managed to scramble in (the chamber is sunk two feet below the bottom passage), and then as he moved around with a candle, we knew we had found something absolutely unique and unprecedented.' They looked for the coffin and mummy but couldn't see it.

On the morning of Monday 27 November 1922, Howard Carter, Lord Carnarvon, Lady Evelyn, Arthur Callender and a representative of the Inspectorate stepped into the first chamber using electric lighting from the main valley system.

'3,000–4,000 years maybe have passed and gone since human feet last trod the floor on which you stand . . . and yet, the blackened lamp, the finger-mark on the freshly painted surface, the farewell garland dropped upon the threshold you feel it might have been yesterday . . . time is annihilated by little intimate details such as these.'

It was richly chaotic scene with overturned, broken fragments all over the floor, suggesting earlier robbers had departed in haste, yet the entire space glowed with a profusion of richness, of grotesque and unknown beasts carved in gold and of practical goods from everyday life. Carnarvon thought that 'one of the finest objects is the chair or throne of the King. It is in wood. The back panel is of surpassing beauty . . . all the figures in this scene are built up by means of semi-precious carved stones . . . the delicacy and grace of this work are indescribable.' Robbers had clearly snatched the jewels embedded in the gold strut work under the chair but so far it seemed as if they had time only to fill their pockets or maybe a knapsack.

Slowly turning round in the space, Carnarvon and Carter could see the outline of a window-sized opening in the plastered wall under the left-hand gold couch stacked by the wall. Crouching, Carnarvon crawled under the couch. Then, lying down, he shone the torch through to see a room in even greater disorder. The floor level dropped down much lower and was covered in a confusion of upturned furniture from beds to chairs, wooden boxes, white alabaster catching the light of the torch and statues of every sort. Earlier robbers were probably looking for jewellery and gold. Carnarvon wriggled carefully backwards to offer his place to Carter and stood up brushing off the dust. Still no mummy.

The careful inspection of the chamber now turned to the wall between the extraordinary black and gold guardian figures presumably walking with confidence to a new world. It was covered in seals and they both noticed that, in the bottom part, a small breach had been made through which a slight person could possibly pass.

The great sun god Ra leaves the Valley of the Kings every day, not much later than 5 p.m. Not wishing to lose the chance, as well as feeling the momentous responsibility, Carter, with Callender's help, knelt down in the corner behind the figures and pulled out the loose plaster. He carefully shone a torch through the gap. Eve was the smallest and slipped through first. It was a sight surpassing all precedent; the impression was entirely overwhelming. The whole chamber filled with gold, a huge gold chest with doors closed and knotted along the side nearest them. Breathing in to slide past the shrine, Carnarvon could just see into another room, his torch catching the eyes of huge dark sculpture of Anubis. The darkness seemed to highlight the unreality of it all but it was clearly a veritable treasury again. Carnarvon had always been fascinated by the representation of the spiritual religion of ancient Egypt, the substitution of statues in lieu of the decaying mortal body. Their legends and processions were woven in art and script through temples and works of art and now, in front of him, in life and death.

In silence, they carefully filled the aperture back up and replaced the rushes, broken pottery and propped up the flat woven baskets. Walking back along the valley floor sometime later, no one said a word, not even a whisper. Carnarvon called it 'The Tabernacle, The Holy of Holies' and wrote a long letter to Almina the same night.

Engelbach returned later the next day on his motorbike as they all prepared for the formal opening. Carnarvon had scribbled a quick list from the Allenbys (Lady Allenby attended) to Egyptian notables such as the Mudir (Governor) of Kena province, Wise Bey of the police, Abdel Razik Bey from the agricultural ministry, Nina and Norman de Garis Davies, the Keown-Boyds (he was Oriental Secretary to Lord Allenby in Cairo and played an indispensable part in the British 'indirect rule') and Mrs and Mrs Arthur Merton – he was the Cairo correspondent for *The Times*. Carnarvon needed the help of the local police, with whom he got on well and always made sure they were welcome at the Winter Palace Hotel to share his enjoyment of smoking the best Turkish cigarettes and drinking his favourite coffee. News travelled like wildfire. Every hotel in Luxor was filling up and visitors were even prepared to camp in the gardens.

Eve helped her father organize a lunch by the tomb of Ramesses VI after the opening. The Winter Palace had provided the waiters and the food, which arrived by camel. In addition, Lord Carnarvon suggested he would like to throw a large party at the Winter Palace Hotel within the next few days. Pierre Lacau arrived the following day and was equally astounded by the richness of the find. In fact, Carnarvon wrote that Lacau 'was so impressed that he could scarcely speak for some time. For beautiful work and absolute art nothing has ever been comparable to this.' On a stone at the entrance to the steps to the tomb, Carter painted the antiquity number surmounted by Lord Carnarvon's crest: the coronet and two intertwined 'Cs'.

Arthur Merton had, for better or for worse, already filed a report for *The Times* and rumours began to spread. As in the past, the biggest risk at this point were the tomb robbers, hiding in the night-time and waiting for a chance. As well as beginning the extraordinary and arduous task of assessing the extent of the job that lay before them, Carnarvon and Carter knew that they first had to make the tomb secure. They also made a statement to the accumulated press who had made their way to Castle Carter saying that they hoped to find the mausoleum of the pharaoh behind the false door.

Tired, Carnarvon sat down the following evening to write to Gardiner acknowledging that the tomb had indeed been plundered in a minor way but extolling the sheer variety and wealth of objects still within it. He also wrote that he thought it would cost at least £2,000 to preserve just these objects. There were endless staves, four chariots, 'the most miraculous alabaster vases ever seen', papyri, the throne of the king, two life-size figures of the king bitumised, all sorts of religious . . . I reckon I'm having to spend £2,000 or more preserving in packaging then there is a bricked-up room which has not yet been opened properly . . . I hope to be back soon Carter has weeks of work ahead of him. I have between 20 and 30 soldiers, police and gaffirs to guard yours C."

Carnarvon's reaction under pressure was calm, although he admitted to Gardiner 'that the whole thing is so tremendous that it rather frightens one'. Without doubt the discovery transcended anything that had ever occurred before, but in fact it was the practical concerns of conservation that were Carnarvon's priority and he asked Gardiner to enquire about the best scientists and methods of preserving the fabrics, paintings, wood and so on. Carnarvon felt somewhat isolated and clearly wished that Gardiner were there already but he asked him to convey all the news to Maxwell. Inundated with congratulations from all parts of the world, among the first batch of telegrams received was a very warm message of appreciation from King Fuad of Egypt.

By 5 December Lord Carnarvon was having various meetings with officials in Cairo. There was an immense amount of work to do and Carter managed to join them two days later. Carnarvon ensured he had lines of credit with his bank while Carter noted in his diary that he had ordered from Rostaing a steel gate for the inner doorway of tomb. He then 'purchased wadding & calico for transport and packing of antiquities' as well as 'nests of cardboard boxes . . . Bandages, calico, wadding, photographical supplies' and Carnarvon had asked him to buy a car, he suggested a Ford and provided the funds to do so. Carnarvon knew he would find using a car so much easier and his knee was a real bore again at the moment – riding a donkey was really not helping it.

Albert Lythgoe, the Curator of Egyptian Art at the Metropolitan

Museum, sent Carter a telegram offering the resources of the museum as needed and Carter replied asking if they would lend Harry Burton as the excavation photographer. 'Only too delighted to assist in any possible way. Please call on Burton and any other members of our staff cabling Burton to that effect.' Carnarvon suggested that they needed chemical and conservation advice, preferably from Alfred Lucas who worked in Cairo. Carnarvon asked General Allenby if Lucas could be loaned from the Chemical Department of Egyptian Government and Carter went to see Lucas who was delighted to offer his services over the winter.

Carnarvon knew they would need to assemble a team of world experts to help them record and preserve the tomb's contents on a hitherto unknown scale and that he would also have to negotiate any deal with the Department of Antiquities and Inspectorate. Meanwhile, Carter carried on in Cairo and then in Luxor with the many practical details that had to be addressed. Arthur Mace cabled and also offered his help. Mace had grown up in England, leaving for Egypt to work with Flinders Petrie, then the American Georges Reisner, before working for the Metropolitan Museum of New York. He had become an expert in the preservation of fragile materials and was now involved with the restoration of ancient Egyptian artefacts for the museum. Carter was delighted to accept his offer.

Carter then returned to the valley to fit the gates on the tomb. Breasted was also present to examine and record the seals along with Walter Hauser and Lindsley Foote Hall (Metropolitan Museum archaeologists) who were to help draft plans of the tomb and scale drawings, respectively. The plan would record where each object was placed in the tomb by the ancient Egyptian officials and each object was then labelled with its excavation number. Some of the objects were outlined in red to make the plan easier to understand and the drawings show how Tutankhamun's objects had been layered upon one another.

Pursued by the press, Carnarvon and his daughter left Cairo for England on 4 December 1922. Reporters who met him en route commented on his calm and 'matter of fact way' and furiously scribbled down anything he said to cable in for the next edition. Carnarvon believed 'that in all human probability the tomb of King Tutankhamen lies beyond the wall'. Outside his own circle and interests, Carnarvon was a little-known figure to many but, extraordinarily, once again it was his sartorial style to which attention was drawn. Lord Carnarvon 'almost rivals Mr. Churchill in his taste for nondescript hats, and he prefers overcoats with loud checks. He is one the most versatile members of the peerage. Besides being an ardent archaeologist, he is a racehorse breeder and owner, a farmer . . . world traveller, and photographer.'

Carnarvon arrived back at Highclere on 18 December. Happy to be home and delighted to see his wife, who was still unwell, he found a letter from Lacau congratulating him on behalf of Comité d'Egyptologie, not only for the discovery but also for the method so far of conducting the excavation. Lacau added that it was the most astonishing reward that any archaeologist could have and congratulated both Carnarvon and Carter for their scientific methods, their dedication to ancient art as opposed to a foremost interest in financial gain. Carnarvon was appreciative but did not entirely trust Lacau, who was already trying to force his hand over the discovery.

Carnarvon spent much of the following month in London, where he could more easily avail himself of the advice of, above all, Alan Gardiner, as well as that of Dr Wallis Budge. Very conscious of the fragility of relations between Britain and Egypt, Carnarvon also wanted to see General Sir John Maxwell and Arthur Balfour.

Gardiner had already arranged various visits and consultations with conservation experts beginning with those at the Victoria and Albert Museum. Carnarvon enjoyed the lucidity and deep knowledge of Gardiner and hoped he would continue with the team in the future. Another port of call was the Royal Geographical Society on Kensington Gore, opposite Hyde Park. Earlier in the year a team of climbers had attempted the first ascent of Mount Everest which, sadly, had not been successful. What was interesting, however, was that, before they had left, the mountaineers had sold the rights to their story to *The Times* for £1,000, to be conveyed in the form of fifteen long cables. Carnarvon was very aware that any such deal for the tomb of Tutankhamun could demand a far higher figure but it gave him a starting point. He wrote to Carter saying that although he thought the *Daily Mail* might pay more 'yet *The Times* is after all the first newspaper in the world'.

Carnarvon also met with another of his friends, the industrialist Hugo Cunliffe-Owen, at Seamore Place. Cunliffe-Owen was a successful businessman who had also worked in the Ministry of Information during the war and Carnarvon sought his help with approaches from film companies such as Pathé. No money had yet been mentioned but Carnarvon had been thinking it through and was proposing a programme that covered the approach to the excavation, inside the chambers and unveiling the mummy. Practical as ever, he thought they would have to bring their own dynamos to provide power and, of course, lighting. He also asked Cunliffe-Owen to propose various recces and hoped there might be a good deal of money in it. Cunliffe-Owen suggested he meet Pathé at their Wardour Street office.

In addition, Carnarvon arranged to meet Bertram Parke at the Dover Street Studios and sought his help in managing the sale or free distribution of various photographs. Some of these were by now actually two years old but, in the light of the discovery, definitely worth something. In fact, Parke was able to sell two of them to the *Illustrated London News*.

Regardless of the potential riches awaiting him back in Egypt, Carnarvon was particularly delighted to collect two tiny, exquisite animal figures, a prancing horse and an ariel gazelle, which he had bought in Cairo. He thought they looked very good and, while 18th Dynasty, he was not certain whether they came from Saqqara or not.

At the end of the week, on 22 December, another cold, clear, dry day, Carnarvon's car swept slowly through the tall wrought-iron gates, past the policemen and into the forecourt of Buckingham Palace, then on through the arched entrance to the courtyard behind before sweeping round to pull up at the grand entrance. He made his way up the magnificent gilded and crimson staircase, following the footmen to the Yellow Drawing Room, to be received in audience by King George V and Queen Mary.

Like everyone, they wanted to hear about this extraordinary discovery and the treasures nonpareil. Immaculately dressed, Carnarvon bowed to the King and Queen before being invited to sit and give an account of his remarkable discovery among the royal tombs of ancient Thebes. Carnarvon described the stifling heat inside the tomb and how the precious objects were scattered across the floor in utter confusion. He related in detail some of the extraordinary pieces propped against the walls, including the golden couches which were out of this world.

Carnarvon said he very much hoped that it would stimulate interest in Egyptology in Britain and lead to further support for uncovering the past. He said that he considered the art of Amarna to be exceptional and that he was fortunate already to possess a few pieces in his collection at Seamore Place. This style of art was continued in the tomb of Tutankhamun and yet some pieces reflected a new era, one which blended into the art of Thebes. He hoped it might lead to further funding for work at Amarna where the Egypt Exploration Society did not have the resources to continue their work. This he found most regrettable.

His Majesty was exceedingly interested and congratulated Carnarvon most warmly. The audience lasted more than an hour before the King and Queen bade him farewell and wished him all the best for Christmas and, of course, the forthcoming year and hoped he would return to continue the story of the treasures in the next royal chambers.

Like everyone, they had read the long cables sent back to British newspapers giving background and detail, but were also anticipating the debate about whether Carnarvon had any rights to the works of art in the tomb.

In the meantime, the Metropolitan Museum which, like other museums, had in the past received gifts from Carnarvon, felt that anything they might gain in return for help would far outweigh the immediate costs. Albert Lythgoe had commented that he was sure Lord Carnarvon would see them all right.

Even before any further discoveries had been made, the news piqued the interest of psychics and mediums. Ancient Egypt has the ability to reach into the collective imagination: ancient times, tombs, processions, priests, gold and forgotten rituals. Popular culture referred to the Book of the Dead and the words suggest the start of horror book or movie, magical incantations. In fact, it is more reassuring funerary text to help you move into the next world, the world of the resurrection.

A fashionable seer and palmist known as Chiero claimed he had received a message, which he passed on to Lord Carnarvon, warning that should anything be removed from the tomb of Tutankhamun it would lead to sickness and death. Velma the Seer asked to read his palm and said that his 'Life Line was perilously near his present age'. Lord Carnarvon later shared such predictions with his colleagues and Professor Breasted noted that perhaps the interest was in response to the 'profound boredom with news of reparations, conferences and mandates'.

In order to dissuade robbers, the pharaohs of Egypt had long threatened retribution to anyone entering a tomb. It was written down as spells and anyone caught would be punished. Obviously given the dearth of unrobbed tombs, the threat had not worked very well: the lure of gold to be enjoyed here and now outweighed any fear for the next life.

Meanwhile, back in the Valley of the Kings, unaware of such doom-laden predictions, on the same day, 22 December, Carter had proposed a press day for all the newspapers, after which he hoped to close off visits for a while in order to continue with the conservation work. It was impossible to make the press happy: Carter had admitted one journalist the evening before to try to 'spread' the viewing, but that led to furious letters from those who entered the next day.

Arthur Mace took the train to Luxor, arriving on Christmas Eve 1922, where he joined Herbert and Helen Winlock in the American House which overlooked the Nile towards Luxor. It was a comfortable expedition house with large, well-equipped rooms courtesy of J. P. Morgan who, as President of the Metropolitan Museum, believed that a well-provided base would aid efficiency and enthusiasm.

Despite the pressure of work, they all gathered for the holidays, Winlock having asked Carter and Lucas to join them for Christmas evening. Carter, surveying the Christmas table decorated with crackers and tiny vases of flowers, the evening filled with candles, light and the sound of happy voices, smiled, looked across at Alfred Lucas and raised his glass. Mrs Winlock was unfortunately not feeling well but the rest of the party was there and in good form.

All the characters in the team were quite different and keeping them together was a challenge but, curiously, they were all very fond of Carnarvon. As Mace put it: 'in spite of his oddities, very lovable.' As the year continued, relations became more fragile, however: Winlock, continuing with the Metropolitan Museum excavation at Thebes, felt sidelined, his team diluted and loaned out to Carnarvon. Mace wrote to his wife, 'relations in our camp are excellent, although Winlock is a bit grouchy sometimes'.

Also present that evening were the two draughtsmen Walter Hauser and Lindsley Foote Hall, the American Charles Wilkinson and the British couple Norman and Nina de Garis Davies, both of whom worked for the Metropolitan Museum as expert illustrators and offered invaluable experience in giving context to hieroglyphs. The latter lived every season nearby in a house loaned to them by Robert Mond, whose philanthropy towards exploration and conservation of the Theban tombs was so generous. Mond combined his career as a chemist with a passion for archaeology; his company would eventually became ICI when it merged with three other British chemical companies in 1926. Finally, of course, there was Arthur Mace in immaculate white linen who sat next to Carter. It was a good opportunity to talk since they barely knew each other. They all enjoyed the trimmings of a Christmas dinner with excellent wine, they pulled crackers and put on paper hats and enjoyed the warm evening.

The overwhelming feeling around the table was still one of disbelief that the artistic treasures and knowledge of another world had been unearthed. Arthur Mace wrote to his wife Winifred: 'Here I am in the thick if it . . . it is simply stupendous, so much so that it takes one's breath away.'

If Christmas offered a moment for pause and reflection, the very following day the intensity of media interest and an incessant stream of tourists, notables and visitors claiming kinship or friendship returned to inundate the excavation. Luxor Post Office was soon overwhelmed with telegrams and fan mail. Every distant relative, it seemed, wrote letters of introduction to try to get a visit to the tomb. The constant interruptions and persistent hunger for news created a very difficult working environment for Carter and the team who were working in very confined spaces, in great heat and considerable discomfort.

On Boxing Day Mace accompanied Carter to the tomb to discuss and prioritize their plans, which were often worked out *in situ* given the monumental nature of the task. Again, Mace wrote to his wife: 'Carter was extremely friendly . . . Reporters are thick in the valley and pop out from behind rocks to photograph and interview . . .'

On 27 December the first object, Box 21, was removed from the tomb and carried to the nearby tomb of the Pharaoh Seti, which was to be used as a laboratory both for restoration and for photographic work. Box 21, which had lain in front of one of the guardian statues to the right of the entrance, was a painted chest, exquisite in its own right but which contained garments and shoes covered with beadwork. Mace later wrote that each such box revealed 'all sorts of unexpected treasures but they take an infinity of time to work out'.

At this point, Carter decided the best step would be to seek collaboration and help from Lacau. Like Carnarvon, Carter was wary of Lacau and very aware that his opinion of private excavators was unfavourable. 'I am being pestered daily by an immense number of applicants . . . to visit our new discovery, the mere answering of which impedes the progress of our work. Would it therefore be asking of you too much to issue an order of service to the extent that under no condition can permission be given to visitors to visit the new tomb. I ask this of you, dear Mons. Lacau, for (1) the preservation of the treasures therein; and (2) to allow the recording, conservation and removal of the objects to proceed. Believe me, Etc. Signed: – H.C.'

Fortunately, Arthur Mace and Lucas got on well as they spent many hours together in the workshop focusing on conserving every possible tiny detail. It was painstaking work. Every single item found in the tomb was 3,500 years old so each presented its own, unique difficulties: how to stop it disintegrating, how to restring beads or recreate the wooden bracelets, how to stop the wood shrinking as it was exposed to the dry air, and so on. Wax was often employed to help in the work: one of the key processes was to melt wax to set beads so that the design could be preserved. Sometimes they would have to go into the tomb to treat works of art with wax *in situ* and they would find Harry Burton taking photographs, Hall and Hauser drawing and recording and Carter under pressure to show yet another visitor in.

In very contrasting wintery weather, Carnarvon took the train back to Highclere where Almina was organizing a quiet Christmas with only a few friends as the family gathered their strength and composure for the coming year, given the extraordinary interest in the discovery. Winifred joined them for Christmas lunch and announced that she was determined to go out to Egypt, as did Carnarvon's jockey Steve Donoghue and Sir William Garstin, whose enthusiasm was perhaps more to be expected. Arriving at Highclere church in good time for matins, Carnarvon was treated like a celebrity. The newly married Lord and Lady Porchester were absent, having sailed for India from Tilbury on Christmas Day 1922. Carnarvon had hoped they might have spent a little more time at home or even accompanied him to Egypt, but at least he had Porchey's dog Susie for company.

Carnarvon was tired but, with the fire comfortably burning, he settled down in his study with a cup of tea to begin a long letter to Carter.

'My dear Carter,

At last, I can sit down and write to you. This letter will come out with Gardiner who arrives on the 3rd at Luxor . . .

I got your cable yesterday and was delighted with the contents especially as you were reported in the *Daily Telegraph* as saying that the whole outfit must go to the Cairo Museum. I saw Lythgoe who has really behaved better than it would be possible to imagine also a nice cable from Robinson whom I answered thanking him and the trustees.

I think that I shall have to have a press agent who will deal with matters and shall bring him out he would deal with all press communications i.e., bulletins gratis and special articles to be paid for. I saw Robinson, editor of *The Times*, yesterday as his paper is quite reasonable. I explained I could <u>not</u> give all news first to *The Times*. He is writing to me about it after thinking it over.'

General Sir John Maxwell was also at Highclere and had agreed with Carnarvon about making some money: 'I think for my part I should be able to sell some books which is what I am writing to Carter.' Maxwell asked what offers Carter had received and Carnarvon told him that they were far lower than those Carnarvon had received in London. Carnarvon also said that he had proposed very strongly to Carter that he 'must reserve the best of objects for [himself] to paint' if he produced it in colour and 'he could get a lot of money' and he had to 'think <u>this out</u>'. Carnarvon was entirely unsure where the next few years would take them and, while the treasures were to stay in Egypt, at least there might be some peripheral opportunities for each of them to explore.

The letter to Carter continued: 'I think that outside books possibly three or more volumes at £5 to £8 a volume and then we should have a popular edition perhaps at 20,000 copies to be sold at 10/6. I fancy this would go alright I have talked the matter out with Gardiner and I think that [Carter], I and [Gardiner] could muddle it out.'

Carnarvon also received a slightly harassed cable from Carter who was struggling with the press, for whom he just did not have any time at all.

Traditionally, at this time of year Carnarvon and his guests would set out into the pale winter light to walk and shoot some of the hedgerows and coverts. Carnarvon enjoyed the fresh air, the pleasure of fading rosehips and bare trees, the curling, misty breath and the stomping of feet of people trying to keep warm. He loved Highclere, even the frosty, desolate days, but his lungs were out of love with such damp bleakness. At the end of the short day, he walked back along Lime Avenue in company with Tommy Richardson, the under-keeper. Where their ways parted for Carnarvon to turn through the gardens, he handed over his shotgun: 'You had better oil this up Tommy, I am heading back to Egypt and I won't need it again this season.' Tommy took the gun, 'Yes Milord, thank you and goodbye then'. This was truer than he knew.

Almina and Evelyn also wrote to Carter. Almina had realized she was not well enough to accompany Carnarvon to Egypt and had arranged instead, on her husband's advice, to go to Paris for an operation on her jaw.

'My dear Howard this is a line is to send you my love and every blessing in the coming year. I have not written a lot of congratulations . . . you are being inundated with correspondence of all kinds. How truly I rejoice . . . your patience and long-suffering perseverance has been rewarded and rewarded well.' She explained the press were not easy here (in England) either, that her husband was 'pestered morning noon and night'. She felt sure 'the sooner C gets back to Luxor it'll be easier for you to get things done'.

Almina also let Carter know she had had the pleasure of seeing his brother and sister-in-law at lunch two days before and that he was the subject of endless conversation. Given she was staying behind, she did hope she could be of some use even in England in any case.

Eve also wrote hoping her letter might reach him on the threshold of a new year. 'My dear I wish you just the very best of everything. May you be as happy as you are successful and for many, many years – bless you – you deserve it. By now you are world renowned and your name, dear, will be added to the famous men in the annals of history. It is wonderful.' She added that her father had had a lot of work to do and was somewhat fatigued. 'However, he revels in it all and, when slightly weary, calls me in to tell him again of the "Holy of Holies" which acts like a magnum of champagne! I cannot thank you sufficiently for allowing me to enter its precincts, it was the Great Moment of my life.'

As the year drew to a close Carnarvon's restless mind was turning over the challenges that lay ahead and, to that end, on 31 December 1922, he began a letter to Carter into which he could add his thoughts and the results of the various conversations he had had.

Carnarvon was concerned with seeking the best advice about stabilizing the works of art. The British Museum experts were somewhat against collodion 'because of nitric acid whose action is uncertain. I hope you understood my cable. It meant the cellulose acetate diluted with acetone to a 2% solution should be first applied and then, if necessary, carried further out as a stronger percentage.' Carnarvon thought he should ask the respected conservationist Langhorn to come out to Cairo where he would set him up in a workshop.

As ever thinking outside the box, Carnarvon had asked Pathé to quote 'terms to me and I think we could certainly do business on it 50-50 of profits'. Equally he saw a buyout as a different option and he updated Carter on his conversations with both Pathé and *The Times*. Pathé had told Carnarvon that it would cost him £20,000. 'I have of course not given up trying – I'm a little surprised.' 'You will have had a letter from Merton (I insisted it should go in cypher . . .) offering £5,000. They're willing to pay for a gentlemanly way and I think we can't do better. £5,000 is minimum with further payments of profits.'

In the meantime, Carnarvon was extremely careful in terms of which photographs he allowed to be used in the press. He had met the editor of *The Times*, Geoffrey Dawson (he had been reappointed in 1923), and he also interviewed Sir Percy Robinson 'who would come out and take all the press matters off our hands which will be a great advantage otherwise life will not be bearable. I think he will come as my agent and not as *The Times*. I shall consult lawyers before signing.'

Carnarvon had also telephoned Gardiner before leaving for Egypt and he wanted to relate their conversations. 'Neither of us having much experience of the Press.'

Carnarvon finished up by saying that he hoped to reach Alexandria from Monte Carlo on about the 24th, perhaps even the 23rd, and reiterated that his wife 'was not at all well and certainly will be unable to come'. Carnarvon also hoped that Carter had sorted out the Ford car – 'you have but to tell Maudsley when it's required' and could Carter please order 'rooms for me and Eve at the Winter Palace. If you want anything cable . . . God bless you'.

37

WONDERFUL THINGS

CARTER WAS SPENDING every day at the tomb. Gardiner arrived in Luxor on 2 January bearing letters and reports from Carnarvon to Carter, but first he wanted to see the tomb.

Carter was working more or less as his own man now and had the challenge of managing the daily schedule and morale of a team, working under intense scrutiny in a confined space, in heat and dust. A steel gate was firmly in place to protect the treasures with round-the-clock security organized by Carnarvon with the chief of police, who was only too pleased to have such an important role in helping to safeguard the treasures of Egypt.

The plan of the antechamber was being drawn to scale by Lindsley Foote Hall and Walter Hauser, and Arthur Mace and Alfred Lucas were working on the immediate conservation issues as the antiquities were brought out. Meanwhile, James Breasted and Alan Gardiner contributed their experience and philological expertise with reference to the seals and inscriptions. Harry Burton was taking photographs and Arthur Callender was acting as a reliable assistant for Carter. Later on, when he returned to Egypt, Professor Newberry would record the botanical specimens and his wife would use her seamstress's skills to help with the textile conservation.

Carter was completely focused on clearing the antechamber methodically, recording, photographing and then preserving each item, allowing further work to be done on the objects before they were transported to Cairo. A host of journalists and thousands of fascinated visitors made the trip to Luxor just to gaze on the site. They would appear in the cool of the early morning, sitting as close as they were allowed to by the police, hoping that they would see at least one object being brought out and up the steps before being taken to one of the neighbouring tombs. As well as the laboratory in Seti's tomb, Harry Burton had set up his photographic studio in the tomb of Queen Tiye.

Some visitors produced letters of introduction from people so important that Carter felt he had no choice but to admit them to the tomb but, in such a narrow space, they held up the work and were a danger to the fragile objects. Such visitors seemed unending and tempers became frayed. Carter was outstanding in his ability to overcome and manage practical problems, but socially he was less adept. The local tradesmen, however, took a different view. Life had never been so good and as one put it: 'Inshallah [please God] they find a new tomb next year also.'

Carnarvon had told his youngest brother Mervyn that he thought they might be able to have the grand opening of the tomb on 10 February, Mervyn having said that he and wife Elizabeth were keen to be there. They were staying in Portofino and decided to sail to Egypt via Genoa and Marseilles, arriving in Luxor with time to spare for some sightseeing.

The antechamber was indeed cleared by the first week of February, leaving just the two guardian statues either side of a bricked-up doorway. In the event, Carnarvon was proved slightly optimistic in his timing: it would be a week later.

The left-hand-drive, black-radiator, Model T Ford tourer motor car, whose purchase Carnarvon had commissioned before he left the previous year, arrived and immediately brought great improvement in day-to-day movement. Another tomb was immediately pressed into service to act as a garage for the car which facilitated travel between the tomb and Castle Carter and the houses of the other team members and saved considerable time and discomfort. They had nearly lost the car when it arrived; it was balanced in a boat and, as they tried to disembark it, it got stuck. Just as it was about to roll backwards into the Nile, they somehow managed to push it up the bank, to the delight of a large audience of local fellahin.

Meanwhile, on 10 January 1923, Carnarvon finalized an exclusive reporting deal with the chairman and owner of *The Times*, his old friend J. J. Astor. The paper paid Carnarvon £5,000 and agreed to give him 75 per cent of the fees for syndicated reports and photographs excepting cinematograph and coloured photographs.

As a practical aid for both parties, *The Times* was to place one or more members of its staff at the disposal of the 5th Earl, to join his party from England to Egypt, his salary and expenses paid by the paper. All photographs taken by Howard Carter and Dr Alan Gardiner were to be supplied to *The Times* after discoveries as the newspaper might think desirable for publication and to give interviews accompanying these photographs (excepting colour and movie film), all to be approved by Howard Carter as agent for the Earl. In terms of distribution of news articles, *The Times* might offer 50 per cent of all interviews and photographs of such material to British newspapers as a matter of goodwill.

Carnarvon wrote to Carter the same day saying, 'it was impossible to go on as we were doing. It made small difference whether one was in the country or not. There are always telephones, telegrams and taxi cabs beside cameras etc.' He did not see the benefit of an auction: 'it's a very curious thing how this discovery has excited the public. All the most unlikely people from the king down to the policeman taxi driver and . . . labourer.'

The day after signing the *Times* agreement, Carnarvon remained in London and spoke to a massive audience at a specially convened meeting of the Egypt Exploration Society at Westminster Hall. Chaired by General Sir John Maxwell, Professor Newberry made the first address after which he introduced Lord Carnarvon. Ever since his terrible car accident, Carnarvon had felt nervous about public speaking. He was never sure if his voice could be heard and was acutely self-conscious of the problems he had with his jaw and the roof of his mouth. He had undergone a number of operations and all was much better, but for a man who wished to do everything well it was a challenge.

To a hushed audience he explained that he had been working in the Valley of the Kings for eight years and shifted perhaps 60,000 tonnes of rock and cuttings. That he and Carter had been excavating the area in front of the tomb of Ramesses VI and had wanted to explore further for some time but were reluctant to interfere with the tourist traffic, hence they had commenced work in the earlier, quieter part of the season. He related Carter's reaction to seeing the treasure for the first time: 'Yes, yes! It is wonderful.' 'When I put my head in, I saw the most extraordinary sight. In the light of the candle, I saw straight lines which were caused by the gold on the state couches.' Carnarvon concluded that while a certain quantity of gold and jewels had been taken, the tomb would help us to 'elucidate a great many questions which are now great mysteries'. On a practical note, he said he had bought a mile and half of wadding in advance of the next stage.

Carnarvon had wanted the Egyptian press to have early and free access to all the information and had cabled Carter to say 'have definitely arranged native Egyptian press receive copy regarding the discovery for publication the same day', but this was not properly expressed in the agreement and the Egyptians were excluded.

All in all, however, it was not Carnarvon's finest hour. *The Times* deal catastrophically alienated every rival newspaper as well as the Egyptian press and, even worse, the nascent nationalist government. Mass-circulation newspapers in England instructed their correspondents to do everything possible to scupper the exclusive. A. H. Bradstreet, the special correspondent at Luxor for the *Morning Post*, first expressed disbelief at the notion of a London deal, dismissing 'an amazing rumour . . . of which no definite knowledge can be obtained here' that might even go as far as closing the whole Valley of the Kings. If this happened, he warned, 'it is proposed to hold protest meetings'.

Once the nature of the deal had been confirmed, Bradstreet also expressed disbelief that the Egyptian Government, officials at the Antiquities Service or the Egyptian press would countenance their being reduced to bystanders, simply to be given second-hand news, and openly agitated in Cairo for the exclusive deal to be broken. Bradstreet was said to have told friends that he would 'drive C. and C. out of their minds for having sold a piece of the world's ancient history to the *London Times*'.

Carnarvon was not immediately aware of these reactions but over the next few weeks he had to deal with the increasing rancour and ill feeling from every other newspaper, American and European. If there was a chance of crossed wires and misconstructions, they were blown out of all proportion and he remained front-page news as he returned to Egypt for the official opening of the tomb of Tutankhamun.

All the family were keen to go out to Egypt but the timing was problematic. Aubrey wanted to go as much as his other siblings but was having such serious problems with his eyes that it was not possible. He and his wife had travelled to Germany to see his oculist,

Dr Pagenstecker, who was now rather elderly, but there was no good news. He also felt that, as an MP, it was not a good time to be away from either his constituency or the House of Commons. He had offered to resign as MP as his sight deteriorated but this had not been accepted and his majority stayed ridiculously large. Winifred had made arrangements to go to Rome and, through Elsie's family, had manage to gain an audience with the Pope. So, in the end, Carnarvon travelled just with Evelyn, setting out on 19 January for Marseilles and then Egypt.

Arriving in Cairo on Friday 26 January, Carnarvon was delighted to see Carter again. The first thing they did was to attend a meeting with the Prime Minister Nassim Pasha, the Minister of the Public Works, Sirry Pasha, the Under Secretary, Abd El Hamid Suleman Pasha, as well as Pierre Lacau and Alexander Keown-Boyd. It was now a new era and an Egyptian Government and, while Carnarvon was a good and sensitive listener, he was surprised by the furore over the *Times* deal. Nationalist politicians all proclaimed Tutankhamun to be the symbol of the new nation's proud and ancient roots. The leading poet and playwright Ahmed Shawqi, for example, said, 'We refuse to allow our patrimony to be mistreated'. Born of a diplomat and politician, Carnarvon's calm and quiet helped establish that in fact the key issue was access.

Sirry Pasha had issued a government communiqué which stated that the Egyptian authorities naturally had no concern with any agreement concluded by Lord Carnarvon with any journal for the publication of his own information or opinions about the treasure, but that they intended to maintain an attitude of strict impartiality towards all correspondents. Instructions were to be given by the Director-General of Antiquities Service to furnish all correspondents requesting it with such information as might properly be published. Moreover, all journalists were to enjoy equality of treatment in the matter of admission to the tomb whenever circumstances permitted.

This announcement gave great satisfaction in Egyptian circles who were strongly critical of the proposed monopoly. Carnarvon was keen to return to Luxor and agreed that the local press could visit the tomb one day each week. In the end they agreed on Tuesdays but, in reality, the arrangements were more flexible and visits often took place on other days.

Carnarvon also explained that the Queen of the Belgians had sent him a telegram asking if she could see the tomb. King Fuad and the Egyptian Government organized her visit with the help of the British High Commissioner, Lord Allenby. The Queen had always stated she had a 'passion for ancient Egypt' and would be travelling with her son and Professor Jean Capart, an eminent Belgian Egyptologist.

Financially, Carnarvon was now beginning to feel the strain. The Rothschild money had all gone and he had received a letter from Lloyds Bank concerning his overdraft just as he left London. He had written back asking the bank to copy in his agent Rutherford, but was not sure he could resolve the arrangements from Egypt. Before leaving for the tomb, therefore, Carnarvon quickly wrote to Rutherford asking him again 'to cut down the expenses as much as possible, what with the super tax, it will be most difficult to make ends meet. I am so rushed here and there have been so many bothers with the wretched press, the matter having become a political one that I cannot for the moment write more, but when I am at Luxor in comparative peace I will communicate fully.'

Carnarvon and his daughter Evelyn were met by a number of local notables at the railway station in Luxor and he invited them back to the Winter Palace Hotel. He was always delighted to sit for a smoke on the terrace of the Winter Palace Hotel, in this case with His Excellency Abd El Aziz Yehieh Bey, Mudir of Qena province, Mohamed Fahmy Bey, Mamur Markaz of Luxor and Sheikh Ahmed Shaker, a judge in Luxor.

Carnarvon was very keen to return to the tomb and see the progress made and to express his gratitude to one and all. As he approached the entrance to Seti's tomb where the workshops and laboratory were situated, he later remarked, 'the smell of chemicals was distinctly discernible and on entering the odour of acetone collodion was very strong. It was a long passage and all the way down on either side the boxes were lined up' containing the precious objects collected from the first chamber. Luckily, Seti's tomb had electricity and this made it easier to see the objects. The throne was even more beautiful than he had first thought, the delicacy of the precious stone work quite extraordinary. However, he commented that what caught his eye most was a wooden box which had contained some of the pharaoh's clothes – 'the painting on this box was so very fine that it more nearly resembles miniature painting than anything else'.

Carnarvon kept in touch with Rutherford back at Highclere, writing frequently not just about the finances but about the wellbeing of the staff. The head keeper Henry Maber was not well, which was worrying, but of more concern was the change of government in Egypt: the 'government which by the way was very weak resigned yesterday'. He knew he would have to start again and build new relationships, all of which was likely to further impede work on the tomb.

The Times itself noted that 'malicious' rumours were beginning to circulate in Egypt against Carnarvon and Carter – 'the mass of Egyptians is firmly convinced that Lord Carnarvon has stolen the more valuable pieces in the chambers' – and there were stories of aircraft landing in the desert in the dead of night to carry the hoard away. Carnarvon and Carter grew increasingly strained and tired: Carter was simply trying to focus on the stewardship of the items and Carnarvon on that of the project.

Arthur Weigall had returned to Luxor as the correspondent for the *Daily Mail*. He would regularly wire the Egyptian authorities in Cairo protesting against the *Times* agreement, and every Tuesday would produce an official permit signed by the Minister of Interior to gain entrance. Numerous evenings were spent plotting at champagne dinners presided over by Mrs Valentine Williams, who was apparently now becoming a sort of news editor for the rival press. Engelbach, chief inspector of antiquities in Luxor, joined in the champagne dinners and seemed to have thrown in his lot with Weigall and co.

Weigall wrote an impassioned letter to Carter setting out how disastrous the *Times* agreement was, that it was now a different world and the old British order was on the wane. Each day on their return from the tomb, the press correspondents would adjourn to Weigall's room and apparently get his views from a scientific point of view, discuss the general abuse of Lord Carnarvon and *The Times* and then disperse to cable their day's story. The aim was 'to do everything possible to break *The Times* agreement'.

Carnarvon returned once more to Cairo to meet with Engelbach, Tewfik Effendi Boulos and, again, Sirry Pasha. Boulos was an experienced man who had worked with Maspero and Carter for nearly two decades and was much liked by both Carnarvon and Carter. However, Carnarvon never warmed to Engelbach, who was the more traditional academic having studied Egyptology, Coptic and Arabic at University College London and who had worked with Flinders Petrie. For his part, Engelbach, like so many others who had devoted their lives to academia, found it galling that it was Carnarvon who had had such spectacular success

From a practical point of view, Carnarvon needed to ensure that everyone was happy with the next stage. A considerable number of guests had to be invited by both Carnarvon and the Egyptian Government and Carnarvon had been drawing up a list of who should be asked, an invidious task.

Evelyn had remained at the Winter Palace Hotel. With so many visitors staying at the hotels or on private dahabiyas, there was a thriving social life with tennis matches and dances. General Sir John Maxwell, Richard Bethell (Carnarvon's private secretary), Mervyn Herbert and his wife Elizabeth had all arrived along with Sir Edward and Lady Beauchamp and their son Mr Brograve Beauchamp.

An American film company also turned up at the site of the excavation and attempted to film some footage and the workers were instructed to cover up and thus hide the objects from view. If nothing else, Carnarvon intended to keep his film rights. He had also positioned himself with his own camera to capture some of the work.

38

HOLY OF HOLIES

THE DAY CHOSEN to break through the doorway was Friday 16 February. Carnarvon was staying with Eve at the Winter Palace as was his brother, who was up early and consequently went with him and Eve across the Nile to pick up the car. Eve quietly told her father that she wanted to let Mervyn know that they had both sneaked into the burial chamber. They could not resist it but had then filled up the hole again. An immense gold chest, like a holy of holies, filled the entire space so that it was very hard to squeeze round the walls. Given the political temperature, Carnarvon was worried in case anyone learned of this and Mervyn promised to keep the secret.

Perhaps twenty people were already assembled at the entrance to the tomb. Apart from themselves, those present included Richard Bethell, Howard Carter, Arthur Mace and Arthur Callender, both of whom were trying to remove the stones, Harry Burton with his camera, Sir Alan Gardiner, Mr Lythgoe and Mr Winlock from the

Metropolitan Museum, Sir William Garstin, Sir Charles Cust from the government, Rex Engelbach and Ibrahim Effendi, Inspector of the Service des Antiquités at Luxor, Tewfik Effendi Boulos, H. E. Abd el Halim Pasha Suleman and, of course, M. Lacau, the Director General Service des Antiquités.

Rows of chairs had been set out in the first chamber, now entirely empty except for the guardian statues which were screened off and a small wooden platform conveniently built so that the wall could be comfortably taken down from the top.

Carnarvon was both excited and slightly on edge – this was a great moment after eight fairly fallow years of mostly clearing up after other excavators. He made a short speech thanking all the workmen: Ahmed Gerigar, Hussein Ahmed Said, Gad Hussein, and Hussein Abu Awad and all the men and boys, as well as Mr Lythgoe and the Americans for their support. They had been most generous and Carnarvon was grateful. Carter spoke next, very nervous and talking about conservation and security. Then he knocked away at the mortar and Callender began carefully lifting down the stones and rubble. After half an hour, the hole was large enough to look through and Carter said he could see a huge gold and blue box. Each guest had a look, then the work continued.

A further two hours and there was a big-enough opening to let people through. Led by Carnarvon they took it in turns to drop into the tabernacle room which was some three feet below the first chamber. Lacau was one of the first, helping pay out the electric cable to give themselves some light. The entire tomb was brightly painted and in one corner stood the seven oars needed by the dead pharaoh to ferry him across to the underworld.

Passing through the shrine they found the entrance to another chamber. It was a treasury containing a canopic shrine, one of the most awe-inspiring works of beauty Carter had ever seen.

Lady Evelyn and Sir William Garstin entered next, and then the rest of the party. Carter describes how each was overcome and unable to express their awe at the sight of this past world. Sir John Maxwell tried to get through and became stuck and was eventually pulled out with much teasing by Carnarvon. He said he had hurt his chest but no one else thought that particular part of his anatomy was his chest.

Carnarvon helped pass back out some beautiful alabaster vases before Carter carefully undid the binding holding the great doors to the tabernacle hut. Inside was another nested gold box, seals intact. It was the most extraordinary day.

The press waited all day, sitting on the parapet around the tomb. There was a cell of disgruntled journalists who never ceased bombarding either Lacau or Engelbach and Weigall remarking, 'I'm not leaving that Tomb for the next 48 hours.' Of course, they could all hear the inner wall being taken down. Then there was the gossip and rumour. One of the native workmen during the afternoon said eight mummies had been found, another that it was three, all false information specially sent out by Mr Carter as a blind.

Exhausted, they left for tea at Carter's house before most of the party returned to the Winter Palace. At dinner that evening, Carter and Callender heard a commotion outside. A cobra had got into the house and 'grabbed the canary' given to Carter by Eve. Despite the snake having been killed, the canary died, probably from fright. The incident spooked the superstitious Egyptians who claimed it was a warning from the spirit of the departed pharaoh against further intrusion into the privacy of his tomb.

There was one more day to prepare for the official opening of the tomb by the Queen of the Belgians on Sunday 18 February, along with Lord and Lady Allenby and other 'distinguished visitors'. Eve was there every day for her father, taking some time out sitting on the steps enjoying a cigarette, just like him, and always well dressed like her mother.

The first visitor was the Dowager Sultana who arrived early in the morning. The Royal Princess, widow of the Sultan, was staying in Luxor and arrived, accompanied by her ladies, in a carriage escorted by guards, both mounted and on foot. An enthusiastic Egyptologist, she described the tomb as 'a dream of beauty.'

After luncheon, Lord and Lady Allenby arrived and waited at the entrance to receive the Queen of the Belgians. Her Majesty was welcomed by Lord Carnarvon, Colonel Watson and Abdul Suleiman Pasha, Under Secretary for Public Works. Prince Leopold arrived slightly later by car. Rather impractically, the Queen had chosen to wear a cream silk dress with a cloth coat and white fox-fur collar to visit an archaeological dig. The Belgian Crown Prince and Lord Allenby opted for shirtsleeves.

Again, Carnarvon sought to refute any quarrel between himself and the Egyptian Government and assure everyone that relations were most cordial. Once more there was a message of congratulations from King Fuad. 'A l'occasion de la découverte des inestimables trésors, dont vous enrichissez la science et l'Egypte, il m'est très agréable de vous adresser le témoignage de mes félicitations les plus vives au moment où vos efforts sont couronnés de succès, et où vous cueillez si justement le fruit de vos longues années de travail.'

The political difficulties were balanced by the sheer excitement of it all. To quote a *New York Times* article of 18 February, 'There is only one topic of conversation . . . One cannot escape the name of Tut-Ankh-Amen anywhere. It is shouted in the streets, whispered in the hotels, while the local shops advertise Tut-Ankh-Amen art, Tut-Ankh-Amen hats, Tut-Ankh-Amen curios, Tut-Ankh-Amen photographs, and tomorrow probably genuine Tut-Ankh-Amen antiquities. Every hotel in Luxor today had something a la Tut-Ankh-Amen . . . There is a Tut-Ankh-Amen dance tonight at which the piece is to be a Tut-Ankh-Amen rag.'

So many ideas were circulating. Professor Petrie made the suggestion that the mummy, if found, should not be removed to Cairo but that instead it should be placed, together with the other treasures, in a new museum built in the vicinity of the Valley of the Kings. Carnarvon, in contrast, wrote that 'those associated with me, are most anxious that arrangements should be made to leave the body in the sarcophagus, its present resting-place. This certainly will be done, unless, in the most improbable contingency, the Egyptian Government insist on its removal to Cairo . . . I have not yet discussed the point nor do I view with favour the . . . morbid taste which some people seem to enjoy of looking at mummies exposed.'

A cabled report from Cairo stated that Mr Tom Terries, representing the film organization Gaumont and Co., Ltd, had entered Tutankhamen's tomb with Lord Carnarvon, and that 'a section of film has been dispatched to London'.

39

THE MOSQUITO

FROM 19 TO 25 February, the tomb would be open to the press and public. Carnarvon and Carter hoped, thereby, to take the edge off the press's rancour. Among those who visited the chambers were Lady Somerleyton and Lady Ribblesdale and, more importantly to Eve, Sir Edward and Lady Beauchamp.

Carter was not feeling well and Eve offered to pop over and see if there was anything she could do. Sadly, Carnarvon and Carter's previously close and amicable relationship had collapsed under the stress. Carter was intensely frustrated with both the continued social visits and the relentless press rancour. He had asked Professor Breasted to his house for a long talk at which time he asked him to prepare all the historical work for the publication of a book on the tomb. Carnarvon had already tried to carve out the future projects and set them out to Carter but the book, however, was something Carnarvon wished to produce himself. They had a furious argument and Professor Breasted reported that Carter told Carnarvon to leave his house and not come back. It was no doubt an explosion of pent-up emotions on Carter's part, a symptom of his intense and exhausted frustration, but everyone needed a break.

In turn, Carnarvon was too tired to consider how the *Times* deal might have been better handled, and was now simply trying to manage what was in front of them. Gardiner and Mace were trying to keep Carter calm. Carnarvon wrote saying, 'I have been feeling very unhappy today and I did not know what to think or do and then I saw Eve and she told me everything.' Carnarvon vowed he would always remain a steadfast friend to Carter: 'whatever your feelings are or will be for me in the future, my affection for you will never change.'

Eve was so often the one person who tried to keep the peace and mediate, whether between her brother and her father or now, in this case, between Carter and her father.

On 25 February the tomb was shut up. It took two days of careful work and Carter commented, 'it has been daily visited by hundreds in the past week, whether personal friends or persons with permits from the Egyptian Government. It was sensible to suspend all work for the time being.' The press were endlessly making mischief and Carnarvon was grateful for the real support of the excavation team. Arthur Mace wrote an open letter to the various papers pointing out how cordial the relations were in the team but it was old news.

Carnarvon hired a dahabiya and sailed south to Aswan, finding peace, as ever, on the water. Evelyn joined him along with Arthur Mace and Sir Charles Cust, an old friend of Carnarvon's who was equerry to King George V. Mace later wrote he much enjoyed it and felt rested. They went to Elephantine Island and to Philae, visited bazaars and generally pottered. It was very refreshing with lots of royal gossip. By this time, Brograve Beauchamp and his parents had left Luxor to return to England. Eve hoped her father had liked the young man but nothing had really been said.

Meanwhile, on 28 February, Callender went south to Erment where he had a small farm just fifteen miles south of Luxor. Carter joined him there as an escape from the valley.

Returning to Luxor and the Winter Palace on 6 March, Carnarvon suggested meeting with various of 'his team' to make plans for the following season. Sir John Maxwell was still there and Callender, Mace and Carter all joined him in the private dining room. Mervyn Hebert was still in Luxor but now said several goodbyes to his brother whom he thought looked tired 'tho' I don't think more so than was reasonably to be expected'.

Exhausted, worried, stressed and feeling permanently rushed in every aspect of his life, Carnarvon cut himself shaving; he nicked a mosquito bite on his left cheek with his razor and carelessly failed to dab it with iodine. He had continued to feel tired and despondent and the doctors prescribed rest and bed.

On 11 March, Eve had left for Cairo with her lady's maid, Marcell, who had undergone an operation for appendicitis and was now well enough to travel home. Eve decided to wait for her father in Cairo. Despite feeling 'a bit seedy', Carnarvon travelled back to Cairo on 14 March and stayed at the Continental Hotel overlooking a garden square.

He had spent much of his life as an invalid of sorts and, as a result, had got used to disregarding his doctor's advice. He ignored it now and went out to dine with Alan Gardiner at the Royal Mohamed Ali Club and then see a 'moving picture'. He said that his face was hurting but refused to go back to the hotel, staying to see the film until the very end. By now he was feeling 'very seedy'. Lady Evelyn called in the doctors and was his constant nurse. Three days later, Eve wrote to Carter saying that Lacau was laid up with influenza in Cairo (Harry Burton was also suffering in Luxor) but, far more importantly, 'the old man' was really ill and 'incapable doing anything . . . yesterday quite suddenly all the glands in his neck started swelling and last night he had a high temperature'.

Before the letter even arrived, Eve, very alarmed, telegrammed Carter to come to Cairo and on 19 March she had wired for her mother. In addition, General Sir John Maxwell sent a cable to Sir Charles Monroe, Commander-in-Chief India: 'urgent will you please expedite intermediate passage for Lord Porchester to the Continental Hotel Cairo where his father Lord Carnarvon is seriously ill – three months compassionate leave'. Lord Inchcape immediately arranged passage on *Narkunda* to Suez.

Almina was ever practical and innovative. At times of grave illness, every hour could count and, with the help of Rutherford, she contacted Geoffrey de Havilland who had set up a aircraft rental business after the Great War. He arranged the flight from Croydon terminal building, just outside London, in one of his converted First World War bombers (a DH.50) which had room for a pilot and three passengers. Together with the best pilot and the best surgeon available, she managed by plane, steamship and finally train from Alexandria to arrive in Cairo on 26 March.

Richard Bethell, who was a friend as well as Carnarvon's private secretary, wrote to Carter: 'My wife and I are moving to the Continental Hotel to be near Eve and if he does not get better, we will cancel our passage for she must have someone to look after her.' Gardiner was also staying and wrote to his wife on 1 April: 'My darling Heddie, I saw him on Tuesday for five minutes, and on Wednesday came his relapse . . . I have just come back from seeing Evelyn . . . why am I so fond of him? And that poor little girl it breaks my heart with her devotion . . . I do so want him to pull through.'

Carter arrived at Cairo on 21 March where he received the news from Sir John Maxwell, President of the Egypt Exploration Society, that the Society hoped that Carter would accept an honorary membership, belatedly, and in all likelihood orchestrated by Carnarvon, as a public sign of appreciation of his contribution. By that stage Carter had worked in Egypt for thirty-two years and had been with Carnarvon for nearly half of that time.

Carnarvon was by now suffering from pneumonia, weakened and exhausted before the age of antibiotics, and a message of encouragement from King George V fell on ears unable to hear.

Almina immediately created a sense of hope by his bedside. She had had so much success with so many wounded men before. Carnarvon was conscious and the depth of affection between them was clear to everyone in the room. Briefly at times he seemed to rally. Winifred had cabled wishing she could be there but she had her audience with the Pope in Rome and wrote on 4 April: 'we heard the Papal Mass this morning. I think it must be good for me just to be in his presence, for he really radiates holiness. I was very pleased, as you may imagine, for he enquired after Carnarvon's discovery & said it had been a great addition to knowledge & sent him his blessing.'

Lord Carnarvon's health had been the subject of daily news bulletins around the world over the last ten days. Gardiner continued to stay with Carnarvon and his family in the hotel and in fact wrote and witnessed a codicil dated 3 April at his request, on a cable form. It read: 'Give all my bearer bonds to my dear daughter.' Gardiner later wrote to his wife: 'Darling, this is a very unpleasing letter, but I am dreadfully depressed and worried about old Carnarvon. I just live under the shadow of his illness these days. Best love from your own Alan.'

Almina spent every moment at the patient's bedside. Porchey arrived late on 3 April and went straight in to see his father: his face seemed so taut and angular, his hand burning hot. 'Papa, it's your son Henry I've come from India to see you.' Carnarvon seemed delirious and Porchey could only sit and wait with Eve and Carter.

Later as Almina leaned over her beloved husband's bed, she thought she heard him say 'I have seen Papa'. Almina knew the Bible verses so well, perhaps recalling the death of the 4th Earl: 'In my Father's house are many mansions: if it were not so, I would have told you. I go to prepare a place for you', and knew that this was it. It was nearly two in the morning and Henry had hardly fallen asleep when he heard a knock and one of the nurses put her head round the door. 'Lord Porchester, I'm so sorry, your father has just died. Your mother has closed his eyes and would like you to go in and say a prayer.' Porchey scrambled into a dressing gown and headed for his father's room. Suddenly, the hotel was plunged into darkness. Carefully, he made his way along the pitch-black corridor and into the suite. His mother was kneeling at his father's bedside crying softly. He knelt down beside her and put his arm around her as he offered a small prayer of his own. 'He fought so hard to live,' whispered Almina, between tears, 'but just at the end he said, "I have heard the call; I am preparing".' Dr Johnnie had already taken Eve back to her room to give her a sleeping draught. She was beside herself.

Newspapers around the world announced the death of Lord Carnarvon, 'Tutankhamun Tomb Discoverer', and hundreds and thousands of column inches were devoted to the journey from treasure to tragedy. Winifred wrote to a friend, 'You will have had the news . . . and will remember enough of the old days to know what it means to me. Thro' all the changes & chances of life we have remained true friends. I adore him now as much as I did more than 40 years ago . . . Almina has fought to keep him.'

40

Aprocession of miscellaneous vehicles made its way up the long sloping shoulder of Beacon Hill in the centre of the Highclere estate. The square, puffing outline of a tractor pulling a covered motor with a Red Cross on either side set the pace for the line of cars which followed. Bumping along the tussocked grass, the track led them up the ancient windswept hill, tiny wild flowers falling down the sides and skylarks circling overhead.

Twelve years before, Carnarvon had excavated here with Leonard Woolley, wondering whether they would find any clues about the Iron Age settlement which had existed there in 1350 BC. This was where he had walked with his father looking back at the Bronze Age tumuli, where he had had ridden his pony and raced against his sister Winifred. To one side, in the valley, were all his broodmares and the stud which had given him such interest and pleasure. Just under the hill was the golf course where he found a game that forced him to have patience, to relax and just be in the present. To the north was his home, Highclere Castle, which Almina had cared for with a never-ending welcome for every guest. And in all directions were the farmland and woods in which lay the houses and villagers that were so much part of his community and life.

Three long black cars brought Almina, Evelyn and Catherine, Lord Carnarvon's three beloved sisters Winifred, Margaret, Vera and his half-brother Mervyn and, of course, Dr Johnnie. Aubrey was not well, lying ill in Portofino having had an eye removed, and could not attend.

Carnarvon's son, now the 6th Earl, and Rutherford, with the rectors of Highclere and Burghclere, chose to walk up the steep side of the hill from the golf course. They were followed by many of the Highclere staff: Mr Streatfield, Mr Fearnside, Mr Grove, Mr Blake, Mr Thirkhill, Mr Storie and Mr Maber. It was a stiff climb and a bit of a scramble up along narrow sheep and rabbit trails which wound between scrubby juniper and thorn bushes.

They gathered at the top by the grave which had been 'hallowed' on the previous day by the rector of Burghclere. Eight men from the estate bore the coffin from the ambulance to the graveside, laying it on the wooden bearers over the grave. The coffin had been made from an oak tree in the park and was covered in the late Earl's purple and ermine coronation robe and coronet.

At 11 a.m., Rev. Jephson and Rev. Best led the simple burial service that Lord Carnarvon had requested. At its conclusion, the robe and coronet were handed to the late Earl's valet. The breastplate on the coffin was inscribed: 'George Edward Stanhope Molyneaux Herbert, 5th Earl of Carnarvon, born June 26th 1866, died April 5th 1923'. A small, wrapped bundle was quietly placed by the foot of the coffin. The little dog Susie slept in the housekeeper's rooms at Highclere when Carnarvon was away. Otherwise, she slept in his bed with him. At the same time as Carnarvon died in Cairo, Susie stood up, howled, and before the housekeeper could get out of bed to see what was the matter, she was dead.

The family had asked to be left in peace and a cordon of police and black-coated cottagers surrounded the hill so that no stranger could get within half a mile of the hill until the ceremony was over. Undeterred, a biplane from the *Daily Express* buzzed overhead taking pictures of the widow, bent over in grief, kneeling at her husband's grave. Entirely on her own, Almina stayed there until late that spring afternoon, tears hard to stop: no one knows the span of how much you love until it is gone.

Before dusk, before the sun god Ra left the world in darkness, the grave diggers returned, filled in the grave and put a simple fence around it.

A memorial service was arranged at Highclere church for personal friends and estate employees and tenantry for two days later and a further service was held by the Mayor and Corporation of Newbury at St Nicolas church. In addition, a memorial service was held at St Margaret's Westminster on Monday 30 April, where Lord and Lady Carnarvon had been married twenty-eight years earlier. 'Largely attended', mourners included Captain Sir Charles Cust, Colonel H. G. Lyons (representing the Egypt Exploration Society), Sir Edward and Lady Marshall Hall, Mrs Percival Griffith (aunt of the new Lady Carnarvon), Professor Newberry, Sir William Garstin, James Rothschild, Sir Wallis Budge and many, many more.

On the same day a most impressive memorial service was also held at All Saints Cathedral in Cairo. The Egyptian newspapers had continued to publish articles about Carnarvon. Abbas Hilmy el-Masri, a well-known Egyptian poet, paid a beautifully worded tribute to him, claiming that Carnarvon had contributed to Egypt's past glory in a manner which 'Saḥbān, the greatest Arabic orator, could not have equalled'.

The congregation included Lord and Lady Allenby, Nulfibar Pasha, representing King Fuad; the Prime Minister Yahaya Ibrahim and the Ministers of Public Works and Communications, Adly Pasha and a number of prominent Egyptians, General Herbert, commanding the Egyptian Army; Colonel-Commandant Grant and M. Lacau, Director-General Service des Antiquités, Alan Gardiner and many others. Howard Carter could not bring himself to go: he had simply withdrawn into himself to mourn privately.

'My beloved friend and colleague Lord Carnarvon who died in the hour of his triumph. But for his untiring generosity and constant encouragement our labours could never have been crowned with success. His judgement in ancient art had rarely been equalled. His efforts which have done so much to extend our knowledge of Egyptology will forever be honoured in history and by me his memory will always be cherished.'

'The widow of the late Lord Carnarvon now to be known as Almina Countess of Carnarvon wishes also thank her many kind friends for their affectionate messages of sympathy, which she hopes in time to acknowledge personally.'

Queen Alexandra, the widow of King Edward VII, wrote to Lady Carnarvon. 'I offer you and your family heartfelt sympathy in the terrible sorrow you have sustained in the death of your husband whose name will be remembered with pride by his fellow countrymen.' The new young Lord Carnarvon received a telegram from King George V and Queen Mary: 'The Queen and I have learnt with deep regret of the death of your father especially after the splendid fight which he made for his life. We offer you and your dear mother and family our sincere sympathy in your great loss.'

For many of his friends he was a hero, an Edwardian adventurer, traveller, innovator and he became one of the foremost excavators of the time. A man of many small acts of kindness and one who despite his illnesses persevered with good humour at all times.

His will was dated 29 October 1919, with two codicils. Probate was eventually granted to the 5th Earl's executors, General the Right Hon. Sir John Maxwell, GCB, KC, MGO, 103, Lancaster Gate, London, Major General Sir Robert Hutchinson, KC, MGO, 57, Catherine Street, Buckingham Gate, London, and Mr Arthur Fitzhardinge Berkeley Portman, of 29, Montague Square, London.

His Egyptian collection was dealt with in his first codicil, made on the same day as his will, but written in his own hand. He left this collection to his wife, adding: 'I would like her to give one object to the British Museum, one object to the Ashmolean, and a fragment cup of blue glass (Tuthmosis III) to the Metropolitan Museum.'

He stated that he wished to be buried, if possible, on Beacon Hill, and directed his executors to erect on Beacon Hill a mound of earth, with trees or stone, which, however, was not to cost more than £50.

He expressly desired that there should be no black horses, or any sort of mourning used at his funeral, or any mourning afterwards; that the funeral should be exceedingly simple, and that two doctors should view his body before burial to make sure that life was extinct. One legacy had been omitted: there was no mention of his concession to excavate in Egypt.

'Let Me Go'

When I come to the end of the road
And the sun has set for me
I want no rites in a gloom filled room
Why cry for a soul set free?

Miss me a little, but not for long
And not with your head bowed low
Remember the love that once we shared
Miss me, but let me go.

For this is a journey we all must take
And each must go alone.
It's all part of the master plan
A step on the road to home.

When you are lonely and sick at heart
Go to the friends we know.
Laugh at all the things we used to do
Miss me, but let me go.

Christina Rossetti

41

LEGACY

'Life is a journey to be experienced,
not a problem to be solved' – Winnie the Pooh

THE EARL AND the pharaoh each found peace within the secluded majesty of ancient landscapes. The settlements and cultures from each place of burial dated from the same time, 1500 BC, although ancient Egypt was a far more sophisticated culture than Iron Age Britain.

Equally, each man was forgotten and at times written out of history. Tutankhamun would have been heralded in his lifetime as the most famous man in the land, but his reign was brief and took place at a time of immense change. Unlike many other pharaohs, he was completely buried and passed by in history, simply a name on a list and a few partially obscured references on broken statues, faience glasses or jars. Lord Carnarvon found fame, which he did not seek, and died, somewhat sensationally, at his moment of triumph in the middle of what could be called the first global media event.

Both were dashing men born into a gilded lifestyle. The work of art from Tutankhamun's tomb that was most admired by Lord Carnarvon was the beautiful painted chest illustrated with chariots and scenes from the hunt, indicating that both probably had a love of fast vehicles in common. Both seem to have suffered from inherent ill health. Recent analysis of Tutankhamun's mummy suggests he was not always well – his skeleton appears far from perfect, one of his knees looks fractured and various comments have been made about the shape of his head. Carnarvon was almost certainly an undiagnosed asthmatic who then completely compromised his health in a terrible car crash and who was renowned for his hats which disguised a slightly domed head. There was no likelihood of anyone borrowing them as they all had to be specially made for him.

Carnarvon was bitten by a mosquito on the left cheek which he then nicked with a razor, which in turn led to septicaemia. Tutankhamun may have had malaria and, moreover, coincidentally the famous golden mask is of perfect hammered gold, except it is thinner at one point: the left cheek.

Every pharaoh buried in the Valley of the Kings tried to deter robbers from breaking into their tombs and disrupting their journey to the afterlife. It was therefore routine to threaten all sorts of curses and retribution on anybody contemplating theft. Very few people now believe in such things but, nevertheless, the lights in Cairo did go out when Carnarvon died, while back at home, at Highclere, his beloved Susie died at the same time as he did. It is perfectly plausible that Cairo's lights failed many times but Carnarvon's son, the 6th Earl, loved a good story and claimed it was the only time. Nevertheless, such was the fascination and awe that rumours swirled and seren-dipitous comparisons were drawn between the Earl and the Pharaoh. Everyone had a view. Sir Arthur Conan Doyle said: 'An evil elemental may have caused Lord Carnarvon's fatal illness.' And the stories of Tutankhamun's curse continue today.

Possibly there was bad bacteria in the tomb but, if there were, the rest of the excavation team were strong enough to fight off any infection without succumbing to it. After Carnarvon's death, Carter stayed on at the Continental Hotel with Lady Carnarvon. Rumours soon spread that he was also ailing and that Lady Carnarvon was nursing him. In fact, he was depressed and sad, having lost his closest friend but not otherwise suffering from any pharaoh's curse. Lady Carnarvon had no choice but to stay on as she had to wait for her husband's body to be embalmed before booking her passage home. It was a human rather than a supernatural tragedy: the Earl's family and friends loved him and missed him, his kindness and sense of humour, and he died too soon at only 56. Once the Carnarvon party left for England, Carter returned to Luxor and later in the year once more stayed part of the summer at Highclere.

If Carnarvon's death was foretold and deemed portentous, it left Howard Carter and Carnarvon's widow Almina in a very challenging position as Carnarvon had failed specifically to mention the concession to excavate in the Valley of the Kings in his will. However, Almina wished to honour her husband and dedicate her life to completing his work and stated she would use his notes to publish a book. She therefore applied to continue the concession, appointing Carter to carry out the work on her behalf.

At first, the excavation continued in a spirit of acceptance and teamwork until a year later, in 1924, Carter snapped. Suffering from exhaustion and the endless pressure of trying to balance conservation with unrelenting visitor interest, he went on strike. As a result, the Department of Antiquities deemed Almina, Lady Carnarvon's concession to be broken. The resulting court case became an international incident. Carter's personality was such that he failed to be sensitive to the sensibilities of others: the single-minded focus which had been essential in discovering the tomb was no longer mitigated by the diplomacy of Lord Carnarvon.

Neither were worldwide public opinion or Egyptian politics on Carter or Almina's side. However, on 19 November 1924 the British Commander-in-Chief of the Egyptian Army, Sir Lee Stack, was assassinated and a new, more pro-British government installed in Egypt. A concession was once more granted to Almina, Lady Carnarvon, for Howard Carter to carry out the archaeological work. On this occasion, they both had to declare that they assumed no rights whatsoever to the treasures within the tomb: 'The Tomb of Tutankhamun and all the antique objects coming therefrom shall be reserved in their entirety to the Public Domain of the State.'

In October 1925, Carter began to reveal the first of the nested coffins in which Tutankhamun's body lay. On the 28th they lifted the innermost solid gold coffin lid to find the mummy encrusted with jewels and royal regalia. The face of the pharaoh was portrayed in the solid gold mask which has since one of the most recognised icons in the world. Every year the concession was renewed and Carter returned to his painstaking and meticulous work, carefully removing each object from the tomb and transporting them to Cairo by river. By 1929, the greater part of the work was done and the job finally declared complete by 1932.

Despite the immensity of the discovery, Carter's life thereafter was one shadowed by disappointment and contention. When he died in 1939, only nine mourners turned up to pay their respects, among them Lady Evelyn Beauchamp who came to bid farewell to a dear friend of her beloved father.

Evelyn had married her beau, Sir Brograve Beauchamp, in October 1923. He was 6 foot 2 inches, and she 5 foot 2 inches. Their daughter Patricia was a force of nature and it is her knowledge and notes that have provided so many insights into these remarkable lives.

Almina had lost her father and her husband and both her children were now married. A further family tragedy followed six months after the death of Lord Carnarvon: his brother Aubrey died. He was hugely missed, leaving a very young family. On hearing the news his friend the celebrated novelist John Buchan wrote: 'I am greatly saddened this week but will be happy to mourn the most delightful brilliant survivor from the days of chivalry, he was the most extraordinary combination of tenderness and gentleness with the most insane gallantries I've ever known, a sort of survivor from crusading times. I drew Sandy in *Greenmantle* from him.'

Almina's money had always been provided and managed by the men in her life but everything was different now. At first, she wished to support Carter and his team, the most experienced and suitable archaeologists in the world, to continue the work of her husband. While she renounced unconditionally all claims to the tomb and its treasures, she did not, however, renounce the estate and her claim for duplicate objects and the accumulated costs of the excavation. Before his death, Carnarvon had spent some £45,000 on the excavation of the tomb and a further £36,000 was invested in his legacy by his widow.

In 1930, negotiations undertaken by Carter on behalf of Almina led to a settlement between the Government of Egypt and the Carnarvon family. King Fuad signed a decree to pay £35,979, which represented the Carnarvon investment since 1923. For all the question of money, Almina's legacy should not be underrepresented – she continued to fund the best archaeologists to work on the tomb in order to leave the world the legacy that was as much her husband's contribution as it was Carter's.

Sadly, the Rothschild money was gone and the death duties on Highclere immense. Almina sold her husband's Egyptian collection, not to the British Museum but to the Metropolitan Museum of New York whose staff had been so instrumental in helping Carter and Carnarvon with the excavation. Edward Harkness, who had been present in Luxor in spring 1923, offered the funds. The money allowed the family to continue to live at Highclere but much of

Carnarvon's life's work was gone. Carter catalogued the collection for Almina but left out a few unimportant items. They were tidied away in cupboards, forgotten about and only rediscovered in 1987 by the 7th Earl after his father died.

Both Lord and Lady Carnarvon knew and valued the Egyptians who worked with and for them in Egypt. Nineteen twenty-two was a time of change in Egypt and thereafter the protocol for excavating among the tombs of ancient Egypt would be less encouraging for foreign excavators. Lord Carnarvon's era had spanned a turning point and he valued his relationship with the Egyptian Cabinet as well as influential English colleagues.

Zaghloul Pasha also telegraphed his condolences to Lady Carnarvon. Numerous obituaries in the Egyptian press were sympathetic and honoured Carnarvon who, in his easy-going fashion, managed to bridge two wholly different worlds and, in so doing, found a window into an ancient one. The question of the ownership and rights to the treasure of ancient Egypt, the works of art and the interpretation of them, were at the centre of the politics of modern Egyptian independence and identity. In January 1924, at the first free parliamentary elections, the heroic figure of Saad Zaghloul with the nationalist Wafd swept to power.

It is worth quoting the Egyptian newspapers from the time of Carnarvon's death on the subject of his role in the discovery of Tutankhamun. He was described as a 'Benefactor to Egypt' and in 1923 was lauded as having put hundreds of thousands of pounds into Egypt by attracting countless tourists. It was further observed by one Egyptian editor that he had contributed thousands from his own pocket.

As an extraordinarily visible record of an ancient civilization which spanned 5,000 years and created wonders of the world still admired today, ancient Egypt stands above all others, if only for its curious mixture of beauty, romance and the macabre. Even amid this wealth of splendour, Tutankhamun's iconic mask shines out like a beacon. For a century now, innumerable magazines, papers and television programmes have used it to encourage visitors to Egypt, which in 2019 contributed a revenue of over $13 billion.

Quite apart from rumours and curses, both Carnarvon and Tutankhamun contributed an extraordinary legacy to the world. Carnarvon was one of the last private excavators committing his own money under terms that allowed him to at least break even and thus continue. Nor was he a mere dilettante who stood by while others did the work, paying someone else while grabbing the glory. Carter not only became a friend but he was, more importantly as far as history is concerned, also a colleague. Carter may have been an expert but Carnarvon shared his passion and worked on the digs alongside him; he learned through the adventure of life. Importantly, he provided the diplomacy and contacts that Carter's prickly personality and birth could not reach and continued to fund their shared dream after everyone else had given up. Their partnership created the foundation for success and subsequently the most able team to ensure the tomb and its contents would be preserved for the future.

The era of the amateur philanthropist was passing. Museum bene-factors wanted results, preferably almost immediately, and were risk-averse. It is unlikely that another excavator would have taken the risks and committed so much. The very unconventionality of the 5th Earl was intrinsic to Tutankhamun's discovery.

In the decade following the discovery of the tomb, Tutankhamun and the Amarna style influenced fashion, art and architecture throughout Europe and America. Tut-mania coincided with the birth of Hollywood and the building boom of great movie theatres, which is why so many cinemas from that time resemble Egyptian temples.

If Lord Carnarvon's name gathered dust, that of Tutankhamun came to the fore. In 1972, the British Museum's exhibition of Tutankhamun's treasures broke all records with over 1.6 million visitors. The lending of some of their treasures to the wider world has been a multi-million-pound industry for both Egypt in terms of license fees and locally for the museums and cities involved in terms of visitor numbers.

The influence of ancient Egypt on modern times cannot be understated. From grand Art Deco structures to something as seemingly simple and ubiquitous as a smoky eye shadow, our culture is steeped with references, artefacts, imagery and characters from the ancient Egyptian Empire. Egyptian mythology has inspired films, countless novels, television series, comic books and games. The Louvre in Paris is entered through a pyramid, while obelisks stand sentinel in many capitals across the world.

For those who seek some version of an afterlife, Egypt really laid out the journey in colour and pageantry, and none more so than the boy pharaoh Tutankhamun. Carnarvon did not live to write his book or to share the story through cinema, but, having read his letters and notes, and steeped myself in his life and times, I have tried to recreate his part in an extraordinary story, and write the book.

ACKNOWLEDGEMENTS

Writing is a peculiarly solitary endeavour. Where I write is a beautiful room high up on the third floor of the castle. It is called 'Orient' and is painted in the strong yellow colours of Egypt, whilst an old CD player keeps me company during long evenings usually with Mozart, Bach or similar. Various people, however, have thankfully entered my world to help in writing this book.

Smiles (Susannah de Ferry Foster) was a tremendous aid with detailed research into the 5th Earl's passion for horse racing and motor cars, as well as returning to fact check during long evenings. Sally Popplewell helped once more to edit, smooth and remove repetition, and fortunately had a good working knowledge of Egyptology, whilst David Rymill (Highclere's archivist) investigated various archive sources for me. Much of this book reflects first source research. My husband contributed throughout, correcting and encouraging, whilst my son Eddie read the opening chapter and said he could not wait to read more.

As ever I owe a huge thank you to everyone at Highclere. Researching and telling this story has been a challenging effort and as ever it is an emotional and mentally demanding journey. I am so grateful for their support – John Gundill, Luis Coelho and Charlotte Sheridan all picked up some of my other work whilst I wrote. Hannah Gutteridge is always offering help to promote the book. Thank you to all.

Some time ago the Metropolitan Museum in New York and The British Museum in London allowed me access to letters and notes, all of which have never been properly read, to incorporate them into this extraordinary story. I also used the archives of the British Library and St Anthony's College, Oxford, plus the Somerset archives, the Winchester archives and the Griffiths Institute. I am grateful to all for access to these resources. I have been most fortunate to meet and discuss elements of my research with eminent archaeologists, so again, thank you. The original discovery is one of collaboration and working together and I am grateful to continue this culture.

Through a very special friend, Karen Hambro, I spoke with Charlie Redmayne at HarperCollins who introduced me to Arabella Pike and her team, who have all believed in this project and book. Thank you all very much.

Karen, this book is also for you.

GENERAL BIBLIOGRAPHY

There are many books concerning both the time period in general and the discovery of the tomb, as well as books on Tutankhamun himself and the treasures found with him. For those interested, here is a selection of publications that may be of interest.

Adams, J.M., *The Millionaire and the Mummies: Theodore Davis's Gilded Age in the Valley of the Kings* (St Martins Press, 2013)

Ades, Harry, *A Travellers History of Egypt* (Interlink Books, 2006)

Ahmed, J.M, *The Intellectual Origins of Egyptian Nationalism* (Oxford University Press, 1960)

Bell, Gertrude, *The Letters of Gertrude Bell, Volumes 1 and 2* (Ernest Benn, 1927)

Carter, Howard and Mace, A.C., *The Tomb of Tutankhamun, Volume 1: Search, Discovery and Clearance of the Antechamber* (Bloomsbury, 2014)

Carter, Howard, *The Tomb of Tutankhamun, Volume 2: The Burial Chamber* (Bloomsbury, 2014)

Edwards, Amelia, *A Thousand Miles up the Nile* (Cambridge University Press, 2010 [1877])

Gardiner, Alan, *The Egyptians: An Introduction* (The Folio Society, 1999)

Hawass, Zahi, *Tutankhamun: The Treasures of the Tomb* (Thames & Hudson Ltd, 2018)

— *Discovering Tutankhamun: From Howard Carter to DNA* (The American University in Cairo Press, 2013)

— *The Golden King: The World of Tutankhamun* (National Geographic Society, 2006)

Herbert, Aubrey, *Ben Kendim: A Record Of Eastern Travels* (G. P. Putnam & Sons Ltd, 1925)

— *Mons, Anzac & Kut: a British Intelligence Officer in Three Theatres of the First World War, 1914–18* (Edward Arnold, 1919)

Howell, Georgina, *Daughter of the Desert: The Remarkable Life of Gertrude Bell* (Macmillan, 2006)

Humphreys, Andrew, *Grand Hotels of Egypt in the Golden Age of Travel: Classic Suites, Picnics on the Pyramids, and Verandahs on the Nile* (The American University in Cairo Press, 2011)

James, T.G.H., *Howard Carter: The Path to Tutankhamun* (Routledge, 1992)

Keown-Boyd, Henry, *The Lion and the Sphinx: The Rise and Fall of the British in Egypt 1882–1956* (Memoir Club, 2002)

Lewis, Bernard, *The Middle East: A Brief History of the Last 2,000 Years* (Prentice Hall & IBD, 1996)

Nicholson, T.R., *The Birth of the British Motor Car: Last Battle, 1894–97* (Macmillan, 1982)

Platt, J and Wilkinson, T., *Aristocrats and Archaeologists: An Edwardian Journey on the Nile* (The American University in Cairo Press, 2017)

Powell, David, *The Edwardian Crisis: Britain, 1901–14* (Macmillan, 1996)

Reeves, C.N. and Taylor, John. H., *Howard Carter: Before Tutankhamun* (Harry N Abrams Inc, 1993)

Reeves, Nicholas, *Akhenaten, Egypt's False Prophet* (Thames & Hudson Ltd, 2001)

— *The Complete Tutankhamun* (Thames & Hudson Ltd, 1990)

— *The Complete Valley of the Kings* (Thames & Hudson Ltd, 1997)

Ridley, Jane, *The Heir Apparent: A Life of Edward VII, The Playboy Prince* (Random House, 2013)

Royle, T, *The Kitchener Enigma: The Life and Death of Lord Kitchener of Khartoum, 1850–1916* (The History Press, 2016)

Tvedt, T, *The River Nile in the Age of the British: Political Ecology and the Quest for Economic Power* (I.B. Tauris, 2004)

Wallis Budge, E.A., *The Book of the Dead* (Benediction Books, 2010)

Westrate, Bruce, *The Arab Bureau: British Policy in the Middle East 1916–1920* (Pennsylvania State University Press, 1992)

Winstone, H.V.F., *Howard Carter: and the Discovery of the Tomb of Tutankhamun* (Barzan Publishing, 2006)

— *Woolley of Ur: Life of Sir Leonard Woolley* (Martin Secker & Warburg Ltd, 1990)

LIST OF ILLUSTRATIONS

All chapter opener images taken from the Highclere Castle Archives.

Plate sections:

The Sphere's front-page report of the discovery of the tomb (Highclere Castle Archives)

The drawing room of Highclere Castle (Highclere Castle Archives)

Highclere Castle, c.1900 (Highclere Castle Archives)

A shooting party outside the castle (Highclere Castle Archives)

A shooting party including the Prince of Wales (Highclere Castle Archives)

Lady Evelyn Stanhope (Highclere Castle Archives)

The 5th Earl Henry Herbert (Highclere Castle Archives)

The Countess of Carnarvon Almina Herbert with the 6th Earl Henry Herbert (Highclere Castle Archives)

Colonel the Honourable Aubrey Herbert (Highclere Castle Archives)

Lady Winifred Herbert (Highclere Castle Archives)

The inauguration of the Highclere Golf course (Highclere Castle Archives)

Lord Carnarvon on the cover of *The Tatler* (Mary Evans Picture Library)

Geoffrey de Havilland's first flight (Highclere Castle Archives)

Geoffrey de Havilland in his aerial motor (Highclere Castle Archives)

The examination of an Iron-Age fort on Beacon Hill (Highclere Castle Archives)

Driving through the Valley of Kings (Highclere Castle Archives)

Lord Carnarvon with his daughter, Evelyn (Pictorial Parade / Getty)

Lord Carnarvon with Howard Carter (Hulton Archive / Getty)

A self-taken portrait of Lord Carnarvon (Highclere Castle Archives)

Susie the dog (Highclere Castle Archives)

The Colossi of Memnon (Highclere Castle Archives)

A portrait of Howard Carter (Highclere Castle Archives)

The pyramids in flood (Highclere Castle Archives)

Various photos of excavations in Egypt c.1910 (Highclere Castle Archives)

Coffins from Deir el Birabi (Highclere Castle Archives)

The entrance to the Tomb of Tutankhamun (Highclere Castle Archives)

The tomb's interior (Getty)

The canopic chest (The Print Collector / Alamy)

Unrolling wadding in the tomb (Hulton Archive / Getty)

Howard Carter examining the mummy of Tutankhamun (Apic / Getty)

The treasures of the tomb loaded on the Nile (David Cole / Alamy)

Lord Carnarvon's death certificate (Highclere Castle Archives)

Howard Carter opening the inner golden shrines in the tomb (Hulton Archive / Getty)

INDEX

201, 205, 206, 216; Gorst's 'Egypt for Egyptians' speech, 197; Antiquities Laws (1912), 216–17; policy regarding share allocated to excavators, 216, 217, 290–1, 312, 351, 352; during First World War, 237, 238–41, 264–5, 279, 282; 5th Earl returns to (1919), 278–80; postwar political unrest, 279, 281–2, 284–5, 286–7; the Wafd (mass political party), 279, 281, 286, 353; 5th Earl's sympathetic interest in nationalism, 281–2, 286, 288; British protectorate over recognized at Versailles, 282; Lord Milner's commission, 282, 284–5, 286–7, 288; independence (February 1922), 294; change of government in (1923), 328; Dowager Sultana of, 333–4; Carnarvon family settlement with (1930), 352; ownership/rights to ancient treasure as key issue in new state, 353

Egypt, ancient: mummies moved to secret caches, 128–9; funerary practices, 128, 143, 156, 175, 176–7, 191, 212–13, 305, 312, 332; shabtis (figurines), 129, 143, 205, 240; Tel el-Amarna, 134–5, 141, 158, 203–4, 296, 311; art, 134, 292, 296, 306, 311, 312; writing/script, 135, 149–50, 155–6, 158, 176, 191, 200, 203–4, 214–15, 284, 305, 321; expulsion of the Hyksos, 150, 183, 192; embalming process, 177; rishi coffins, 177, 191; spells/curses aimed at tomb robbers, 312–13, 349; Book of the Dead, 312; allure/attraction of, 353–4; influence on modern times, 354, 355 see also Egyptology; Thebes (ancient Egyptian city); Tutankhamun, tomb of; Valley of the Kings

Egypt Exploration Fund/Society, 134–5, 172, 214, 280, 311, 324, 339–40, 344

Egyptology: 5th Earl's growing fascination, 124–5, 126–7; Department of Antiquities in Cairo, 124, 126, 127, 216, 301, 303–4, 308, 325, 332; Director of

Antiquities as always a Frenchman, 127, 211; German influence in Cairo, 127; Luxor antiquity dealers, 128–9, 201, 204–5, 263–4; and modern tomb robbers, 128–9, 130–1; Amherst collection in Norfolk, 133–4, 204, 284; Carnarvon Tablets (1 and 2), 149–50, 183; Manetho's lists, 158, 213; antiquities trade, 191, 194–5, 201, 204–5, 263–4, 291, 292, 310–11; antiquities room at Highclere, 193–4, 284; 5th Earl's *Five Years at Thebes*, 195, 217; 5th Earl's growing expertise, 203; Amenophis III bracelet plaques, 204; Amherst Papyri, 204; Abbott Papyrus, 214–15, 284; during First World War, 239–41; Amherst Papyrus, 284; 5th Earl's collection at Seamore Place, 289; exhibition at Society of Antiquaries (1922), 296 see also Egypt, ancient; Tutankhamun, tomb of and under archaeology

Elveden Hall, Norfolk, 26, 48, 64, 71

Elwes, Simon, 288

Engelbach, Reginald (Rex), 301, 305, 329, 332, 333

Eton College, 21–5, 27, 28, 32, 33, 34–6, 37, 38, 66, 94

Evans, Sir Arthur, 202–3

Everest, Mount, 310

Fahmi Pasha, Mustapha, 286

Fahmy Bey, Mohamed, 327

Falkland Islands, 80

Fearnside, George (valet), 62, 65, 91, 164, 168, 170, 343

Ferdinand, Archduke, assassination of (June 1914), 219

First World War: Maspero's loss of son in, 214; build-up to, 219–23; outbreak of (August 1914), 223–5; British Expeditionary Force (BEF), 224, 225; medical services during, 225–6, 232–5, 236, 241–3, 247, 261–3; and Aubrey Herbert, 227, 228–30, 237, 239, 244,